Christmas 1974
from
Diane & Dick.

Babe Ruth

BABE RUTH

His Life and Legend

Kal Wagenheim

PRAEGER PUBLISHERS
New York · Washington

Published in the United States of America in 1974
by Praeger Publishers, Inc.
111 Fourth Avenue, New York, N.Y. 10003

© 1974 by Praeger Publishers, Inc.

Library of Congress Cataloging in Publication Data

Wagenheim, Kal.
  Babe Ruth; his life and legend.

  Bibliography: p.
  1. Ruth, George Herman, 1895–1948. 2. Baseball.
I. Title.
GV865.R8W3   796.357'092'4 [B]   73-13049
ISBN 0-275-19980-0

Printed in the United States of America

to
June, Becky, Lowell . . .
and Jeff

Contents

Contents

Sections of illustrations follow pages 84 *and* 180.

Acknowledgments

The following books were helpful in providing the basic outline of Babe Ruth's life: *Babe Ruth's Own Book of Baseball* (G. P. Putnam's, 1928); *Babe Ruth: The Big Moments of the Big Fellow,* by Tom Meany (A. S. Barnes, 1947); *The Babe and I,* by Claire Ruth with Bill Slocum (Prentice-Hall, 1959); *The Babe Ruth Story,* by Babe Ruth as told to Bob Considine (E. P. Dutton, 1948); and *The Golden People,* by Paul Gallico (Doubleday, 1965). I also consulted numerous biographies of contemporary figures and found particularly useful information in *My Fifty Years of Baseball,* by Edward Grant Barrow with James M. Kahn (Coward-McCann, 1951) and *Adios to Ghosts,* a brief autobiography privately published in 1937 by Christy Walsh. For invaluable data on the period in which Ruth lived and played, I am particularly indebted to *A Tower in Babel*: *A History of Broadcasting in the United States,* by Erik Barnouw (Oxford University Press, 1966); *The Good Years: From 1900 to the First World War,* by Walter Lord (Harper & Row, 1960); *Only Yesterday*: *An Informal History of the 1920's,* by Frederick Lewis Allen (Harper & Row, 1931); *The Lawless Decade,* by Paul Sann (Crown, 1957); and *The Great Depression,* by Robert Goldston (Bobbs-Merrill, 1968).

Much of the information on Ruth's career was found in the newspapers and periodicals of his era. For access to these, I am indebted to the New York Public Library and its Newspaper Division on West 43d Street, the library of the Baltimore *Sun* (which had many items about Ruth's origins), the Boston Public Library (which had very good material on his years with the Red Sox), the Newark Public Library, the library of Newark-Rutgers University, and the Baseball Hall of Fame Library in Cooperstown, New York (where librarian Jack Redding was most cooperative in showing me clippings, photos,

Christy Walsh's old scrapbooks of Ruth's tours, and many other items).

But above all I'm indebted to the many people who shared with me their personal memories of the Babe. It's impossible to name everyone, but I can't fail to mention Jumping Joe Dugan, still spry and witty, of Walpole, Massachusetts; Whitey Witt, still down on the farm in Woodstown, New Jersey; Harry Hooper, now in his eighties, who was out duck hunting the first time I called at his home in Santa Cruz, California; Babe Ruth's sister, Mrs. Wilbur M. Moberly of Hagerstown, Maryland; William Laidlaw of Saint Just, Puerto Rico; Pete Sheehy, still with the New York Yankees—and a very special note of gratitude to Marshall Hunt, formerly of the *Daily News,* the "Ludwig Consumo" of the press corps, who spent years riding the rails with Ruth. It was in listening to Mr. Hunt and reading the microfilms of his dispatches that I began to appreciate the verve, madcap humor, talent, and poetry of the sportswriters of the 1920's, who introduced Babe Ruth to his vast, admiring public and helped to make that decade the great time it surely was.

KAL WAGENHEIM

PROLOGUE

Keep lean and strong and clean,
Keep spirited and keen.
"Play ball!" means something more than runs
Or pitches thudding into gloves!
Remember through the summer suns
This is the game your country loves.

GRANTLAND RICE

"He Fell from a Tree"

"Born? Hell, Babe Ruth wasn't born! The sonofabitch fell from a tree!"

Joe Dugan takes a slug of his Early Times Bourbon on the rocks and lets go with a high-pitched, wheezy laugh. We're sitting in the crowded, talky bar of the Copley Plaza Hotel in downtown Boston. Glistening chandeliers, potted palms, sunlight through the tall windows. He looks around. "They didn't let ballplayers and actors into this joint back in the old days," he says.

"Jumping Joe" Dugan, third baseman for the '27 Yankees, greatest team ever. Anyone will tell you. He is seventy-eight years old, tall, thin, erect. The rhythms of his piping voice remind you of W. C. Fields.

"So you wanna know about Babe Ruth, eh? Ruth, Ruth, Ruth. He was like a big baby; a lovable devil. Grin on his face alla time. He was an animal, a *great* animal. Fell from a tree! Didn't *look* like anybody else. He had a nose! Ever see his nostrils? You could drive a Ford right into one o' them! Smoked cigars. Chewed snuff. Snorted it through his nose. He'd chew anything. Jesus!

"I batted against the Babe when he was a pitcher. He was one o' the greatest. When he was up at the plate, he swung from Port Arthur, Texas, at every pitch. Everything was go for broke. It was like Dempsey, the old knockout punch. When he got hold o' one, it was a homer in *any* park, including Yellowstone National, y'hear?

"Whitey Witt and I, we shared a room next to the Babe for a few seasons on the road, back in the 'twenties; that's when a shave and a haircut was a quarter. Lawton W. Witkowski was his real name. A little bowlegged Polack. Still lives down in Jersey. Oh, the Babe loved Whitey, because he was his kind o' guy. I was no altar boy either! We were *all* good drinkin' men.

"It was prohibition then. They said you couldn't do it, so we *did* it!

3

Ruth had a bootlegger in every town. 'Babe here, send up a case o' scotch, case o' rye, and fill the bathtub up with beer.' Standing order. And Whitey and I would help him drink it all! He didn't have much trouble getting me an' Whitey over there. Hell, the bastard was gettin' fifty or sixty thou a year, and we were making ten or so. He loved anybody who wanted to hang out with him. But geez, that was dangerous. Tough. He was an animal, he fell out of a tree. He never was born! Never forget the day in Chicago. Babe calls up this guy. 'Charley there?' 'No,' says the guy on the other end, 'but I'll take your order. What is it?' This is a true story now. So Ruth says, '*You* know what it is. Rye, scotch, beer, have it up here right after the game.' Then he asks, 'Say, what happened to Charley?' The guy answers, 'He's got amnesia.' 'He's got what?' 'Amnesia!' So Ruth says, 'Fer chrissakes, send me a case o' that, too!' He thought it was an after-*dinner* drink, the sonofabitch! Oh, it was really somethin' on the road. The things I saw him do on and off the field—unbelievable! We were supposed to be in breakfast by nine o'clock. Half of us'd go down, sign in, and go right back and sleep it off. Not the Babe, though. He'd be out all night, and next morning his eyes'd be clear as a little baby's.

"One day, we went to Belmont. I bet fifty and Ruth bet five hundred across. The horse fell at the first jump. 'Dugan.' he says, 'you dirty Irish sonofabitch, fifteen hundred bucks—we coulda been drunk for a week!' But by the end of the day he won plenty. 'You in a hurry to get home?' he says to me. Sonofabitch takes me to a speakeasy. Got home at three in the morning. Next day, I played one inning and Huggins takes me out. 'You don't look too good,' he says to me. Ruth? The bastard hit two home runs. Never had a hangover.

"Babe was a broads man. Met lots o' girls in his life. Beautiful and unbeautiful. Hell, he was no Clark Gable. No Rhodes Scholar either. But with that kind o' money, they came right to the hotel! The Babe had a phonograph in his room all the time. Silk bathrobe on, in come the broads, great dancer.

"He was one in a million. We're playin' at the stadium one day and who comes in but President Coolidge. So we line up to meet the President. I say to Waite Hoyt, 'Let's stick around. Ruth'll have something to say.' I was third from last. I say, 'Hello, Mister President. It's a great honor to shake hands with you.' Ruth takes his cap off and says, 'Hot as hell, ain't it, Prez?' What the hell you gonna do with a guy like that? Coolidge looked at him, thought he was nuts!

"Al Capone? I met him, too. He invited Ruth to this big night club in Cicero, Illinois, and I tagged along. Never saw anything like that in my life. All kinda booze, beer, broads. He went for those broads.

Now this fellow Aaron today, I guess he's great. He's *gotta* be great. But Babe Ruth was number one in America. Bigger than the President. There was never anyone like him. Nobody *close*. He was more than an animal. He was a god."

* * *

March, 1929. Saint Petersburg, Florida. Babe Ruth, the Sultan of Swat, meandered about the spring training camp, his huge torso wrapped in a thick shirt, trying to sweat off a winter's worth of good living. Carl Sandburg, then a reporter-columnist for the Chicago *Daily News,* inquired:

"If some kid ballplayers asked you for five rules, five big points to watch, what would you tell them?"

"Cut out smoking and drinking, get enough sleep, get the right things to eat."

The Babe, says Sandburg, "wouldn't think of two more and was willing to let it go at these three." The rest of their colloquy went something like this:

SANDBURG: If some boys asked you what books to read, what would you tell them?

RUTH: I never get that. They don't ask me that question. They ask me how to play ball.

SANDBURG: What's your favorite flower?

RUTH (*laughing*): I don't care about flowers.

SANDBURG: What's your favorite horse?

RUTH: Oh, I quit that. I quit playing the ponies long ago.

SANDBURG: If some boys asked you for a model of a man to follow through life, would you tell them President Coolidge is pretty good?

RUTH: Well, I always liked President Harding . . .

SANDBURG: Is there any one character in history you are especially interested in, such as Lincoln, Washington, Napoleon?

RUTH: I've never seen any of them.

* * *

On April 8, 1974, at 9:07 P.M. Eastern Daylight Time—when Henry Aaron hit his 715th home run in Atlanta Stadium—35 million television viewers across the nation saw the historic shot, and watched the ecstatic explosion of 53,000 spectators, as a huge electronic sign blazed with the letters: "MOVE OVER BABE, HERE COMES HENRY."

By some eerie coincidence, Henry Aaron and Babe Ruth were born just a day (and thirty-nine years) apart: Aaron on February 5 and Ruth on February 6. But here the similarity ends. More than a contrast between black and white skin, the difference between Ruth and Aaron is one of opposite personalities performing on vastly different stages; America and Americans have changed far more than we realize in the past four or five decades.

In 1920, Babe Ruth hit more home runs than fourteen of the sixteen *teams* in the major leagues. He beat at least one entire team in twelve different seasons.* But statistics don't begin to tell the story.

Ruth was a mythmaker's dream. To begin with, he looked the part. At the peak of his power and fame, he was 6 feet 2 inches tall and weighed about 225 pounds—an extraordinary size for a man of his epoch. His massive shoulders and arms—and the big potbelly that made his legs look thin by comparison—formed a body that was recognizable from afar. His moon-shaped face, with the broad, flat nose, the small brown eyes, and the perpetual grin, was homely and unforgettable. It was an earthy, good-natured mug that almost cried out for caricature. He was a big swinger on and off the field; he *was* Zorba before Kazantzakis created him.

In contrast with the cool science of Aaron's batting technique, Ruth, in a rare moment of self-analysis, once said: "I swing with everything I've got. I hit big or miss big." He appealed to a deeply rooted American yearning for the definitive climax: clean, quick, unarguable. Ruth and his pitching adversary squared off like two Western gunslingers, as fans cheered for the symbolic annihilation of one man—either Ruth, twisting himself into a pretzel shape as he took a murderous swing at a third strike, or the pitcher, standing forlorn as the Babe's smash rocketed out of sight and he made his ritualistic tour of the bases.

On opening day of 1974, when Aaron hit his 714th homer, a man was arrested for "streaking" nude through the stands of Cincinnati's stadium; in 1927, the year Ruth hit his 60 homers, a female school teacher in New Jersey lost her job when she was seen smoking a cigarette after school hours. But the difference is far deeper than mores alone.

There was no radio until the middle of the 1920's, and television was a remote dream. Most Americans had never seen a big league star in the flesh. Unless you lived in, or traveled to, the ten Eastern or Midwestern cities where the teams played, your chances of seeing a star were slim. The legend of Ruth's heroic home runs grew by word of mouth, buoyed by the hyperbole of the sports press—America's

---

* In Henry Aaron's best year (1971), he hit 47 home runs, while the weakest club hit 71 and the average club had 120.

epic poets—who called him the Sultan of Swat, the Bambino, the Prince of Pounders, the Wizard of Wham, the Bazoo of Bang, the Maharajah of Maul.

"The train would come puffing into the station in some small town," says a fellow who often made the trip, "and there on the platform would be dozens—sometimes hundreds—of people, all wanting to catch a glimpse of the Yankees, but especially of the Babe. Guess they had nothing *better* to do! The Babe usually sat near a window, and he'd really mug it up for 'em. If he was eating a hot dog, he'd wave it at 'em. If he was playing hearts, he'd show 'em what a great hand he had; then he'd wink and put his fingers to his mouth—a big secret between him and them. Oh, they loved it, they ate it up."

Jimmy Cannon could rightly claim a few years ago, "It is part of our national history that all boys dream of being Babe Ruth before they are anyone else." The adults dreamed, too. When Ruth was earning more than one hundred thousand nearly tax-free dollars a year—and spending more than that on liquor, women, horses, cars, and every imaginable caprice—a factory worker brought home about twenty-five dollars a week to feed his family and pay the rent. Even in 1929, the boom year before the crash, only two out of ten American families earned more than sixty dollars a week, and the savings of the richest sixty thousand families were equal to those of the twenty-five *million* families below them. The gap in life-style between a celebrity like Ruth and the average American was more like a yawning canyon. "The poor could wrap their dreams around him," said one writer. Today, a skilled blue-collar worker—with a carpeted home, color television, a phalanx of electrical gadgets, and a late-model car or two—lives a life that is at least comparable to that of the star athlete; comparable, certainly, to Henry Aaron, who dresses in quiet good taste and drives an economy car.

Today, in our more egalitarian society, with films and magazines that leave little for the inner eye to fancy, with television sets that show us the most remote corners of our world village—with zoom lenses and instant replays that capture, live, not only the 715th home run or the acrobatic end zone catch, but even the murder of Presidents' assassins—Americans have apparently lost their capacity to be awed. And, with 105 different professional sports teams, shifting franchises too quickly for loyalties to mature; with divisional playoffs and league playoffs and championship playoffs; with Monday Night Football and mid-week reruns of last Sunday's game; with Saturday afternoons devoted to Wide World camera-skipping from motorcycle races to roller derby to golf to figure-skating to demolition derbies—Americans have no opportunity to focus their passions on a single figure. As Russell

Baker recently noted when he announced he'd "stopped being a sports fan": "there was just too much of it . . . it was like having a banana split with every meal."

The age of kings is over. The "star" has been eclipsed by the "superstar" and even that word has dimmed in meaning. Henry Aaron is the rightful heir to Babe Ruth's crown, but he seems to have come along at the wrong time.

So! To borrow a line from Babe Ruth's favorite radio program, *The Lone Ranger,* "Return with us now to those thrilling days of yesteryear!"

FIRST INNING

The person born under the sign of Aquarius is
very sociable . . . although he loves his home
and family, he does not want to feel tied down.
With children, the Aquarian is likely to get
along very well; he does not treat them as in-
feriors. . . . He is easily moved by hard-luck
stories . . . the weak part of the Aquarian's
body are his ankles and his calves . . . his joy
of life usually impresses members of the opposite sex. . . . Money in itself has very little
interest for him . . . routine work is not apt to
hold his interest for very long . . . employers
may find him a bit trying and unreliable . . .
the Aquarian usually has his own set of laws
to live by. He hungers for freedom and may,
to some, appear slightly mad.

from a popular guidebook
to astrology

"Little George"

As one might expect on such an occasion, the earth shuddered when Babe Ruth was born. February 6, 1895, was one of the coldest days in memory. Frost slew the orange and olive crops of the Mediterranean, blizzards raged wildly through the American Northwest. In Baltimore, where the mercury hovered near zero, tramps stuffed newspapers inside their shabby clothes and banged at the doors of homes and stores, pleading for shelter.

In a grimy working-class district of South Baltimore, Katie Ruth waited to bear her first child. She lay in bed in the second-floor front bedroom of her parents' house at 216 Emory Street, near the corner of West Pratt. The house was one of four connected row dwellings, numbered 212 through 218, with the red brick façade and white marble steps so typical of Baltimore. It was a narrow home, barely 12 feet wide and 59 feet long, facing a street that is more like an alley.

If it's a boy, Katie had long ago decided, she would name him after her husband, George Herman Ruth, a big, dark-haired hulk of a man who today was working in his father's grocery-saloon a few blocks away on Frederick Avenue. George and Katie lived over on Frederick, but today she wanted to be near her mother. In the remaining seventeen years of her life, Katie would give birth to four boys and four girls, including two sets of twins, but only two would reach adolescence: "Little George," to be born today, and Mary Margaret, who came five years later.

In pain, frightened, Katie looked over at her mother, who sat nearby and spoke soothingly to her in German. There, too, was Minnie Graf, a midwife who had pulled dozens of yowling babies into the tough world of South Baltimore. Outside, snowflakes fell to the cobblestones of the narrow street. A few heavily bundled women scuttled along with bags of groceries. The men of the neighborhood—European immigrants or the sons of immigrants—were off at work in the nearby factories, railroad yards, and docks that made Baltimore one of America's most important cities.

He was a big child and nearly tore her apart. A few hours later, after Mrs. Graf had gone, "Little George" lay sleeping beside his exhausted mother. His father, after coming from work early that evening, fussed and cooed, smiling proudly. There was a great resemblance that grew with the years. "Dad had a mustache. Old Germans always did," said Ruth's sister recently. "And the Babe was bigger than his dad—but the *face,* oh my goodness!"

The grandparents were also proud to see Kate's firstborn. Her father was Pius Schamberger, a Catholic, born in Germany, who had lived in the house on Emory Street for seven years. He had been a saloon keeper and a grocer, and now he worked as an upholsterer. Kate would list her maiden name on her son's birth certificate as "Kate Shamberg." Either she had "Americanized" the surname, a common practice among first-generation Americans, or a careless city clerk saved her the trouble, also a common practice.

Babe Ruth's paternal family roots are more obscure. As late as 1944, ten years after he retired from baseball, *Current Biography* said, "His name was reportedly George Herman Ehrhardt. Just when and why the Babe's name became Ruth is not clear." But Ruth always vehemently denied this. An official in the Baltimore Bureau of Vital Statistics recently confirmed—"for the millionth time," he added—that a George Herman Ruth is, indeed, shown as the father on the Babe's birth certificate. Local directories of the era list "Big George" as a driver, an agent, a salesman, and a gripman on a cable car. His daughter adds that "for a time Dad was in the harness business, and later he and his brother John sold and installed lightning rods for barns, schools, and farmhouses." According to the biography by his second wife, Claire, the Babe's paternal grandparents were a Peter Ruth, of German descent, born in 1801 in Bucks County, Pennsylvania, and Kaziah Reager, of part-Irish descent, born in 1805 in Lancaster, Pennsylvania. The dates seem unrealistic, because Peter Ruth would have been ninety-four years old when his first grandson was born. If anything, he may have been the Babe's great-grandfather. Another, more likely source refers to the grandfather as a John A. Ruth, a Lutheran, who founded a lightning rod business in Baltimore in 1873 and had two sons, John A., Jr., and George Herman, the Babe's father.

* * *

It was a smaller, simpler, and far poorer America in 1895 (Jack Dempsey was also born that year, and F. Scott Fitzgerald and John

Dos Passos the next). Grover Cleveland presided over a nation of 65 million people in forty-four states. The fortunes of the rich were not yet threatened by a federal income tax, and the typical worker labored ten or more hours a day for ten dollars a week—when he found work. A severe recession, starting two years before, had caused widespread unemployment.

Baltimore, a thriving port on the Patapsco River near Chesapeake Bay, was a stimulating place for a young boy. "Little George" spent his earliest years with his parents at 339 South Woodyear Street, not far from the Baltimore & Ohio yards, but by the time he was six his father owned a saloon with an upstairs apartment at 426 West Camden.

He came of school age shortly after the outbreak of the Spanish-American War, the nation's first big venture into imperialism. Textbooks taught children that the United States was the "freest, most enlightened and powerful government on earth," and that "half-civilized peoples, like the Chinese and the Mexicans, have towns and cities . . . but have few arts and little intelligence." The young Ruth, however, spent little time in school. His earliest memories were of the dirty, hectic streets, of cart drivers whipping their horses and cursing at the urchins who made a playground of the narrow thoroughfares, of shopkeepers who chased and beat them when they stole fruit from the stands. "It was a rough, tough neighborhood," he once said, "but I liked it." He must have been exposed to the German language, at home and perhaps on those teeming streets. Years later, writer Fred Lieb recalled chatting in German with Lou Gehrig and "Ruth got into the conversation . . . he spoke it surprisingly well."

Ruth rarely spoke of his parents. Once, however, shortly before his death, he bitterly confided to Bob Considine, "My mother hated me, didn't like to see me chewing"—tobacco, not gum, of course. But his parents were victims of their own impoverished circumstances. His mother was constantly ill and constantly pregnant. His father worked long hours behind the counter of a small saloon. So Little George roamed the streets of South Baltimore with dozens of other young urchins, rarely attending school. By his own admission, years later, he was "a bum." Once, he stole a dollar from the saloon till and bought ice cream for all his pals. When he confessed to the theft, his father (who apparently had never heard the tale of another George who was rewarded for admitting that he'd chopped down a cherry tree) dragged the boy down to the cellar and beat him with a horsewhip. So Little George took some more money.

One night soon afterward a brawl erupted in the saloon, and shots were fired. When police came running, a neighbor complained, "There's a young kid living there; it's no place for him."

So on June 13, 1902, George Herman Ruth and his seven-year-old son got off a streetcar in front of Saint Mary's Industrial School for Boys of the City of Baltimore, at the corner of Caton and Wilkens Avenues. The courts had committed the boy there until age twenty-one. Inside the office, while his father made the arrangements, Little George broke down and cried. A pleasant man in clerical garb tried to soothe him. He told him that he'd be given a fine home and made a useful citizen. But Little George didn't want to stay. He already missed his parents, and he liked the freedom of the streets.

But he stayed. Saint Mary's was a Catholic protectory run by the Xaverian brothers. It was a training school for orphans, delinquents, children of poor parents who could not support them, and strays picked up on the city's streets (one such stray who boarded briefly at Saint Mary's during Ruth's tenure was a youth named Asa Yoelson, later known as Al Jolson). Spread over several acres, the school held eight hundred boys in six interconnected gray stone buildings. Little George shared a dormitory with two hundred roommates.

Many Americans think of Ruth as an orphan because he lived so much of his youth in Saint Mary's. Of the dozen years from age seven to nineteen (1902 to 1914), he spent eight inside its walls. He was sent back home after his first month there, but his parents returned him to the school in November. When Considine asked why, Ruth snapped, "What do you think? My old man had a saloon. For me, when he wasn't looking, the stuff was free." His mother softened and begged for her son's release, but when he came home she lost patience with his wild behavior and beat him until she herself was near collapse. He came home again just before the Christmas of 1902, when the family moved to Hanover Street, and stayed for more than a year. But back he went at age nine and was confined for four years. Brother Herman, the head of the school's recreation program, recalled the twelve-year-old Ruth as "pretty big for his age, on the wiry side. He was full of mischief, nothing timid about him; an aggressive, shouting boy, always wrestling around with the others."

The Xaverian brothers called him George, but his friends had choicer sobriquets.

Because of his gaunt face, large, flat nose, and fleshy mouth, they called him Nigger Lips, according to Louis J. "Fats" Leisman, a former pal of Ruth's at Saint Mary's.

Released again around 1908, Ruth stayed home until 1910, when his mother died. A year later, his father took him back once more but sent him away for keeps in 1912, when he was a big, gawking seventeen-year-old. It was about that time, one cold winter day, that Brother Paul, the superintendent of Saint Mary's, spotted Ruth sitting outdoors, wearing a thin shirt that was unbuttoned. "Aren't you afraid you'll catch cold, George?"

"Naw, not me, I'm too tough."

He had to be tough. His old pal Fats Leisman doesn't recall a single time in all their years together when the elder Ruth came to visit his son. "Guess I'm too big and ugly for anyone to come see me," he would say to Fats with a smile.

However, Ruth always spoke warmly of his years at Saint Mary's and with great affection for the Xaverian Brothers, who became his surrogate parents. The child of a mixed marriage between a Catholic and a Lutheran, he was given little religious direction at home. He became a Roman Catholic at Saint Mary's, where he was given his first Holy Communion, regularly went to confession, and had the faith drummed into him daily. When he was about fifteen he even confided to one of the brothers that he wanted to be a priest, but his statement expressed admiration more than commitment.

Unlike his aimless existence on the streets, he led a rigid, orderly life. A bell woke the youngsters at six sharp, and they attended Mass each morning before breakfast. Afterward they made their beds and hurried off to class. Once a boy reached fourteen years of age, he was assigned three hours of class and three hours of work daily. Young Ruth was assigned to the third floor of a four-story stone building on the school grounds, where he made work shirts for a private company called City Tailor. (Years later, while earning $80,-000 a season, Ruth reminisced, "I was the best shirtmaker in the school!" Then, fingering the silk of his tailor-made shirt, he said, "That's why you can't fool me about shirts to this day. I worked on an electrical machine that stitched the parts together; cheap shirts, those blue and gray cotton ones that in those days went for a dollar. Say, it's quite a trick getting a collar just right on a shirt!")

The boys worked at their jobs five and one-half days a week and were allowed to play in the big yards every afternoon and all day Sunday—after Mass, of course. During recreation time, every boy was required to take part in some team sport. It was a busy life.

Brother Gilbert, one of the men who helped to discover Ruth for the big leagues, later recalled that "when most boys are spending their leisure in the movies or standing around corners smoking cigarettes, Babe Ruth was getting ten hours' rest every night and from two to three hours' batting practice every afternoon for at least ten months out of the year. . . . Unconsciously, he was being molded into the longest hitter of all time."*

Brother Matthias, the prefect of discipline at Saint Mary's, was perhaps the biggest single influence on the young Ruth. A giant of a man who stood six feet six and weighed more than 250 pounds, Matthias seems to have been the ideal father figure that Ruth needed. He seldom raised his voice, but his stern, imposing presence earned the respect of all the boys, who called him the Boss. Ruth was awed by the big man's gentle strength and often spoke with reverence of how Matthias stood at one end of the yard and batted baseballs clear over the school fence in center field. Soon, he tried to emulate Matthias's every gesture, even the way he walked. The short, pigeon-toed stride, body leaning forward, which became the Ruth trademark, was nearly identical to Matthias's manner of walking. They spent hours together, catching baseballs. Once, Ruth was transferred to the Saint James Home, also operated by the Xaverian Order, an institution without walls in the City of Baltimore where the boys had more freedom. They worked in local factories, and their paychecks were delivered to the home, which deducted the cost of board, insurance, and laundry and deposited the remainder—minus spending money—in the boys' savings accounts. But somehow George got into trouble and was returned to Saint Mary's.

"The day the Babe returned," says Leisman, "he was dressed in a gray suit and was wearing a black baseball cap. As he entered the big yard, he walked very slowly and didn't seem to hear the voices of the three or four hundred boys screaming, 'Welcome back, Nigger Lips!'" But Brother Matthias was also there to greet him, with no scolding or recriminations.

During his last year at Saint Mary's, George escaped through a window and was gone for three days before school officials tracked him down. As punishment, he had to stand on the road between the little yard and the big yard for five days during recreation period. Then Matthias handed him a ball and a glove and told him he could join the boys once more.

Baseball was already the national pastime (the National League was formed in 1876 and the American in 1900) and was by far the major sport at Saint Mary's, which had forty-three teams. There were leagues according to age group. There were also "dormitory" teams, and "floor" teams, and "shop" teams, where the cabinet makers

---

* Gilbert was the baseball coach at nearby Mount Saint Joseph's College. In 1928 he published a long memoir in the Boston *Globe* about Ruth's early days. During the height of Ruth's career, the garrulous Brother Gilbert was a much sought-after speaker at men's club smokers.

played against the shirt makers or the boys in the print shop. Then there was the "main" team, the cream of the crop, which represented the Saint Mary's colors against other schools. The Babe soon became the star of the main team. He also played handball and football, and even fancied that he might become a boxer.

He started out on the team as a left-handed catcher, using a right-hander's catcher's mitt. In an elaborate ritual, which he soon perfected, he would catch the pitch in his gloved left hand, flip the ball in the air, stuff the mitt under his right armpit, seize the ball in his throwing hand, and fire it back to the pitcher.

Ruth's pitching career began by accident, Matthias recalled. One day the team's star pitcher was knocked out of the box and every relief pitcher that Matthias sent in was promptly mauled by the opposing batters. Ruth, "who always had a strange sense of humor, thought it was funny!" So Matthias handed him the ball and said, "If you're so smart, let's see how well you can do." He came in and didn't allow a hit for the rest of the game.

He was quite a batsman, too. One season, young George kept track of his home runs and estimated that he hit more than 60 in over two hundred games; they sometimes played as many as three games a Sunday. In 1912, the *Saturday Evening Star,* the Saint Mary's newspaper, published the account of a game where seventeen-year-old George Ruth batted leadoff; divided his time on defense as catcher, pitcher, and third baseman; got three hits, including a home run; and struck out six men.

"He Is a Fork-Hander"

A big red roadster glided through the front entrance of Saint Mary's Industrial School and stopped in the front yard. It was a cold day in late February of 1914, just a short while after George Ruth's nineteenth birthday. The driver of the car was Jack Dunn, owner and manager of the Baltimore Orioles of the International League. Two friends rode with him: Fritz Maisel, third baseman of the New York Yankees, and Brother Gilbert, the baseball coach of nearby Mount Saint Joseph's College. Dunn needed talent to stock his team for the coming year. He was eager to sign the Mount Saint Joseph's star pitcher, "Rube" Meadows, but the obstinate young twerp refused to leave school. To placate Dunn, Brother Gilbert promised to show him "the greatest left-handed pitching prospect outside of organized baseball."

The previous fall, at the urging of a catcher on his college team, Gilbert had gone to Saint Mary's to observe the "batting prowess of one George Herman Ruth." As he sat in the bandstand behind first base, Gilbert watched Ruth catch the warm-up throws of the Saint Mary's pitcher, and in his customary ritual take off the glove and return the pitch.

" 'He is a fork-hander,' I remarked, realizing that a left-hand catcher is the equivalent of a bone out of joint, or a misfit in society."

In the first inning, with a man on third base and two out, Gilbert recalls, "I had my first vision of George Herman Ruth as a batter. . . . Clad in a uniform that was a trifle small for him, there strode up to the plate one of the most graceful big men that I have ever seen. . . . The opposing pitcher turned his back to home plate and waved his outfielders back." Moments later, "simultaneously inclining his body forward and jauntily thrusting his right leg backwards . . . George Ruth . . . took a lusty cut at the ball . . . and all eyes on the big campus followed the pellet as it fairly screamed over the right fielder's

18

head. . . . That same day he hit three home runs." So strong was the fork-handed catcher's arm, adds Gilbert, that "a jest prevailed at Saint Mary's that unless a base runner had both feet on the sack, Ruth would throw him out."

A few days later, Brother Gilbert was introduced to Ruth, who, Gilbert recalled in his 1928 memoir, "was the same great big, good-natured kid that he is today. Free from guile and deceit of any kind . . . he looked out on the world with the grave and solemn wonder of a child."

It seems that Gilbert was not the only one to tell Jack Dunn about the Saint Mary's star. Joe Engel, then a pitcher for Washington, had gone to Emmitsburg, Maryland, in the summer of 1913 to pitch for the alumni of Mount Saint Mary's College on Commencement Day. As he later related the story to Tom Meany, there was a preliminary game in progress between the Mount Saint Mary's freshmen and a rowdy bunch from a "Baltimore orphanage," which was also called Saint Mary's. Pitching for the orphans was a tall fellow whose dark hair was clipped close on the sides and "roached" on top, a bristly straight-up style that was popular in the late 1890's. "Roach" and all, he struck out eighteen or twenty of the frosh batsmen, and after the game he sat around banging his left hand against a huge bass drum. The next day, on the train back to Washington, Engel saw Dunn and told him he'd seen a big left-hander "who's got real stuff," adding as an afterthought, "He can also beat the hell out of a bass drum."

So on that raw winter morning in 1914, Dunn, Maisel, and Brother Gilbert sought out Brother Matthias, whom they found clad in over-alls, working in one of the Saint Mary's shop buildings. When they sp spoke of Ruth, Matthias—never one to waste words—said, "He can hit."

"Can he pitch?" asked Dunn.

"Sure, he can do anything."

Off they went in search of Brother Paul, the superintendent. By now, rumors had swept through the play yards that Jack Dunn was there to sign Ruth to a professional contract, and a crowd of youngsters fell in step behind them.

Then they spotted George, who by now measured six feet two inches and weighed nearly 170 pounds. He wore tight blue overalls and, along with one of his buddies, was sliding across an ice pond in the windy yard, whooping and yelling.

Nudging Dunn, Gilbert said, "There's our victim."

"He's a Rube Waddell in the rough," said Dunn, his eyes popping wide.*

---

* Rube Waddell was an eccentric, fireballing left-hander who was one of base-ball's top pitchers at the time.

"George!"

He came running and sliding over, breath steaming from his broad nostrils, three shiny metal rings on the fingers of his pitching hand.

The first contract was for $600 a season, not bad at a time when sirloin steak cost twenty-seven cents a pound and boys worked in sweatshops for forty cents a day. There were "certain legal difficulties," Brother Paul explained, because "George is supposed to stay here until he's twenty-one." But these were ironed out, and Jack Dunn, owner of the Baltimore Orioles, also became the guardian for his newest pitching prospect.

On March 2, 1914, Dunn waited outside the gate of Saint Mary's in his red roadster. There had been a terrible storm the night before, tearing the roofs off many homes, knocking down trolley car lines, making a shambles of the harbor. But the trains south were running. George Ruth, carrying his few possessions in a cheap suitcase, stood behind the barred gate and shook hands with the Xaverian brothers. Matthias's last words to him were, "You'll make it, George." As for the boys at Saint Mary's, we rely once more upon Brother Gilbert, who tells us, "Yes, friends, and those whole-souled youngsters, even in the loss of their idol, experiencing as they were commingled feelings of joy and sadness, sincerely meant all that was contained in their ardent wish . . . a sonorous chorus rent the air with, 'Best of luck, George!' "

As Dunn's car headed for Union Station and the train that would take them southward to the spring training camp in Fayetteville, North Carolina, one of the Xaverian Brothers, in a neat, flowing script, wrote the final entry in George Herman Ruth's record at Saint Mary's: "He is going to join the Balt. Baseball Team."

And George Herman Ruth, wiping a tear from his eye, looked out the car's side window at the gray walls of Saint Mary's receding in the distance. And then, yes friends, came the grand revelation: Holy shit! No more slop on the supper table and fighting for seconds, no more sneaking a puff on a cigarette in the john, no more whacking off under the sheets after dark! Yoweeeeeeeeeee! Jack Dunn, his new guardian, was so terrorized by the barbaric yawp that he nearly drove his shiny red roadster off the road.

* * *

This was George Ruth's first train trip, and probably his maiden voyage beyond the city limits of Baltimore. The train left Union Station the evening of March 2, 1914, bound for Washington and points south, and would reach the Orioles' spring training camp in Fayetteville, North Carolina, the next day. Aboard were twelve Orioles, a scout by the name of Sam Steinman, trainer Walter Fewster, three Baltimore sports writers, and a few trunkloads of bats, balls, and other paraphernalia.

Jack Dunn—who would head south the next day with the rest of the team—accompanied George to the train and, just before he climbed the steps, slipped him a five-dollar advance. He felt rich.

Dunn's "babysitter" during the long train trip was Ben Egan, a big, jovial catcher, recently sent down to Baltimore from the major leagues. The prankish Egan ordered a few of the naïve recruits to "keep watch" on the Pullman porters during the night and prevent them from stealing the players' shoes left out in the corridor. "And don't let 'em give you any crap about they're only taking 'em off to give 'em a shine," Egan said, without the slightest trace of a smile. Another young player was told to maintain an all-night vigil, in order to assure that the team wouldn't ride past its destination. As for Ruth, Egan shipped him off to bed early, warning that he might have to pitch the next day. Pointing at the little clothes hammock that stretched from one end of George's upper berth to the other, Egan confided, with an insider's wink, "That's for pitchers to rest their throwin' arm." Several hours later, "as the train clickety-clacked southward," George lay sleepless while young voices rang out: "Stop! Thief! Hey, he's tryin' to make off with the shoes!" His arm, suspended in the tiny hammock, was stiff and hurt like hell. Sighing, he wondered whether he'd ever get the hang of being a professional pitcher.

George was never one to pay attention to his geography lessons at Saint Mary's. It had been near freezing in Baltimore. When the train pulled into Fayetteville the next day, he was amazed at the balmy weather. Last night's storm had left big puddles on the ground, but the temperature was in the seventies. He just couldn't get over it! The players took a bus to the hotel, checked in, and trooped toward the dining room for breakfast. "Order anything you want, kid," said one of the older men. "The club pays our feed bill during the spring." George was pouring maple syrup on his third helping of wheatcakes and ham when he sensed that some of the other men were staring at him. Chewing vigorously, he looked up, shrugged, and went back to his food. "I wouldn't have believed it if I hadn't seen it," said Roger Pippen, the young correspondent for the Baltimore *Sun*.

After the first spring workout, Pippen filed a story to his paper, calling Ruth "a promising twirler." And after watching Ruth hit one practice pitch after another over the outfielders' heads, Pippen wrote, "He takes a long lunge at the ball and hits it on the nose. He holds his bat down at the end and puts all his weight behind his swing."

When Ruth smacked one ball into a distant cornfield, Gilbert, in his memoir, assures us that the right fielder yelled, "Hey, Dunnie, if you want me to chase that pill, you'll have to provide taxi fare!" And, he adds, "one of the little colored boys" watching the workout shouted, "Molly Moses! Dat's sure a hittin' man!"

Fayetteville was like a wonderland to young George. He awoke at dawn, strolled down to the station—still marveling at the balmy weather—and watched the trains roar through. He was always first in line when the dining room opened for breakfast. His next stop was the hotel elevator; up and down he went, watching fascinated as the old Negro operator magically stopped the car level with the floor every time. One morning, he could stand it no longer and slipped the man one of his five dollars to let *him* run the thing. "A few minutes later," he recalled, "I left the door open on the third floor and was rubbernecking up and down the corridor, while I made the elevator go up another flight." Suddenly, a player screamed, "Pull your goddam head in there!" He did, just in time, but got a bawling out from Dunn, who soon heard of the near-decapitation.

"He was a wild one," said Ben Egan. "Had a habit of just taking off without telling anyone. He'd see a horse and buggy standing around, just anybody's, and he'd be off with it, full gallop, just for the ride. The same with other folks' bicycles." As Egan and Dunn chatted outside the hotel one day, "the Babe comes tearing up in a bike, swerves suddenly and goes smack into the back of a wagon load of hay. He bounces a few feet up in the air and comes right down on his back. Dunn runs over, shakes his finger and hollers, 'You wanna go back to that school? You behave yourself, y' hear? You're a ball-player, not a goddamn circus act!' "

There are several versions of how Ruth got his nickname. A former Saint Mary's inmate swears that he was called Babe the first day he arrived at the school, a frightened seven-year-old, and began to bawl. The most popular tale—and the one endorsed by Ruth himself—is that, on the first day of spring training, "Dunn practically led me by the hand from the dressing room to the pitcher's box. I was as proud of my Orioles' uniform as I had been of my first long pants. . . . 'Look at Dunnie and his new Babe,' one of the older players yelled." But it's also said that scout Steinman and newsman Pippen were out for a walk one evening when they spied Ruth tearing around town on a "borrowed" bicycle. "Roger," said the scout, "Dunnie didn't get that fellow from Saint Mary's, he got him from an infant asylum. We've got some real kids on this trip, and that Ruth is the biggest Babe of the lot." Whatever the true story, by the time the 1914 season got under way, articles by Pippen and other Baltimore writers frequently referred to the young phenomenon as "Babe" Ruth.

By March 6, just three days after the Orioles began training, the Baltimore *Sun* published a large photo spread of the team's promising recruits. Among them is one George Ruth, solemnly gazing at the camera, a tall, skinny fellow with a baggy uniform, a small fielder's mitt, and a tiny cap atop a shock of hair that dipped close to his right eye. His face looked gaunt, with heavy shadows under the eyes, a broad nose, and big, prominent lips. More ham and pancakes, and plenty of everything else, would soon fill in those features.

That very night, when rain forced the Orioles to cancel outdoor practice, they challenged a local high school team to a game of basketball, and the big, rawboned Ruth led them to an 8–6 victory. A day later, as the weather cleared, the Orioles divided up into "Regulars" and "Yanigans" and played their first practice game. Ruth, playing left-handed shortstop for the "Yanigans" and batting fourth, got three hits, including a mile-long triple. After the game, he sent a note to Brother Albans at Saint Mary's, gleefully reporting that "I am making good in basket-ball, baseball and everything else that they've got down here." Well, not quite. A few days later, a *Sun* dispatch noted that the Oriole rookies, Ruth among them, "were down in spirits." It seems that a "friend" of the players who came to the park each day brought a rig "similar to a roulette wheel" to the hotel one night. "He did a rushing business . . . the game was used again today, and at 5 o'clock the youngsters were like the farmer who bought the gold brick."

Soon the dispatches from Fayetteville were calling Ruth "a real find" who "has a world of speed and handles himself like a veteran." Manager Dunn was "all smiles" over Ruth, who was "smashing long flies to the cornfields." Within two weeks, Dunn announced that "Babe Ruth definitely will be staying with the team" and called him the "most promising player I have ever had."

Less than three weeks after leaving Saint Mary's, Ruth got his first taste of big league competition when he came in as a relief pitcher to snuff out a rally by the Philadelphia Phillies. A show called "Along Came Ruth" was playing on Broadway at the time, and one Baltimore paper used that as its headline to describe his triumphal entry. "His speed and benders called a halt to the merry-go-round," said the *Sun*. A week later in Wilmington, North Carolina, Ruth pitched brilliantly for nine innings in an exhibition game against the world champion Philadelphia Athletics. The Athletics' cleanup batter had touched Ruth for three hits, and while Baltimore batted in the seventh, the Babe, who never read the newspapers, scratched his head and said, "Dunnie, who's that big stiff on third base? I can't seem to get him out." The older players on the bench roared with laughter. The "big stiff" was Franklin "Home Run" Baker, who the previous season had led the American League with twelve home runs.

On April 13, a few days before the 1914 season opened, the New York Giants came to town and beat the Orioles 3 to 2. But the New York *World* reported that Baltimore's young left-hander, "Baby Ruth," had pitched a fine game against the big leaguers. A few days later, on a Sunday, the Brooklyn club of the National League also stopped in Baltimore en route to its official opening game.

Casey Stengel, then an outfielder for Brooklyn, recalls his first encounter with Ruth. "Now, there was no Sunday ball in Baltimore," he says, "but you could play on the racetrack outside the city. . . . A young kid is pitching for the minor league club; you know, in those days, folks was beginning to part their hair on the side, but this kid you could see had sort of dark curly hair and parted it in the middle. Well, I'm playing right field and this kid comes up. . . . I don't play very deep because after all, this kid is a pitcher on a minor league team . . . anyway, the kid hits the ball way over my head and this is a race track, mind you, and there's no fence. I run like the blazes . . . and hold this kid to a triple. . . . Next time the kid comes up . . . I got out about thirty-five feet deeper than any right fielder has any business playin'. Know what happens? The kid hits the ball over my head again. I'm runnin' and runnin', remember this place got no fence, and I'm sayin' this is a heck of a way to spend a Sunday. . . . Well, the next year, we play the Red Sox in the World Series . . . who's pitchin' for the Red Sox but that kid from Baltimore, the one who hit the two balls over my head with his hair parted right in the middle."

Babe Ruth made an auspicious debut with the Orioles on April 22, 1914. He shut out Buffalo 6 to 0, allowing only two hits and getting two of his own, including a single his first time at bat. But only two hundred people came to Oriole Park to see it. "There were nearly as many hot dog and crab vendors as fans," said one witness. In the meantime, some 2,000 fans were across the street cheering for the new Baltimore Terrapins of the "outlaw" Federal League, which had stolen away a number of big league players. That season the Federals would offer Ruth a $10,000 bonus and a salary of $10,000 if he jumped to their side, but he was under age and his "guardian" Jack Dunn would never have granted him permission to abandon the Orioles.

By now, Dunn had doubled the Babe's salary to $1,200 a season.

With his first $100 pay check, he rushed out and bought a motorcycle, the first major possession of his lifetime. Soon, he was zooming about the city of Baltimore, to all his old haunts, taking his friends on joy rides. He raced out to visit the brothers and boys at Saint Mary's and proudly showed off his machine. He dropped in to see his father and stepmother, Martha, who now lived above a saloon at 522 West Conway Street. He took his fourteen-year-old sister, Mamie, for thrilling rides around the block. Except for a few hours at the ball park each day, he spent morning and night zipping about town, terrorizing pedestrians and motorists.

By the second month of the season, Dunn boosted Ruth's salary to $1,800. Wow! Never had he imagined so much money. He went haywire. After one wild night on the town, he staggered into Oriole Park, his teammates held him under an ice-cold shower, and he went out to pitch a two-hitter, winning the game with his own hit in the final inning. On June 27, he faced Buffalo again and beat them 10 to 5. He never bothered to read the newspaper accounts of his victories. He almost certainly missed the front-page headline two days later, with the news that in Sarajevo, the capital of far-off Bosnia, Archduke Franz Ferdinand had been murdered by a pistol-wielding nationalist; within a month, all of Europe, chained together by alliances, would be at war. But the Babe kept pitching, batting, and speeding about on his new contraption, which by now bore the bruises of countless smash-ups. By midsummer, the Baltimore *Sun* was saying, "He is a wonder. . . . During the past few months, his shoots [fastballs] have made the whole baseball world sit up and pay attention."

"They Called Each Other 'Hon' "

Jack Dunn was desperate. His team was winning day after day, and young Babe Ruth had pitched eight victories in a row. But Dunn was losing money every day as Baltimore fans strolled past Oriole Park and filled the Federal League stands across the street. One afternoon, only eleven people paid to see Ruth shut out Rochester.

In dire need of cash, Dunn decided to sell off his best players and start a new club in Richmond, Virginia, the next year, far from Federal League competition. At least seven big league clubs were reportedly interested in Ruth, but Dunn first called Connie Mack of the Philadelphia Athletics (who had lent him $10,000 to buy the Baltimore franchise) and invited him to inspect his "great young left-hander," who would pitch the first half of a doubleheader against Newark a few days hence. Mack took the train to Newark and watched the Babe get blasted out of the box by a hail of hits in the first inning. Frantic, Dunn sent Ruth in for the second game, and this time he shut out the Newarkers. "He's a great pitcher," said Mack, "but he's worth more than I can afford." Next, Dunn tried another creditor, Joe Lannin, owner of the Boston Red Sox, who had lent him $3,000 to pay his salaries the previous month. When Dunn offered to sell his best pitching prospects, Lannin asked former Red Sox shortstop Freddy Parent, who was located in Baltimore, to look them over. Parent reported back that Ernie Shore was "ready to win in the majors right now." Ruth, he said, was "still very crude, but he can't miss with a little more experience." Dunn went to see Lannin at the Ebbets House in Washington, D.C., and—over dinner and drinks—auctioned off Ruth, Shore, and the big, prankish catcher, Ben Egan. In return, the $3,000 debt was canceled and Lannin gave Dunn a sum of money ranging from $8,500 to $25,000, depending upon whose account one believes.

26

A rule of organized baseball required that any player promoted to the big leagues receive at least a 25 per cent raise. So Ruth, whose salary had recently been raised to $500 per month by Dunn, was now a big leaguer earning $625 per month, just a few months after leaving Saint Mary's School. Lannin was so concerned that the Federal League might pirate away his three new properties that he got them to sign three-year contracts. He even insisted that Oriole secretary Bill Wickes accompany them as bodyguard on the Baltimore-Boston train to ensure that no Federal Leaguer would waylay them en route, and rewarded Wickes for his trouble with a $100 check.

Babe Ruth stepped off the train in Boston at 10 A.M. on July 11, and five hours later he was pitching against the Cleveland Indians in Fenway Park.

He went out to the mound "head down, pigeon-toed, walkin' with little short steps," recalls Harry Hooper, who then played in the outfield for the Red Sox and was team captain.

The "giant lefthander," as the Boston *Globe* described him, pitched "like a veteran" in his first major league game, keeping the Cleveland batsmen off balance with his speed and sharp curves. He won the game, 4 to 3, although he was removed in the seventh inning for a pinch-hitter.

If some clairvoyant had predicted Ruth's future in 1914, "he would have been thrown into a lunatic asylum," says Hooper, who recalls him as "an overgrown sweet pea, a big, uneducated rube." Years later, Hooper observes, "he got a little culture, and could even give nice little talks, but when he first came up he couldn't do *anything.*" Actually, he was little different from any typical nineteen-year-old, except that he could outhit and outeat several of them combined. "Lord, could he eat!" says Hooper. Most of the players ordered a sandwich when the train stopped at some town, but the Babe would "grab a half a dozen hot dogs, a few bottles of soda pop—he wasn't a heavy drinker then, mostly pop and a bit of beer—he'd stuff that in, give a few belches and roar, 'O.K., boys, let's go!' Guess they didn't feed him much in that school he went to." Once, during the hop from Boston to Saint Louis—which took nearly two days—the Red Sox were playing cards and killing time when the Babe said, "Boy, I'm still hungry. Who wants t'come to the dining car with me?"

"I'll go with you, Babe," said Hooper. The railroad line was famous for its thick beefsteaks, which were served on an enormous platter. Ruth, says Hooper, "asked for a double order, cold, and cleaned it up. Never saw anything like it!"

Some of the Red Sox veterans were very tough on the young rookie from Baltimore. When Ruth innocently walked up to take batting practice with the regulars, he was rebuffed with harsh insults. Later, in the locker room, he found his bat sawed in half.

Virtually every man went by a nickname, and there was little appreciation of subtlety. Manager Bill Carrigan was called "Rough," for obvious reasons. Clarence Walker, a new outfielder with an odd, tight walk, was dubbed "Tillie." (Cincinnati had a deaf-mute outfielder named Bill Hoy; everyone called him "Dummy.")

Ruth had a handsome physique, with a small waist, broad chest and powerful shoulders and arms. But his round face was homely, thick-lipped, and tanned as brown as a Brazil nut. He was also hairy and loud and naïve, and thought nothing of climbing back into the same soiled underwear he'd left in his locker before the game.

So he became "the Big Baboon." And it really got under his skin. One Red Sox star had a deep voice and during a quiet moment in the clubhouse loved to yell out, "Big Ba-BOON!" One time, they were dressing after a game, and the man bellowed: "Big Ba-BOON!" Ruth, tears in his eyes, rose from the stool in front of his locker and said, "Whoever it was, stand up and fight!" There were no takers. Later, the man was approached by Hooper, the team captain, who said firmly, "You're hurtin' his feelings and it ain't right. Next time you say that, I'll tell him who done it." Soon, the insults of his teammates became more good-natured than vicious. But not so with the other teams in the league. He was the ape, the baboon, the big monkey. And some players, from the safety of darkened dugouts, called him "nigger." This was the supreme insult, given Ruth's poor, lower-class upbringing close to the Mason-Dixon line. The "nigger" epithet became so widespread that, since Ruth was often described as an orphan, some people even today point to his hazy origins and speculate that one of his ancestors was black.

*   *   *

When Ruth first came to Boston, he boarded with a Mrs. Lindberg on Batavia Street, but he soon moved into Putnam's Hotel at Copley Square, where he received his first and only fan letter of the season, a note from Brother Matthias: "You're doing fine, George. I'm proud of you." Lonesome at first, he soon made friends in Boston. One was Michael Crowley, the son of a Boston police officer, who drove a taxicab and prowled about town with the Babe.

A Boston friend confided: "I don't know if the Babe had ever been with a woman before he joined the Red Sox. But after he found out what it was all about, why, he was a *bear*."

It was about this time, says the Babe in his autobiography, that

"I felt rich enough and old enough to take myself a wife. She was Helen Woodring, who came originally from Nova Scotia and was a waitress at Landers Coffee Shop . . . she used to wait on me in the mornings, and one day I said to her, 'How about you and me getting married, hon?' Helen thought it over for a few minutes and said yes." This is a classic example of the Babe's poor memory. The girl who became his wife for fifteen years was Helen Wood*ford,* originally from Manchester, New Hampshire. The nineteen-year-old Babe and the sixteen-year-old waitress, an attractive little girl with dark hair and dark eyes, soon went everywhere together. They often double-dated with Myrtle Durant, also a waitress at Landers, and Myrtle's beau, Parker Hatch. They skated at the Boston Arena. They smooched and listened to "Sylvia," the latest hit, on the Victrola. They thrilled to the adventures of Pearl White, who was starring in an exciting new movie serial, *Perils of Pauline.* They tried dancing the new craze of the day, the tango, which had become so popular that an Oklahoma paper lamented, "The effort of trying to look proper while dancing the tango must be very trying to the facial muscles of the up-to-date man," and a Little Rock editorial worried about "the tango face." It was still an age of public prudery (Chicago banned coed bathing on city beaches that summer, and a real estate man in Atlanta was arrested for wearing a sleeveless bathing suit), but the Babe and little Helen were soon on the most intimate terms, cooing and planning their wedding day. "They got along real nice," recalls Harry Hooper. "They used to call each other 'hon.' "

Then cruel fate—in the person of Red Sox owner Joe Lannin—intervened. By August 20 it was apparent that Boston had no chance to win the league championship, so Lannin shipped Ruth down to his Providence Clams farm team, which was fighting for the lead in the International League. In a tearful goodbye, the Babe promised Helen that he would return soon, and was off to Rhode Island. He raced back to Boston to be with his "hon" at every opportunity. During one of those trips, on a street near Cambridge, the Babe became involved in such a terrible auto smashup that his practically new driver's license was suspended. By September 27, the Providence team had played out its season, but Boston still had ten games to go, so Lannin called Ruth back to the big time, and to the arms of his faithful little Helen.

By season's end, his future looked very bright. Counting his appearances with Baltimore, Boston, and Providence, the Babe had won 24 games and lost only 10; he had pitched in five big league games, winning two and losing one. It was in Providence, on September 5 against Toronto pitcher Ellis Johnson, that he had smashed his first professional home run and beat the Maple Leafs 9-0 on a one-hitter. And on October 2, in Boston, he had made his first big league hit, a double off Len Cole of the New York Highlanders.

The Babe and Helen drove to Baltimore in mid-October. Since he was still a minor, he secured a note from his father giving him permission to marry. They motored to nearby Ellicott City, Maryland, on October 18 and in Saint Paul's Catholic Church the Reverend Thomas S. Doland pronounced them man and wife. The date and circumstances of this unheralded wedding became the source of great controversy in 1929, when Helen died. At the time, one Boston paper claimed that during the summer of 1914, while the Babe was in Providence, Helen took a train there with Myrtle Durant and Parker Hatch, and the four were married in a double ceremony. Another account puts the wedding in Boston, with the Ruths taking an apartment in the Back Bay section before he was shipped down to Providence in August. But the only wedding certificate traced by the press was dated October 18 in Ellicott City.

That was the first of four winters the young couple spent in Baltimore. Now Little George was a well-paid athlete. With his earnings, he went into partnership with his dad in a new saloon at 38 South Eutaw Street, on the corner of Lombard. It was directly across the street from the Bromo-Seltzer plant and a short walk from many other factories. The saloon-restaurant was located on the first floor, and the upper two stories were for living quarters. George and Helen had their own bedroom and ate with the rest of the family. The woman who cooked for the saloon also prepared the family's meals, and she specialized in sour beef and dumplings and other German dishes that Ruth loved. He helped tend bar with his father and also set up a small gym in the back room where young men from the neighborhood worked out on the punching bag and shot the breeze. It was a men's bar, no ladies allowed, and while having a drink a man could practically make a meal of the cheese, crackers, pretzels, hard-boiled eggs, and other free lunch tidbits on the bar. At Christmas, says Ruth's sister, who was a teenager at the time, "Dad and the Babe used to decorate the place with wreaths and streamers. It was a happy time."

SECOND INNING

Baseball is the American success story. It is
the only avenue of escape for thousands of
boys born into a dreary environment of poverty. It is, moreover, a great common ground
on which bartenders and bishops, clergymen
and bosses, bankers and laborers meet with
true equality and understanding. The game has
proved in everyday language that democracy
works.

J. G. TAYLOR SPINK, publisher
of *The Sporting News*

"Two-Head!"

On May 6, 1915 (the day before a German submarine sank the liner *Lusitania* off the Irish coast), young pitcher Babe Ruth stepped up to bat in the third inning of a game at the Polo Grounds. Jack Warhop, the New York pitcher, let loose with one of his exotic underhanded deliveries, and Ruth hit what the *Times* called "a mighty homer" into the upper tier of the right-field stands. It was the first of 714 times during a regular game that the Babe would trot around the bases, tipping his cap and smiling.

His big bat was making him famous. Even then, a paper predicted that he had promise of becoming "one of the greatest drawing cards the game has ever known." On July 21 at Sportsman's Park in Saint Louis, he hit what was described as "the longest home run ever witnessed here"; the ball cleared the right-field bleachers, soared over Grand Avenue, and smashed the plate glass window of a Chevrolet dealer.

But he could only demonstrate his batting prowess every fourth or fifth day. He was a pitcher, and such a good one that he caused as much of a sensation as Sandy Koufax or Tom Seaver when they rose to stardom. When he was right, he was every bit as fast as the great Lefty Grove, many oldtimers insist. That year he helped Boston to win the pennant and led all American League pitchers with 18 victories and only 6 defeats.

Late that August, with Boston's pennant chances at stake and the bases loaded, Ruth faced the heart of the Detroit Tigers' lineup: Bob Veach, Sam Crawford, and Ty Cobb. He struck out the three sluggers in a row. Cobb was furious and protested heatedly that the young Boston pitcher was "doctoring" the ball to make it jump and dip. He pitched another crucial late-season game in Chicago when the White Sox were in second place, close behind Boston. The crowds were so large that an army of carpenters was hired to build extra seats in

33

the outfield. Every batter tried to knock short fly balls into the temporary stands for a groundrule double. But, recalls Harry Hooper, "the Babe blew it right past 'em. We won three out of four games in that series, killed their chances for a pennant, and as we left town all you could hear was the carpenters, hammerin' away, knockin' down the stands again."

Unlike the portly latter-day Ruth, he was rangy and fast on his feet. Earlier in the season, in a winning game against Philadelphia, the Boston *Globe* praised Ruth's "great bit of baserunning," when he dashed from first to third on a sharp single.

His running after hours was also attracting notice. Paul Gallico once described the young Babe's discovery of how life could be lived: "God, life was swell! All the food he could eat, beer and whiskey, girls with red or black or yellow hair and soft lips, baseball every day, nice warm places to sleep, silk underwear, fine warm clothing, plenty of pals, money in the pants pocket, more where that came from, name and pictures in the papers, a big shiny automobile to ride around in—wow!"

He got off to a fast start when the Red Sox trained at Hot Springs, Arkansas in the spring of 1915. It was a wide open town—a crude little forerunner of Las Vegas—with roulette, faro, crap games, horse races and every other imaginable way to risk one's money. One club owner lost so much there that he was forced to sell a pitcher on his team before the gamblers let him leave town. Ruth, says one Red Sox veteran, "had no idea of the value of money, and must've lost more that spring than he had coming for the whole season."

Memphis, a six-hour train ride from Hot Springs, was the next stop on the club's spring tour and offered no less opportunity for diversion. In early April, the *Globe* noted that there had been an early morning meeting of the Boston players, and three of the younger members were "called down very hard for breaking the club rules at Memphis." One young pitcher in particular "was fined a neat sum." During that spring tour, the Babe was spotted wandering about the streets of one town at four in the morning. When manager Carrigan demanded to know why he hadn't observed the midnight curfew, Ruth, a wounded expression on his face, replied, "But I *did*. I got to my room by midnight and went out again at a quarter past."

Ruth's first roommate on the road was pitcher Ernie Shore, a fellow alumnus of Baltimore. Soon afterward, according to a shopworn tale, Shore threatened to leave the team unless he was given a different roommate. "The Babe keeps using my toothbrush," Shore allegedly complained. When confronted with Shore's accusation, Ruth reportedly replied, "Gee, that's all right, he can use mine any time he wants." Here is a bowdlerized version of a much more randy tale. One night on the road, Ruth smuggled a girl into the room. Shore tried to sleep, but the moans, groans, and squeaking springs were impossible to ignore. Finally, with the sun nearly up, Shore dozed off. When he awoke, Ruth was snoring mightily and the girl was gone. Shore noticed four or five cigar butts on the floor next to Ruth's bed. When he inquired later that morning, the Babe smiled, saying, "Oh, that! I like a cigar every time I'm finished."

After Shore, Ruth roomed with Dutch Leonard, another fun-loving lefthander. They so abused the club curfew that manager Carrigan ordered adjoining double rooms on the road. He shared one with Leonard, and Ruth was paired off with an older man, Heinie Wagner, who doubled as coach and utility infielder. Even then he managed to break loose. One Sunday in Washington (ball games were not allowed to profane the Sabbath in those days), Ruth asked permission to be gone overnight so that he could visit his "people" in nearby Baltimore. The next afternoon, Ruth was out on the field, just a few feet away from manager Carrigan, when the Babe's father, sitting in a box near the bench, yelled out, "Nice goin', George; you're down here and never come to see us!"

"To this day I can see the scowl on Carrigan's face as he started for the Babe," chuckles Duffy Lewis, who was also there.

Part of Ruth's "charm," says former teammate Waite Hoyt, "was the utter unconsciousness of the sensation he was causing."

For example, he decided to take up golf. One day he went to a "high tone" course along the Boston shore together with Hooper, Larry Gardner, and Chester Thomas. Ruth could hit the ball a mile, but his aim was poor. He sliced one drive into a sandtrap and got down in there. He kept whacking away at the tiny ball but only came up with great clouds of sand. Soon he was red-faced, sweaty, and frustrated. Thomas just held his sides laughing, and Gardner yelled down into the trap, "Hey, Babe! Look at Thomas!"

"That sonofabitch!" yelled the Babe, and Thomas laughed all the harder. "That goddamn sonofabitch!" he yelled even louder, still flailing away at the sand. Later that afternoon, an official of the golf club icily suggested that the Red Sox players patronize some other course. "We got put off quite a few courses because the Babe cussed so much," says Hooper.

Ruth's presence in the Red Sox clubhouse was impossible to ignore. He loved to yell, play practical jokes, and wrestle around with the younger players. And he always prompted loud laughter when he tried to wrestle Chester Thomas, who weighed only 160 pounds, because the little catcher invariably pinned the big Babe to the clubhouse floor.

Although, as mentioned before, the vicious baiting about Ruth's appearance subsided once he became a Red Sox regular, his teammates couldn't resist kidding him. Now he was called "Tarzan," and he enjoyed the nickname until he found out from a writer friend that Edgar Rice Burroughs's creation was the "king of the apes." From then on, the cry of "Tarzan!" was like waving a cape in front of a bull.

One snowy night in Boston that winter, Dan Howley, another ballplayer, saw Ruth inching his car through heavy traffic along Washington Street. Howley yelled out "Two-head! Two-head!" This was Howley's private nickname for the Babe, "because he had such a big head." Ruth jammed on the brakes. He suspected who it was but couldn't see Howley in the crowd on the sidewalk. When Howley yelled it again, Ruth jumped right out of his car and ran after him. Howley escaped around a corner but snuck back a few minutes later, peeked out from behind a building, and saw Ruth still searching for him among the rush of pedestrians. "And there was his car standing where he'd left it, with the traffic jammed as far as you could see and the cops whistling and swearing awful!"

Gradually, however, Ruth learned to take the kidding with more equanimity. One day in Boston, with umpire George Moriarty behind the plate, the Babe had lost control over his pitches. Angered by the way Moriarty called one ball after another, he stormed toward the plate and yelled, "You've been missing plenty on me!"

"How many?" Moriarty asked.

Taken aback, Ruth stammered, "Well . . . at least fourteen!"

"Fourteen! Why, you big lug, you can't *count* up to fourteen!"

After retiring the side, Ruth went to the Boston bench and moments later yelled to the umpire, "Hey, George, look!" The umpire couldn't help laughing. Ruth was counting up to fourteen, using his fingers.

* * *

In a year, Ruth had gained twenty pounds and weighed about 190. Even when playing a game, he would send an usher for a hotdog, a bag of peanuts, or an ice cream cone, according to John Igoe, a young Boston druggist who later became Ruth's first business agent. Carrigan often bawled out Ruth for eating on the bench and finally issued a firm ban on food during the game. But this didn't prevent Ruth from sneaking off to the clubhouse to gulp down a snack. Late at night, said Igoe, "he'd sometimes cook up a two-pound steak, using a quart of chili sauce as flavoring, and then go to bed and sleep as peacefully as a child."

He gulped down life with the same gusto. The fact that his driver's license had been suspended the previous year was no hindrance to him. On several occasions, said the Boston *Herald,* "he has struck pedestrians while going at a speedy clip," and once, as a pedestrian himself, "he collapsed at Beacon Street and Massachusetts Avenue." But despite all his high living (the highest of which was on the road), he managed to find some time for his young wife, Helen. They went on bowling parties with the other Red Sox players and their wives, visited each other's homes, and played cards. They went to the movies (*Birth of a Nation* had its world premiere that year, and there was a riot in front of Boston's Tremont Theater as local blacks protested the film's alleged racial prejudice). Another pet amusement was to go to Revere Beach during the summer and shoot mechanical ducks. Ruth had a sharp eye and often hit 96 out of 100 shots. He also loved to dunk the African Dodger by heaving baseballs at a target. Once, said his friend Johnny Igoe, "he had seven hits in a row, and the dusky gentleman playing the part retired from business."

That first year in Boston, says Igoe, the Babe showed a fondness for rainbow-hued ties and checked suits. "On more than one occasion part of his raiment was really laughing at the other," Igoe recalled. One slushy afternoon that winter in Boston, Ruth headed to the Red Sox office for a meeting. He started out from home wearing rubbers over his bright yellow shoes. On the way downtown, one of the rubbers was lost in the mud and he came into the office without noticing the loss until someone mentioned it. He grunted, "One rubber's no good to me," and threw the other one out the window.

The Babe's only setback in an otherwise triumphant 1915 season came during the World Series, which Boston won in five games against the Philadelphia Phillies. Manager Carrigan—either because he was piqued at Ruth's wild behavior or simply because he preferred to use his veterans—didn't allow Ruth to pitch a single game. "I grabbed Carrigan's lapels before every game and demanded to know when I was to get my chance. . . . I ate my heart out on the bench," said Ruth. In the first game of the Series, however, Carrigan sent him up to pinch-hit against Grover Cleveland Alexander; he whistled a line drive to the first baseman who got him out on a fine stop. The great Ty Cobb, who covered the series for the New York *Sun,* observed, "I will venture that this series will create a record from one angle. That is for a pitcher to be sent in as a pinch-hitter. Ruth may claim that honor." He also claimed $3,780 as his winning share for the Series, a sum higher than his regular season salary of $3,500.

He did even better in 1916, taking home a series share of $3,910 as the Red Sox again won the pennant and beat Brooklyn in five games for the world championship. The Babe made his World Series pitching debut that October, winning the second game, a 14-inning thriller, by the score of 2 to 1; it was so dark at the end that no one could see the ball. That season established Ruth as one of baseball's finest pitchers. He won 23 games, lost 12 and had the best earned run average in the American League, allowing the opposition only 1.75 runs per game. His bat, too, made him an extra threat. In June, against Saint Louis, he made his first pinch-hit home run. Because of his fine year, the Red Sox increased his salary from $3,500 to $5,000. Just before Christmas, Joe Lannin sold the team to Harry Frazee, a New York theatrical producer. In turn, Rough Carrigan retired (by now he owned a bank and a string of movie theaters in Maine) and was replaced as manager by second baseman Jack Barry.

Ruth equaled his brilliant performance in 1917, the year the Russian Revolution broke out and America declared war against Germany. By May of that year, the Selective Service Act required that all able-bodied men register for the draft, and many were called to war. As a married man, Ruth was deferred and would later join a National Guard unit. That year he won 23 games for the second straight season. He put some of his money into a small Boston cigar factory that manufactured a Babe Ruth nickel cigar with his picture on every wrapper. "I smoked them until I was blue in the face," he said.

That summer, Ruth's temper provoked one of the most unusual situations in baseball history. More than 16,000 fans crowded Fenway Park to see Boston play Washington on June 23. The Red Sox were only 1½ games out of first place. Ruth, who had a 12–4 pitching record, barely warmed up for the contest and spent most of his time chatting with friends in the grandstand. His first two pitches to leadoff batter Ray Morgan were called balls by umpire Brick Owens. The second one was close to the strike zone and Ruth was visibly upset by the umpire's call. The third pitch was high, ball three. When he fired the next pitch and Owens called it ball four, Ruth rushed halfway toward the plate and yelled: "If you'd go to bed at night, you————, you could keep your eyes open long enough in the daytime to see when a ball goes over the plate!"

When Owens threatened to evict him from the game, Ruth yelled, "Throw me out and I'll punch ya right in the jaw!"

"You're outa of this game right now," said Owens, jerking his thumb.

This threw Ruth into a frenzy. He charged the umpire. Chester Thomas, the Boston catcher, tried to stop him, but Ruth ran right over him, reared back, and swung, missing the umpire's jaw but landing a solid blow behind the ear, knocking the man in the blue suit to the ground. This earned him a week's suspension and a $100 fine. When Ruth left he was replaced by Ernie Shore. Catcher Thomas was so shaken up that he had to be replaced by Sam Agnew. Moments later, Morgan tried to steal second base and Agnew threw him out. Shore went on to retire the next twenty-six Washington batters in a row for one of the few perfect games in baseball history.

The young Babe was clearly a creature of impulse. That November, according to a Boston paper, he was returning from an auto ride early in the morning "accompanied by a young lady." Two trolley cars were approaching from opposite directions. Rather than wait, Ruth tried to beat them across the tracks. He didn't make it. His car was caught between them and "smashed to a shapeless mass" as he "heroically stuck to the wheel." By some miracle, he escaped injury, but his lady friend was rushed to the city hospital in an ambulance.

By 1918, Ruth's slugging was the talk of fans around the American League. Never had anyone hit a baseball so far. So vicious was his swing, they even cheered when he struck out. The New York *Times* called him the "caveman of baseball" who wielded his deadly bat "just like the men of the stone age waved their mighty clubs."* He was said to "scoff" when he hit a single, merely "lift his eyebrows" at a double, and take only "a little interest" in a triple, because slamming home runs was becoming his specialty.

Because of the war in Europe, a short season (starting in May and ending on Labor Day) was required by Secretary of War Newton D. Baker's "work or fight" order. Athletes who didn't go to battle had to work in defense plants after the season. The war tax was ubiquitous. In one city, a woman whose yard adjoined a ball park had always sold seats in her tree for 5 to 10 cents, depending on how high the patrons had to climb. The price was advanced a penny, with the extra cent going to the war revenue. Americans were implored to "save all fruit pits" for the Red Cross, because the army needed them to make charcoal for gas masks. Some U.S. soldiers were already back home with wounds from European bullets. Correspondents brought back plaintive accounts of how hard it was to teach baseball to French youth, who perversely insisted upon kicking the small sphere around as though it were a soccer ball. "Throwing, it would seem, is distinctly an American achievement," said one reporter back from the front.

When Boston manager Jack Barry was called to war, Frazee re-

* An alliteration-happy editor headlined this story, "Boston Babe Bumps Big Batting Marks."

placed him with Edward G. Barrow, who had managed several minor league clubs and also served as president of the International League. Barrow, who was born in a covered wagon as his parents migrated westward, was a stocky man with bushy eyebrows, a former amateur boxer who never shrank from a brawl. During his career he had signed up the great Pittsburgh shortstop "Honus" Wagner and also Zane Grey, who played outfield for Washington before he made a fortune spinning Western adventure tales.

Barrow knew little more than the ordinary fan about baseball, and had brains enough to let Harry Hooper run the team on the field, but he did know how to run a business. In the minors he attracted fans by hiring world boxing champs John L. Sullivan, James Corbett, and Jim Jeffries to umpire games. Years later, he proudly claimed that in 1918 he began the practice of allowing spectators to keep foul balls hit into the stands, because he "got sick and tired of watching the ushers wrestling with the customers and building up a thousand dollars worth of bad will over a two-dollar baseball." Later he would begin the practice of marking the distance from home plate to various parts of the outfield fence.

"We called him Simon Legree . . . he was a strict disciplinarian, and merciless with people who didn't produce," says Hooper.

Barrow met Ruth in January of 1918, when the Babe and star first baseman "Stuffy" McInnis came to the Red Sox office to sign their contracts for the coming season. Ruth signed for $7,500, on the promise that he would receive $10,000 the next year if he made good. McInnis also signed up without great dispute. Barrow was so pleased that he gave Red Sox secretary Larry Graver a $5 bill and told him to take both men out to lunch. In those days, such a sum was enough for a sizable lunch for three. But later that afternoon Graver returned and told Barrow, "You owe me $2.85." When Barrow sputtered and asked why, Graver stared at him and said, "Have you ever seen that big guy eat? He had a whole custard pie for dessert!"

Barrow was less concerned about food than about some of Ruth's other passions. Realizing that he would have to keep "a special eye" on his big lefthander, he rehired Heinie Wagner as a coach and roomed him with Ruth, warning the veteran that it was part of his job to see that the Babe obeyed training rules. But Ruth, as always, managed to escape. Early in the 1918 season, the Red Sox had just finished a Saturday game in Washington. Sunday was an open date, and a doubleheader was scheduled in Philadelphia on Monday. En route from Washington to Philadelphia that Sunday, Ruth hopped off the train at Baltimore. Later he explained that he'd been struck by "a sudden longing" to see his sister and didn't have time to ask anyone's permission. Barrow hit the ceiling and immediately sent coach Wagner off like a bloodhound on his trail. On Monday, minutes before game time, the young bon vivant and the older coach showed up together at the ball park, both of them red-eyed and contrite. Barrow gave Ruth such a violent bawling out that his young star threatened to quit and join a team in the Delaware River Shipbuilding League. The Boston club filed an injunction to prevent him from playing elsewhere, and Barrow, calmer by now, reached an understanding with the Babe. He knew that Ruth was a gold mine as a gate attraction and feared losing him. But he almost lost him for good that May. The Babe had a sore throat, and the team trainer tried a remedy that cured the cold but nearly killed the patient. He took a big swab of cloth, poured nitrate of silver on it, and reached deep into Ruth's throat. The Babe began to strangle. Barrow, who was nearby, heard Ruth's gasps and rushed him to a drugstore near Fenway Park, where he had a violent spasm. The druggist managed to neutralize the effect of the chemical. Barrow fired the trainer immediately. It was a week before Ruth could swallow food comfortably, and years later he would claim, "I always had a strong voice, but I believe it was so husky because of that stuff put into my throat."

Ruth was hitting so well by the middle of 1918 that papers around the country called him "the Boston Terror" and predicted he would set a new home run record if allowed to play regularly. But Barrow was reluctant to lose Ruth's pitching talents, despite his young star's pleas for a regular spot in the lineup. That summer, a Boston paper even reported Ruth's "break with Barrow . . . over his desire to be in the game every day." Barrow suggested a compromise, offering Ruth the chance to pitch *and* play the outfield. But after a few weeks of this experiment, Ruth wore a leather strap on his wrist and refused to pitch, claiming that his arm was weary.

"Tired!" Barrow barked at him. "Of *course* you're tired! You're running around all the time! If you'd stop your carousing at night you could play every day and never feel it!"

Ruth begged Hooper, the team captain, to intercede. But when Hooper did, Barrow shot back, "Why, I'd be the laughin' stock of the league if I put its best lefthander in the outfield!" But Hooper kept after him and was joined by Everett Scott and Heinie Wagner and some of the others. One day, after Ruth had pitched, Hooper went up to Barrow and said, "Ed, we had a real good crowd. Have you noticed that every time Babe pitches we have a big crowd?"

Barrow nodded and Hooper continued: "Well, do you think they come out here to see him pitch or to see him hit? Why don't you put him in there every day?"

A few days later Barrow gave in, but he warned, "Mark my words, the first time he gets into a slump, he'll be down on his knees askin' me to pitch again!"

That time never came. From the day that Barrow relented, Ruth appeared in the lineup against righthanded pitchers and took only occasional turns on the mound. The metamorphosis from pitcher to slugger was nearly complete. In his first four seasons as a Red Sox pitcher, Ruth had hit a total of 9 home runs in 361 times at bat. But in 1918, while winning 13 games as a pitcher, he batted 317 times, had an even .300 average, and hit 11 homers, enough to tie Tillie Walker of the Athletics for the league title (Gavvy Cravath of Philadelphia led the National League with only 8 homers that year).

He still had much to learn about the finer points of outfield play. Hooper was the regular right fielder, who contended with a blinding sun field in Boston. There was a big, awkward fellow named Braggo Roth playing left field for the Red Sox that season. So Hooper decided to put Ruth in right and play between the two young outfielders, in center.

"Sakes alive," he says, "if someone hit a ball out to me, I'd hear those footsteps comin' from both sides and I began to fear for my life! Both of them were gallopin' around that outfield without regard for life or limb, hollerin' all the time. I said, holy cripes, I'm gonna get out of here before I get killed! So I shifted Babe to center and moved myself to right, just to keep clear of those two. Sheer self-preservation on my part. But the Babe learned fast. He had a fine throwing arm and did things instinctively."

Ruth would have had 12 homers that season—and a career total of 715—were it not for an archaic ruling. On July 8, the Red Sox were locked in a scoreless tie against Cleveland. Amos Strunk singled for Boston in the tenth inning. Ruth came up and blasted Stan Coveleski's first pitch two-thirds of the way into the right field bleachers. "Believe It or Not" cartoonist Robert E. Ripley later called it "the longest hit ever seen at Fenway Park, although he got credit for only a triple." The rules in those days provided that if a batter drove in the winning run to end a game he received credit for only as many bases as he had actually touched before the run scored. Strunk tarried long enough to allow Ruth to reach third before he crossed the plate. Later the rule was changed so that a game-ending home run would count for four bases, but it was never made retroactive.

On Saturday night, August 24, as the Babe celebrated his 3–1 pitching victory against St. Louis that afternoon, his 46-year-old father lay dying on a street in Baltimore.

It was a strange family tragedy, never adequately explained. That night, George H. Ruth was running the family saloon at the corner of Eutaw and Lombard streets; the same saloon that the Babe had helped him to establish a few winters before. Ruth's second wife Martha had a sister who was married to a man named Oliver Bleefelt. Apparently, he had not been living with his wife for some time. She had recently returned from a hospital and was staying with the Ruths, above the saloon. A few weeks before, Bleefelt had been arraigned in police court and charged with criminally assaulting and enticing a 16-year-old girl from her home. According to Baltimore police, Mrs. Bleefelt's brother—a 30-year-old fireman named Benjamin H. Sipes—came calling to give her some money. His sister "began to cry and complained to him that her husband had been ill-treating her." Then, Sipes told police, he went into the saloon, where he found Bleefelt, and berated him for abusing Mrs. Bleefelt. There was a heated argument and Sipes left, walking across the street, where he stood in front of a cigar store. For some reason never explained, Ruth's father emerged from the side entrance of the saloon, strode up to Sipes, "and hit him on the cheek. He reeled and another blow felled him. While on the pavement, Ruth kicked him, but he managed to get up and struck Ruth, who was on the edge of the curb. The saloonkeeper lost his balance, fell backwards, and cracked his head." Bystanders carried Ruth into the saloon. Unable to revive him, they rushed him to University Hospital, a few blocks away, where he died the next morning. After a coroner's inquest two days later—"the accused told a straightforward story which made a very good impression on the jury," said the Baltimore *Sun*—the coroner found that Sipes "delivered the fatal blow in self-defense." At 2 P.M. on Wednesday, August 28, Big George Ruth was laid to rest in Loudon Park Cemetery. Among the mourners were his wife, Martha; his daughter, Mary (who had married just three months before); and his son, Babe, who had rushed down on the train from Boston. When his dad was lowered into the grave, "it was the first time I ever saw George cry," said a relative from Baltimore. The twenty-three-year-old baseball star was now truly an orphan.

Because the World War continued in Europe, the major leagues curtailed their regular season and began the 1918 World Series on September 5. Barrow surprised the experts by choosing Ruth to pitch the opening game, rather than his 21-game-winner, Carl Mays.

The war was very much in evidence. At one game, a Boston paper noted the presence of "sixty pale and modest heroes who have been invalided home from the horrors of the Marne battlefield; these wounded Yanks had their first taste of enjoyment since they got out of ear shot of the thundering shells of the Huns." During the seventh-inning stretch of the first game, there occurred an event "far different from any incident . . . in the history of baseball." As the crowd rose to take "their afternoon yawn," the band broke forth to the strains of "The Star-Spangled Banner." "The yawn was checked and heads were bared as the ballplayers turned quietly about and faced the music. . . . First the song was taken up by a few, then others joined, and when the final notes came, a great volume of melody rolled across the field." To the players, however, money was of even greater consequence than patriotism. They threatened to strike at one point during the Series because so much of the gate would be contributed to war charities, and—for the first time—players from all first-division clubs would share a portion of the proceeds. But American League president Ban Johnson, "who was drunk out of his mind," according to one witness, made a florid clubhouse speech and managed to bully and cajole the two teams into continuing with the Series, even though the share for each winning player had dropped to barely $1,000.

In the dugout just before the first game, Barrow stressed the fact that Cub outfielder Leslie Mann—a right-handed batter who was so stocky that John McGraw called him The Centaur—was murderous against left-handed pitching. "Don't let up on him at any time, and don't let him dig in at the plate," Barrow warned Babe.

"Don't worry, Eddie. I'll take care of him," said Ruth.

The game began. The leadoff hitter was Max Flack, a fellow about Mann's size, who batted left-handed. Ruth fired one directly at Flack's head and flattened him to the ground. White-faced, Flack stood frozen as Ruth blazed the next three pitches over the plate. After the inning, a smiling Babe said, "Well, Eddie, I guess I took care of that Mann all right, eh?" Barrow scratched his head because Mann, who was third in the batting order, had singled off Ruth. It finally dawned on Barrow in the fifth inning that the Babe had mistaken one player for the other. In that inning, according to one newspaper account, "Flack took the full force of one of Ruth's shoots right on the top of his cap . . . it was a fearful bang which resounded through the stands as the ball and Flack's head met. Three doctors and half a dozen undertakers forgot about the game and were on their toes in a second, thinking that an important case was at hand." After that inning, Barrow took Ruth aside and patiently explained to him the difference between Max Flack and Leslie Mann. Ruth, by the way, pitched nine scoreless innings, and Boston won the thriller, 1 to 0.

With Boston leading the Series two games to one, Barrow chose Ruth to start the fourth game. On the train ride back to Boston the

night before, Ruth—seemingly unconcerned about the next day's crucial test—was roughhousing with a young second-string pitcher. They
playfully punched each other and rolled all over the floor. Ruth took a
roundhouse swing, his adversary ducked, and the Babe's knuckles
smashed against the steel wall of the train. The middle finger of his
pitching hand swelled up three times its normal size.

"You damn fool!" yelled Barrow.

But Ruth pitched and got credit for a 3–2 victory; he held the Cubs
scoreless for seven innings, then was relieved when they rallied for
two runs in the eighth. Until Chicago scored, Ruth had pitched 29⅔
consecutive innings in World Series competition without allowing a run;
this record endured more than four decades.* For the remainder of
his life, even after he'd hit 60 home runs in a season, the Babe was
proudest of his World Series pitching record. He helped to win his
own ball game against Chicago that day by tripling with two runners on
base. It is hard to believe that the *New York Times* correspondent
in Boston was writing about a pitcher when he said: "The Tarzan
of the Boston tribe, Babe Ruth, came to the plate, swinging his savage
looking black bludgeon. . . . Like Banquo's ghost at Macbeth's banquet,
the colossal figure of Ruth cast a sinister shadow over the Chicago club."
On a 3–2 count, Ruth whacked a tremendous line drive that rolled
to the fence, where it "nestled, bruised and lopsided against a sign
which advised the reader to eat somebody or other's bread . . . the
quiet folks of the Fenway stuck their heads out of the windows to
see whether an earthquake had struck their exclusive neighborhood."

Two days later, the Boston Red Sox were world champions, and
Babe Ruth—winner of two Series pitching duels and co-champion
home run slugger of the league—was a national hero. After the Series, he paid a visit to his family in Baltimore (the local press noted
that "the great and only Babe Ruth has fallen victim to the Spanish
flu," whatever that was) and then reported for defense work at the
Lebanon Plant of Bethlehem Steel. On November 11, however, an
armistice was declared—the great war was over—and soon afterward
Ruth returned to Boston.

Aspiring to lead the life of "a New England country gentleman," he
bought the 160-acre Sylvester Perry farm in West Sudbury, twenty
miles west of Boston, where, according to one report, "he cavorted
gleeful as a puppy."

The farm, about a mile and a half from the Sudbury train station,
became the Babe's biggest, newest toy. His wife, Helen, welcomed
the idea and may well have been the guiding spirit behind it. Since

---

* Whitey Ford of the Yankees set a new record that still stands, completing
33⅔ scoreless innings in the 1962 Series.

their marriage four years before they had drifted apart, as Ruth's career was in sharp ascendance, and she remained the plain little waitress, unable to cope with life in a fishbowl. No children had resulted from their union, although there were stories later that a few infants died in childbirth, adding tragedy to an already tragic mismatch. The Babe spent half the season traveling, away from Helen, and led an active life even while at home in Boston. The farm seems to have been Helen's last-ditch attempt to save their marriage. She once told a reporter, "Someday people are going to find I've kidnapped my own husband and run away someplace where we can lead a simple life, away from grandstands and managers and photographers. You know what I'd like to do? I'd like to slip away to a little farmhouse in the hills and have a little garden, and Honey could rest and play with me. We could fish and go on tramps together, and have a glorious time." Ruth entered farm life with the same zest as all new undertakings. The farm, which included a large pond, had cost him about $12,000. The rambling twelve-room house on the property dated back to 1737. There was also a garage, a large hen yard, and the charred remains of a barn. Soon after taking possession of the large home, Ruth paid a man to haul off the "junky old furniture," including many valuable Colonial period antiques. He enjoyed the outdoor life at Sudbury, chopping wood, hunting, fishing through the ice in his pond, skiing a bit, and tramping about in the woods with a pack of howling dogs, searching for rabbits and quail. One weekend he bought several shotguns and a case of shells, and invited a few of his friends up for a "shoot." Most of them were sedentary types who preferred to relax near the fireplace, swap tall stories, and pickle themselves with good whisky. But that night Ruth and two guests got dressed in khaki clothing, grabbed guns and lanterns, and trooped off into the darkness. Moments later, the windows rattled from the roar of gunfire. There was no big game to be found, but they'd discovered a pack of bullfrogs in the pond and were blasting them to bits. Leonard Small, a Boston *Globe* photographer, once visited the Sudbury farm and asked Ruth, "Why's a piece of the chimney missing?" Ruth explained that he was out of kerosene one morning and the fire was dimming. To "help it along," he siphoned some gasoline from his car and poured it on. A large hunk of iron caught him on the head as he ducked away from the blinding explosion, but no serious injury resulted.

"It's a Gift"

By the fall of 1919, Ruth was acclaimed throughout the country as "the greatest batsman the game has ever known," the "mastodonic mauler."

In one ball park after another, throughout the American League circuit and along the exhibition trail, his mighty home runs were called "the longest ever." The old era of bunts, hit-and-run, stealing bases, and scheming for the small advantage was being eclipsed by Ruth's raw power. The home run, as Tom Meany later observed, was like "the lethal knockout punch of Jack Dempsey . . . the broad, direct approach to victory, the shortcut so esteemed by Americans in sport and in business, in recreation and in war."

The year began on a note of uncertainty when Ruth, wintering at Sudbury, warned that his salary demands for the coming season "may knock Mr. Frazee silly, but I think I deserve everything I ask." The demands were humble in comparison with what he would earn in a few years. He wanted $15,000 for a single season (which would have made him the second highest-paid player in baseball, behind veteran star Ty Cobb), or $10,000 on the basis of a three-year contract. Frazee, who would hit the jackpot some years hence with his Broadway production of *No, No, Nanette!*, was now in tight circumstances. Despite Boston's fine showing in the previous two seasons, the attendance figures were disappointing. Frazee swore he would go no higher than $8,000 per season. So, when the steamer *Arapahoe* left New York harbor on March 18 to carry the Red Sox to their spring camp in Florida, Ruth was not aboard. His personal manager, Johnny Igoe, circulated tales that the Babe was working out in a Boston gymnasium and that promoters had offered him $5,000 (nearly five times more than his 1918 World Series share) for a single boxing match against heavyweight "Gunboat" Smith. Three days later, Frazee invited Ruth to a conference in Manhattan. The Babe arrived but didn't

47

appear ready to sign, because he hadn't even brought a suitcase. Finally, they agreed on $27,000, spread over three years. The Babe picked up a phone, asked a friend in Boston to rush down with his baggage, and caught the next available train to Tampa.

Frazee felt better about Ruth's contract a few days later, after a Red Sox exhibition game against the Giants at the old fairgrounds in Tampa. Batting against "Columbia George" Smith,* the Babe walloped a ball so far over right fielder Ross Youngs's head that those who saw the blow were awestruck. After the game, as Youngs stood where the ball fell, a group of writers—including Fred Lieb, Frank Graham, Paul Shannon, and Melvin Webb—observed as someone took a surveyor's tape and measured the distance to home plate: 579 feet!

Ruth still took occasional turns as a pitcher in 1919 (he won 8 games and lost 5), mainly to bolster an injury-riddled staff, but Barrow now conceded that his future lay in being a full-time slugger, and he appeared in all but ten of the team's 140 games that year.

He had quickly acquired all the habits and superstitions of a slugger. For nearly a year he used the same dark ash wood bat, carrying it gingerly on and off the field, not even entrusting this task to the clubhouse boy. Before a game, he would pat his weapon, cure it with tobacco juice, rub it with a piece of bottle—and it responded with one home run after another.

One day Harry Hooper, who had a sense of history, said to him, "When you get done with that bat I want it."

"I will like hell," said Ruth. "I'll keep this baby as long as I live."

But a few weeks later, Ruth cracked the bat slightly. After the game, he tried to repair it with tape and tiny nails. One day, however, he was called out on a third strike and became so furious that he slammed the bat against the plate. That was the last straw. The split in the wood was irreparable.

As Ruth strode back to the dugout, says Hooper, "his eyes were blazing."

Hooper sat next to him on the bench. After a few moments of silence, he ventured, "Babe, how about that bat?"

"Take this sonofabitch, I don't wanna see it as long as I live!"

Hooper took it, kept it, and many years later donated it to the Hall of Fame in Cooperstown.

*   *   *

On April 18, the Red Sox played an exhibition game in Baltimore, and Ruth's hometown fans honored him with a pregame ceremony.

---

* It was still somewhat rare for ballplayers to have attended college, and Smith's nickname meant that he had been a student at Columbia University.

When asked to explain his magical hitting powers, Ruth shrugged his big shoulders, stammered, pawed at the earth around home plate with his spikes, and simply said, "It's a gift!" Then he showed them just how gifted he was, smashing *four* home runs in the game. For good measure, he hit two more the next day.

Ruth didn't neglect his social life while hitting home runs. Barrow had hired Dan Howley as a coach that year, with the understanding that he would be Ruth's "keeper."

"Don't worry, Mister Barrow," he said. "I'll take care of that guy if I have to put a ring through his nose."

But Howley was no more successful than any of Ruth's other "keepers." The Babe was especially hard to find in Washington, where he had many friends. One night early that season Barrow slipped a porter at the Raleigh Hotel a couple of dollars to wake him when Ruth arrived, no matter the hour (the night before, he'd waited until 4 A.M. and finally retired without seeing his young star).

About six in the morning the porter knocked at Barrow's door and whispered, "That fellow just came in." Barrow put on his dressing gown and slippers and trudged down the hall to the room that Ruth and Howley shared. He saw a light through the transom and heard voices. But when he knocked, the voices hushed and the light was doused. Barrow found the door unlocked, so he entered and switched the light on. Howley had ducked into the bathroom, but the Babe was tucked beneath the covers, calmly smoking a pipe. Anger seething in his voice, Barrow asked, "Do you always smoke a pipe at this time of morning?"

"Oh, sure. It's very relaxing."

The manager pulled away the covers and found Ruth fully dressed, "even to his shoes and socks!"

"I'll see you two at the ball park!" he roared loud enough so that even Howley, cringing on the toilet seat, could hear.

Before the next game, Barrow read the riot act to the Red Sox team, warning them about curfews and regulations, all the while eying Ruth, who was bent over tying the laces on his spikes.

The Babe, who had been brooding all morning, shot back, "If you ever come into my room like that, you ————, I'll knock your goddamn head off!" (The space is left blank because no publication of the time would dare repeat Ruth's exact words, but one source assures us that he used "a gutter term than no man, especially a Barrow, could accept without fighting.") There was a shocked silence in the clubhouse. Ruth was only twenty-four; Barrow was fifty, but he was a powerful man.

Trembling with rage, Barrow said, "You fellows finish dressing and get out of here. All except Ruth." But the Babe joined the stampede out the door and was soon shagging fly balls in the outfield.

Moments before game time, Ruth trotted over to the dugout and stared down at Barrow, who sat on the bench scribbling the lineup onto the umpire's card.

"Am I playing today, manager?" he asked humbly.

"Go in and take your uniform off," Barrow growled, never looking up. "You're suspended."

That night, as the Washington-to-Boston train sped through southern New Jersey, the buzzer rang at the door of Barrow's drawing room.

"If there ever was a big, shame-faced kid with a guilty conscience trying to get off the hook," said Barrow, "that was the Babe as he stood framed in the doorway."

"Will you speak to me, manager?" said the Babe, in his most penitent tone.

The Babe sat down, put his head in his hands, and said, "Ed, someday, somebody is going to kill me."

Softening, Barrow said, "Nobody's going to kill you, Babe, but don't you know you can't go around calling people names like that? What makes you act that way?"

"I started to say something about those early days in Baltimore, but I didn't know how to say it," the Babe recalled.

They had "quite a talk" that night, according to Barrow. "He told me about his boyhood and the tough going he had as a kid. My heart went out to this big, overgrown boy, and I understood him better. Most of all, he didn't want to be suspended. That was the greatest punishment I could give him, because he loved to play baseball."

Finally, Ruth asked, "Eddie, if I leave a note in your box every night when I come in, and tell you what time I got home, will you let me play?" For the rest of that year, Barrow found a note in his hotel mailbox, that began "Dear Eddie . . ."

"I don't know whether he ever lied to me or not. . . . I took his word," said Barrow. And besides, who could complain about a few wild nights, when there were all those home runs in the afternoon?

*   *   *

By midseason, Ruth was well on his way to breaking the American League home run record of 16, set in 1902 by Ralph "Socks" Seybold. In Philadelphia on July 5, he hit two homers in a single game, the first time he'd done so in official play, and he repeated the rare feat two weeks later against Cleveland. By July 29, he pulled even with

Seybold's mark and aimed for the modern major league record of 24, set in 1915 by Gavvy Cravath of the Philadelphia Phillies. He matched that achievement on September 1 in a doubleheader against Washington, when he turned in a virtuoso performance, pitching and winning the first game and hitting home run number 24 in the second. Four days later, in Philadelphia, he tied the nineteenth-century record of 25 home runs, made in 1899 by John "Buck" Freeman of Washington, and hit four singles for good measure.

When Ruth appeared with the Red Sox for another exhibition game in Baltimore on September 7, an overflow crowd of 10,000 (quite a contrast with the eleven fans who paid to see him that afternoon five years before) saw him hit two homers, "the first clearing the center field fence and bouncing off a porch of one of the Greenmont Avenue houses." In New York the next day, he beat Freeman's record, whacking his 26th home run into the right field grandstand of the Polo Grounds.

The young slugger was standing on top of the baseball world. "Ruth is quite likely . . . to set an achievement that should last for a generation," said syndicated columnist Grantland Rice.

There was an offer from Hollywood to make a film. His mail in Boston was piling up "to alarming proportions," said a Red Sox official. Even if he spent twenty-four hours a day opening the letters, "he would not reach the bottom of the heap." While most fans asked for autographed photos, "not a few of the letters are perfumed."

Then another hurdle popped up, barring Ruth's claim to supremacy. Some zealot, poring through old records, discovered that way back in 1884 a man named Ed Williamson of the Chicago White Stockings had hit 27 home runs.* The Babe was still one short.

"Babe Ruth Day" drew a capacity crowd to Fenway Park on September 20. The great slugger, it was announced, would not only try to break Williamson's home run record but would also pitch the first game of the doubleheader. The crowd spilled onto the playing area and had to be roped in below the right field bleachers. In a box together with Red Sox owner Harry Frazee sat his old friend Cap Huston, co-owner of the New York Yankees. Before striding out to the pitching mound, the Babe was again honored by the local Knights of Columbus, who gave him several hundred dollars in U.S. Treasury savings certificates and a pile of other gifts, including a diamond ring.

Throughout his career, Ruth demonstrated an amazing faculty for rising to special occasions; this was no exception. He pitched and won

---

* This was a fluke, because Williamson's home park that season had a right field fence only 215 feet from home plate; at different parks in the two seasons before and after 1884, he hit a grand total of 5 home runs.

the first game and, according to historian Robert Smith, who was then a youngster sharing a bleacher seat with his brother, "the crowd set up a noise that sounded like the armistice celebration." It appeared that he would tie Williamson's home run record when he smashed a ball toward the right field bleachers, where the two Smith brothers sat clutching bags of peanuts. The ball struck the seats below them "with a whack loud enough, we thought, to carry even above the yell of the fans." The ball then bounced back over the bleacher wall and into the overflow crowd on the outfield grass, who fought over it wildly. The umpire, watching the mad scramble, decided that the ball had not cleared the fence and called it a triple, which evoked a loud protest. So eager were the Bostonians to see Ruth tie the record that National Guardsmen, who were taking the place of Boston's striking police-men, circulated a petition in the bleachers. They carried the long list of scribbled signatures to the umpire, but he refused to change his decision. The fans, however, didn't have long to wait. In the second game, Ruth reached far across the plate for an outside pitch and with what appeared to be one hand stroked the ball toward left-center field. It was so deep out there that many a ball had bounced between the fielders for an inside-the-park homer, but no one could recall a shot clearing the fence. To Harry Hooper, who was sitting on a bench in the left field bullpen, it looked like a sure double, but it kept carrying toward the fence and then soared right *over* the fence! It was his 27th home run, and the ecstatic fans and players rushed onto the field and carried Ruth from second base across the plate.

Four days later in New York, Bob Shawkey of the Yankees tried to fool Ruth with a slow curve. He "stood firmly on his sturdy legs, like the Colossus of Rhodes," said a New York paper, "and taking a mighty swing . . . catapulted the pill for a new altitude and distance record." It was a "glorious smash," the "longest ever made at the Polo Grounds," which cleared the stands by several yards and landed among the weeds in an adjacent lot. And two days after that, Ruth set a new distance record for the Washington park when he smashed his 29th and final homer of the season.

At season's end, the statisticians announced that Ruth had batted .322 and led the league not only in home runs but in runs scored (103) and runs batted in (112). His home run barrage, during the era of the "dead ball," was a staggering feat, and Boston fans almost forgot that the Red Sox had finished far out of the running. Since the turn of the century, home run champions had averaged slightly above 10 per season in the American League and about 12 in the National. Four of Ruth's 29 homers had been with the bases full, a feat that stood unmatched for four decades. He had hit a homer in every park in the league, another unique achievement. At the Polo Grounds in New York, at Navin Field in Detroit, at Sportsman's Park in Saint Louis, at Fenway Park in Boston, he was credited with hitting the longest drives in history. At Chicago's Comiskey Park, his three shots into the right field bleachers were "as many as the entire collection of American League sluggers has averaged since the park was built," said one paper, which commented: "Ruth stands alone." In a single season, he threatened to revolutionize baseball, but this was just the beginning.

THIRD INNING

When we first heard of the Armistice, we felt
a sense of relief too deep to express, and we
all got drunk. . . . On the next day, after we
got over our hangovers, we didn't know what
to do, so we got drunk. . . . We returned to
New York, appropriately—to the homeland of
the uprooted, where everyone you met came
from another town and tried to forget it; where
nobody seemed to have parents, or a past more
distant than last night's swell party, or a future
beyond the swell party this evening.

MALCOLM COWLEY,
Exile's Return

"The Diamond-studded Ball-Buster"

Colonel Jacob Ruppert looked glumly out the window of his office at the brewery, where the beer flowed like gold at the rate of 1 million barrels per year. A few months hence—on January 16, 1920, to be precise—Prohibition would cut that flow to a trickle. The Evangelist preacher Billy Sunday was already rejoicing in his sermons that "the slums will be only a memory. . . . Men will walk upright now, women will smile and the children will laugh." The Colonel had several million to tide him over until wetter days, but what irked him most of all was that his damned Yankees couldn't win a pennant.

In fact, the Yankees hadn't won a pennant since they'd joined the American League in 1903 as the Highlanders. They were an "orphan" club, who rented the Polo Grounds from the Giants for their home games. Ruppert and Cap Huston had bought the decrepit team for $450,000 four years ago from Frank Farrell, a gambler and politician, and "Big Bill" Devery, New York's former police chief. The new owners, said one friend, were "the strangest pair of men I have ever known in baseball."

Colonel Tillinghast L'Hommedieu Huston, better known as "Cap" to his many drinking pals, had a modest upbringing in Ohio and went to Cuba during the Spanish-American War as a captain with the Second Volunteer Engineers. He stayed on and amassed a fortune by working on large harbor projects in Havana and other ports. He was a big, heavyset, casual fellow who loved to drink and wore baggy, rumpled dark suits and a derby, and loved to drink.

Ruppert, the fifty-one-year-old son of a millionaire brewer whose own father had founded a brewery in Bavaria, wore fastidiously tailored suits and custom-built shoes. His Saint Bernards and Boston Terriers were the pride of the Westminster Kennel Club; his collections of jade, porcelain, and first editions were the envy of his friends. He owned several race horses and a yacht called *The Alba-*

57

tross, and kept a score of monkeys to amuse him at his country estate in Garrison, New York. He belonged to the "silk stocking" Seventh Regiment of the New York National Guard, and at age twenty-two had been appointed a colonel on the staff of Governor David B. Hill. As the Tammany candidate from the 15th District, he had served in Congress from 1899 to 1907. He lived stylishly in a twelve-room Fifth Avenue apartment that was cared for by a butler, maid, valet, cook, and laundress. Although a biographical sketch some years ago assures that "he was distinctly of the masculine type," Ruppert never married and was considered "one of New York's most eligible bachelors." Ruppert viewed the world from heavy-lidded eyes, seemed to regard everyone with an aloof smile, spoke with a Germanic accent, and rarely, if ever, called anyone by his first name. He always addressed the Babe, for example, as "Root."

Thus, the Ruppert-Huston partnership was a union of opposites, their common bond being money and a penchant for baseball as a profitable plaything.

The unlikely man hired to assuage the bruised egos of these two wealthy sportsmen was Miller Huggins, a former major league infielder who was called "Rabbit" by his teammates because of the disparity in size between his large ears and his body, which measured 5 feet, 6 inches and weighed scarcely 135 pounds. Huggins was hired away from the Saint Louis Cardinals to manage the Yankees in 1918. He twice coaxed the team into the first division but never came close to a pennant. Huggins's hiring caused the first serious dispute between Colonel Ruppert and his partner. Ruppert had acted unilaterally, sending a terse telegram to advise Huston, who was with the army in Europe at the time, earning his own right to be called "colonel."

Exactly how the Yankees acquired Ruth in the winter of 1919 is somewhat of a mystery, but Houston and Red Sox owner Harry Frazee had clinked many friendly glasses together, and it's rumored that Boston manager Ed Barrow was in on the deal; he, too, jumped to New York the next year and became the club's general manager. (Muckraking columnist Westbrook Pegler always claimed that "rich promoters" in New York had given Frazee the money to buy the Boston franchise in the first place and that Frazee later sold to "the rich angels of New York a bunch of ivory on the hoof" and "wrecked the team for sordid gain.") The widely accepted version, however, is that in October, 1919, after the Yankees had finished third in the league, Ruppert asked Huggins what was needed to produce a winner.

"Get Ruth from Boston," said the manager, explaining that Red Sox owner Harry Frazee was hurting for cash.

It would not be the first time that Yankee money had bailed Frazee out of a financial crisis. A Yankee–Red Sox deal the previous summer had shaken the foundations of organized baseball. On July 13, 1919, Red Sox pitching star Carl Mays had walked off the field in a huff, disgusted over sloppy defensive play, which had caused him to lose several close games. Despite pleas by Barrow and Frazee, Mays took off on a fishing trip. While the Red Sox management pondered whether to suspend the mercurial Mays, feelers came from several clubs—including the Yankees—to buy him. American League President Ban Johnson had insisted no deal could be made until Mays reported back to Boston. But before he did so, Frazee sold him to New York for $75,-000 and two lesser players. Johnson was infuriated and suspended Mays, warning the Yankees not to use him in their games. But the Yankees obtained a temporary injunction against the league president, and Mays pitched several games. The issue became so acrimonious that three clubs (New York, Chicago, and Boston) even plotted to abandon the American League and form an expanded National League. In a showdown meeting early in 1920, they broke Johnson's autocratic rule and got Mays reinstated, without penalty, as a member of the Yankees.

Thus, when Ruppert sent Huggins up to Boston to speak with Frazee, it was like dispatching someone to a supermarket with a bundle of cash. Huggins reported that Frazee would "begin talking" if the Yankees recognized $125,000 as a "fair price" for Ruth. Ruppert sputtered, "Who ever heard of a ballplayer being worth $125,000 in cash!" But Huggins insisted that Ruth was a bargain. "Bring him to the Polo Grounds and he'll hit 35 homers at least," he said.

One Sunday morning later that winter, Ed Barrow was bathing in his apartment at 644 Riverside Drive when the phone rang. With a towel wrapped about his thick torso, he rushed to answer. It was Frazee, who wanted to see him at 6 P.M. in the bar of the Hotel Knickerbocker.

"Simon," said Frazee, "I'm going to sell Ruth to the Yankees. I can't help it. Lannin is after me to make good on my notes. My shows on Broadway aren't going so good. Ruppert and Huston will give me over $100,000 for Ruth and they've also agreed to lend me $350,000. I can't turn that down."

The sales contract was signed the day after Christmas of 1919. Frazee was handed $25,000 in cash and three promissory notes to be paid over the next three years, which, with interest, would give him a total of $110,000 for selling Ruth. Even more important, Ruppert agreed to lend him $300,000 for crucially needed operating capital. It was by far the biggest deal ever made for a single baseball player.

In the meantime, Ruth—oblivious to all these machinations—was having a grand time barnstorming and playing golf in sunny Los Angeles. His druggist-manager Johnny Igoe, looking ahead to salary talks with the Red Sox, was again hinting that Ruth might give up the game and become a prize fighter. Now, said Igoe, the Babe would challenge heavyweight champion Jack Dempsey! To lend credence to this threat, Ruth held a press conference and, with a straight face, told the reporters: "I have always wanted to be a professional boxer, but I gave up any future I might have had in the game to play baseball."

Shortly after New Year's Day, Huggins went to the Coast to discuss the deal with Ruth. After three days of searching he finally found the Babe at the Griffith Park golf course. In the clubhouse, Huggins told him, "We haven't put through the deal yet," and then, wagging his finger, said, "but I want to know whether you'll behave yourself if we do. . . . I know you've been pretty wild in Boston, Babe, and if you come to New York it's got to be strictly business."

"Yeah, yeah, sure," said the Babe, who was "getting a little fed up" with the sermon.

Then they got down to money. Ruth not only demanded a contract of $20,000 for the coming season but asked for $15,000 of the purchase price. After two days of bargaining and several telegrams by Huggins to New York, Ruth signed a contract that paid him about $40,000 over the next two seasons, but at least half the money was to be in separate installments, almost in the form of performance bonuses. As the ink dried on Ruth's contract, Huggins wired Ruppert, and on January 5, 1920, the news broke that Ruth had accepted a tentative contract to play with the Yankees; the sale price was announced as $125,000. The highest previous price for a single player was $50,000, when Cleveland bought Tris Speaker from Boston, and when Chicago paid a similar amount to buy Eddie Collins from Philadelphia. Red Sox fans were outraged, and Ruth's sale was described as a "second Boston massacre." Newspaper cartoons showed a "for sale" sign on the Boston Public Library and the Boston Common. They also pictured Fenway Park in darkness, with a sign "Building Lots for Sale." Johnny Keenan, leader of Boston's Royal Rooters fan club, fought back a tear and wailed, "Ruth was 90 per cent of our club!" Frazee, the embattled Red Sox owner, tried to justify the sale of his star: Ruth had become "simply impossible" and the Boston club "could no longer put up with his eccentricities." He was "one of the most selfish and inconsiderate men that ever wore a baseball uniform," said Frazee, claiming that twice during the past two seasons the Babe had jumped the club and revolted, refusing to obey the manager's orders. On January 16 the papers carried the Babe's counterattack: He liked Boston and its people, but Frazee was blaming him "to alibi himself with the fans." Frazee was so cheap, he said, that on Babe Ruth Day at Fenway Park, Ruth had to pay for his wife's seat, "and after the game I was called to his office where he handed me a cigar and thanked me."

Frazee swore that with the proceeds from the Ruth sale he would buy more talent and build a pennant contender. But just the opposite proved true. In subsequent months, he sold away Boston's best players; since Frazee was deeply in debt to the Yankees, he reserved the choicest talent for Ruppert, and wags referred to the Red Sox during the next few years as "New York's best farm club." The Boston club, which won four pennants in the years 1910–19, never climbed out of the second division during the next decade, finishing last seven times.

Ruth left the West Coast in late February and stopped off in Boston, where he demanded a share of the proceeds from his sale to the Yankees. But Frazee refused even to meet with him. The Babe then took a train to New York for a conference with his new bosses.

He walked into the Yankee office with a big smile on his tanned face, pulled out a fistful of nickel "Babe Ruth" cigars, and offered them around. Ruppert took one, holding it between two fingers and sniffing it cautiously. Cap Huston, nursing a hangover, paced about the office, warning Ruth that his fabled late-night escapades "will have to stop" and that manager Huggins's word was "law." On and on rambled Huston as Ruth sat there, puffing his cigar and squinting through the smoke. Finally Ruth exploded, "Look at ya! Too fat and too old to have any fun!" Then, glancing at Ruppert, "That goes for him, too!" And, jerking a big thumb at Huggins, who was trying to stifle a grin, he added, "As for that shrimp, he's half dead right now!" End of lecture. After this first encounter, the Yankee owners promptly took out a big insurance policy to protect them against "any accident severe enough to take the home run king out of the daily lineup."

So concerned were Ruppert and Huston about Ruth's welfare that when he took the train south to report for spring training in 1920 they assigned Joe Kelley, an old ballplayer, to accompany him on the trip. Two days after they left, Huston's phone rang at midnight. It was a collect call from Baltimore. "Good lord," Huston groaned, "Ruth must've escaped from Kelley!" But he heard the Babe's booming voice at the other end: "Look, Colonel, it's that old guy Kelley. I can't get him on the train. He met some pals here and don't wanna leave."

* * *

Ruth's joining the Yankees in the spring of 1920 was a perfect marriage of personality and circumstance. Here was the champion slugger of all time, in all his uncouth splendor, walking onstage precisely at the outset of America's most flamboyant decade.

America was ripe for a hero like the Babe. The country had recently ended its involvement in a grim world war. People wanted fun, and fun they got. Westbrook Pegler, then a young sportswriter, called the 1920's "The Era of Wonderful Nonsense." Papers spiced their dull gray prewar formats with bold headlines, eye-catching illustrations, and whimsical story angles, bending the truth whenever fiction was more interesting. Circulation soared.

New York was the ideal—perhaps only—place for the creation of a modern demigod. "When anything happens big in this world, it's gonna happen in New York," said Ruth's former teammate Whitey Witt. Manhattan alone had eleven major daily newspapers in 1920. Its writers were the best-known and most talented in the country, and their columns were syndicated across the continent. The mere sight of a dozen writers and an equal complement of photographers trailing after a star athlete generated excitement by itself.

The New York *Daily News,* founded the previous summer by William Randolph Hearst, was one of the earliest papers to recognize the value of sports coverage as a circulation booster. It became America's first major tabloid and within a few months was selling 250,000 copies a day. *News* publisher Joe Patterson sensed Ruth's potential as "good copy" and assigned reporter Marshall Hunt to cover the Babe twelve months of the year. Patterson "wanted us to write in a kind of bouncy way. Very biff, bang, boom stuff," says Hunt. In a few years, the *News* was selling a million copies daily, and much of the readership was due to the "biff, bang, boom" coverage of Babe Ruth's escapades on and off the field. Of his long relationship with Ruth, Hunt recalls fondly, "I never had a cross word with the big baboon. He was no intellectual . . . but he really liked baseball and he liked people."

All the papers jumped on the bandwagon. The adulation of a handful of sports heroes, says Paul Gallico, soon reached the point "almost of national hysteria." For the first time, professional athletes became millionaires, and the poorer their beginnings the more romantic a tale it made. The writers became infected by their own en-

thusiasm and were swept away by their own ballyhoo. As restaurateur
Toots Shor aptly described the sportswriters and hangers-on of that
era, "Guys like us here are born to have fun and discuss the little
things in life and not get mixed up in discussion of heavy, big-time
arguments." "I came along in a gayer and happier time," said Grantland Rice, the columnist who soon became the "poet laureate" of
sports.

The fun was lucrative, too. Most reporters worked for slave wages
in those pre-Guild days, but some top byliners pulled in $35,000 a
year, and more if they had a column. Before radio and television, the
syndicated columnist was the only press personality whose words
reached millions of people coast to coast. It was a golden era, too, for
the slick magazines, such as the *Saturday Evening Post, Cosmopolitan,
Liberty,* and the *New Yorker.* F. Scott Fitzgerald batted out light
romance tales and peddled them to the slicks for $5,000 apiece.
Damon Runyon, Ring Lardner, Heywood Broun, and others earned
nearly as much for their lively sports stories. Lardner, for example,
received up to $3,500 (about twice the annual wage of a factory
worker) for each story accepted by *Cosmopolitan,* and the magazine
was willing to publish one every forty-five days.

If you didn't make it on salary, you could always pad the expense
account. There was "no limit," says Hunt. "I was brutal. Anything you
wanted. I faked 'em, and never a word. The rule was publish or
perish, as long as you produced. They liked loyalty, they liked enthusiasm, they liked a guy who would work around the clock and later
tell the managing editor, 'That was fun!' although sometimes it
wasn't." The reporters also had good connections with politicians, some
of whom were regulars at the ball park. "If you were on the inside,
what more could you want?" says Hunt. Any newsman, for example,
could get a job with Mayor Frank Hague of Jersey City if he had a
run of tough luck. One reporter happened to mention at the ball park
that he was searching for a type of Belgian building block to adorn his
suburban patio; a few days later, a whole street in Queens was
torn up "for repair" and the blocks were delivered to the writer's back-
yard.

The writers who covered Ruth during the next decade were an
interesting bunch: cynical, fun-loving, and witty. Dan Daniel was already a veteran who had come up when editors paid by the word.
When Daniel covered the Yale-Harvard regatta, says Hunt, "he would
even write about 'all those fine people staying at the hotel,' and list
'those who had an enjoyable lunch,' middle names and all. Then he'd
slip in the manager's name and do a brief essay on 'the history of
this fine old hostelry.' The funny thing, he could lace it together so

tight no editor knew where to cut!" When the time came to face
the typewriter, "Daniel would take off his coat and hang it over his
chair, then he would rub his hair back with both hands, and zoom!
He'd produce five twenty-two inch columns of type. Just the sheer
physical exercise involved was amazing! He made out so well that his
paper finally had to put him on a straight salary."

And Hunt, says Daniel, was "one of the more frolicsome hombres
of the early Yankee years." He remembers the night on the train
when Hunt removed all the paper drinking cups from their dispenser
in the Pullman car, snipped a small hole in the bottom of each, and
deftly replaced them. Hunt and Will Wedge of the *Sun* (later of the
Times) once caused a sensation in a Boston hotel when they dropped
two live flounders into their bathtub and announced a fishing tournament. There was young Bill Brandt, a recent addition to the *Times*
sports staff, who enjoyed sending hotel postcards to his friends and
relatives. He even had made up a special rubber stamp that said:
"Having a wonderful time, wish you were here. Bill Brandt." One
night, while the rookie reporter was out of his room having dinner,
Hunt sneaked in and stamped several cards, sending them to the
President of the United States, to Brandt's sports editor, and to Mr.
Sulzberger, the head of the *Times*. "Nearly got him fired," says
Hunt. "Every once in a while when he looked at me, tears would
come into his eyes."

If other men became Ruth's "ghosts," writing his syndicated columns
and articles, Hunt became his "shadow," following him about, suggesting visits to hospitals and orphanages, and inventing newsworthy situations that resulted in exclusive features for the *Daily News*. "Marsh
is okay," said Ruth once, "but someday I hope that little runt misses
a train. A guy has to have some privacy!" There were two young
writers with like-sounding surnames: Ray Kelly, who had a great
appetite, was called "Carniverous Kelly"; Bob Kelley, who had been
gassed in the war and suffered occasional fainting spells on hot days,
was "Collapsible Kelley." Fred Lieb was also at the Yankee spring
training camp and had brought along his wife; their hotel room adjoined the one shared by Ruth and "Ping" Bodie, a good-natured
Californian of Italian extraction who reputedly could "snore an
opera from start to finish." He slept so loudly that Mrs. Lieb complained to the desk clerk that the elevator was disturbing her sleep.
The clerk replied that the elevator was at the far end of the corridor.
One writer traveled the league circuit that year with an alligator
named Alice. There was a Boston reporter who liked to remove his
false eye during cocktail parties and replace it with one that had a
small American flag in the cornea. And there was Rud Rennie of the

Tribune, who once interviewed a girl who had struck out Ruth during an exhibition stunt in Chattanooga; he solemnly quoted her views on baseball in his column, and concluded: "After her work this afternoon, Miss Mitchell was sent back to the kitchen for further seasoning." Social critics like Heywood Broun were also drawn to the glitter and fun of the sporting scene. Once, when the Babe was in a terrible batting slump, Broun trumpeted in his column: "The Ruth is Mighty and shall prevail." There was Ford Frick (one of Ruth's first ghost writers), who later rose to the presidency of the National League and then became commissioner of baseball). Frick, says one colleague, "could bat out a thousand words of froth ten minutes after the game and then speed off for a good dinner." This infuriated men like Dan Parker, who would "sweat blood" writing his overnight stories, and Will Wedge, an aspiring poet, who went so far as to take his work home, where, "amidst a nagging wife and squawling brats," he'd peck away at his feature story.

Among the "big guns" of the New York sports press were Damon Runyon and Arthur "Bugs" Baer of the *American*. A few days before spring training in 1920, the *American* had a prominent spread atop its front page, showing caricatures of the two. On Runyon it said, "This leading baseball expert of the country is sojourning down at Jacksonville, scanning the daily doings of Babe Ruth and his teammates . . . he will tell you the story so cleverly . . . that every line in his tale will be a gem." There was a similar tribute to Baer, who covered the Giants. The Prohibition era had just begun, and that week the inimitable Bugs informed his readers that during a train trip with the Giants "a stranger came into the car with a bottle of timber alcohol, but nobody knew him well enough to die with him." Runyon, says Hunt, was a "frosty devil, who had enthusiasm for his work and considered himself quite a dude." Runyon showed up at one Southern spring training camp with a special trunk holding so many pairs of shoes that a hotel maid thought he was a shoe salesman from Saint Louis.

"No," Hunt told her. "He writes baseball for a New York paper."

Shaking her head incredulously, the woman said, "They have a man to do that?"

The Yankee press corps members never lost sight of the fact that they were writing about a game. Much of their perspiration was generated in trying to outdo the puns and zany imagery of their colleagues.

Ruth reached the Yankee spring training camp in Jacksonville on a nippy March day in 1920. The "first official motion" of manager Huggins, wrote Damon Runyon, was "to flatwheel himself twice around the behemoth, admiring the graceful proportions of the Babe from his belt down, which was as far up as Miller could see without getting a crick in his neck." From then on, Ruth's name dominated virtually every press dispatch from the Yankee camp.

Calling him "The Diamond-Studded Ball-Buster," and "The Billion-Dollar Fish," Runyon explained to his readers that he couldn't resist writing about Ruth because "all our life we have been poor and the Babe cost so much money that even to talk about him gives us a wealthy feeling."

It was a cold, damp spring and the team had little chance to work out the first few days. In fact, said Runyon, "all a visitor saw of the Yanks was a mighty exhibition of eating and yawning." Babe Ruth and Sammy Vick "already have the waiters at the Hotel Burbridge run flatfooted," he said. (Vick, by the way, was such a glutton that players and writers of the era often described the devouring of a gigantic meal as "doing a Sammy Vick.")

The Babe was in the company of so many big league eaters at the rain-soaked Jacksonville camp that the bored writers organized a Great All-American Table Stakes. Ruth, Vick, and Irvin Shrewsbury Cobb, "the famous eating author," were among the favorites. The gormandizing contest was the talk of the New York papers for days, as every journalist strove for new heights of folly. It was decided, Runyon said, that "Mr. Cobb should start from scratch with Ruth, and that they shall spot their competitors one Virginia ham each, and a double porterhouse." The rules forbade Cobb, a formidable raconteur, from telling stories during the contest, "on the grounds that Ruth cannot do a menu justice if he has to stop and laugh." As for Cobb, Runyon said, "he can emit a raucous guffaw and chamber a dill pickle simultaneously." The contest was canceled "indefinitely" when the Yankee management expressed concern that someone might stuff himself to death.

With the weather too chilly for baseball, Ruth donned a pair of white flannel pants and set out for the golf links of the Jacksonville Country Club. It was a windy day, and at a distance his big frame was mistaken by one observer for "a four-master coming up the harbor with the mains'l set." Out on the golf course, says Runyon, there was a "historic meeting" between the Babe and Rube Marquard, a veteran pitching star who was also considered an oddball.

"Folks gathered close to the noble grouping and inclined attentive ears to hear what burning words as might fall from the mouths of these parties.

" 'Lo, Rube,' said the Babe.

" 'Lo, Babe,' said Rube."

A couple of days later, when the rain and cold let up, Ruth was able to take his first practice swings at the plate. Soon, readers around the country learned that he had smashed "a two-miler . . . into the lap of a small boy sitting on the right field fence; the boy stuck the ball into his pocket and ran all the way home, two miles off."

But Ruth's hits were few and far between in the early practice games, and both writers and fans aimed brickbats at the Yankees' "$125,000 Wonder." During a game against Brooklyn on March 20, a fan in the left field seats kept calling Ruth (according to the family newspapers) "a big piece of cheese." The Babe leaped over the bleacher fence and threatened to "obliterate" the man, a tiny fellow, who soon evened up the match by producing a long, gleaming knife. As the Babe back-pedaled, fans and players intervened to prevent the little fellow from slicing up the cheese.

Part of Ruth's batting troubles that spring may have been due to his strenuous after-hours schedule. But he wasn't alone. In fact, when the Yankee regulars played the second squad in practice, Runyon called them "The Haig & Haigs." Writers still talk about the memorable windup of that 1920 spring season, when the Yankees left Jacksonville for a two-day stand at Miami, which was then one of the rum-running capitals of the prohibition era. The night after the second game, players, reporters, and Yankee co-owner Cap Huston took the launch across Biscayne Bay to one of the Florida Keys for a farewell blow-out, hosted by the Cincinnati Reds. On the way back, two reporters fell into the bay and it took three men to carry Yankee outfielder Ping Bodie to the train bound for Palm Beach. Ruth managed to walk, but the next day in Palm Beach he was so bleary-eyed that, while chasing after a fly ball in the outfield, he ran into a palm tree and knocked himself cold. "This is the last time we train in Miami," declared Jake Ruppert.

"Crack It, Babe!"

The frenzy over Ruth's home run record the previous summer was only a minor prelude to what came in 1920. After installing his wife, Helen, in an eight-room Manhattan hotel suite, the Babe got down to business. By midyear it was obvious that he would break his own 1919 record with plenty to spare. He did, with sixty-one games left in the season, and each blow thereafter was like a moon shot, carving out unexplored territory, changing the whole concept of the game.

"He was the picture of power," says Harry Hooper, who was traded from Boston to Chicago. After pregame batting practice, players usually retired to the clubhouse to change shirts and rest for a few minutes. But Hooper recalls how he and the other White Sox players would "hurry and change just to go out and see the Babe hit in practice." They were awed by the way he handled his big bat as though it were a toothpick, and blasted the ball out of sight.* Sometimes, just for fun, he'd slap a practice pitch *one-handed* into the nearby right field stands of the Polo Grounds. But when he was serious he took a murderous swing at the ball. He swung so hard, says Hooper, "you know how a woman has marks on her stomach when she has babies? Ruth had one on his shoulder, a big red splotch. 'Howdya get that, Babe?' I asked him once. 'Oh,' he says, 'I swung at one and missed.'"

When he hit one on the nose, there was no mistaking the ball's destination. "I've heard a lot of players and writers say there was a distinctive noise—like a metallic click—when Ruth really hit a home

---

* It's often said that Ruth swung a 54-ounce bat, but John Hillerich, part owner of the company that makes Louisville Slugger bats, said that Ruth ordered a set that size only once, to limber up in spring training. There's no need to gild the lily, because he normally swung a 35½-inch bat that weighed from 42 to 46 ounces, about half a pound heavier than the bats used by most big league hitters. Only when he grew older and his reflexes slowed did he order lighter bats. He swung a 37-ounce bat when he retired.

run," says Marshall Hunt. "It was like two billiard balls, like a sound of solid things crashing together."

Ruth himself attributed his batting prowess to "timing, the one secret you can't teach; it's born into a man." But there were also his exceptional confidence and poise. Former teammate Jimmy Reese recalls how he and some of the other Yankees watched with fear as Lefty Grove blazed his warmup pitches into the catcher's mitt. But Ruth would say, "Baby is going to hit one today." He'd strike out the first time up, and perhaps the second, but then he'd wallop one over the fence, trot back to the dugout and say, "Baby got his today." When he rounded third after one of those homers, says former opponent Jimmy Austin, "there was always time for a laugh or a wisecrack . . . he'd never pass me without giving me a wink." Writers and players always marveled at the fact that, of all the sluggers, Ruth was the only one who never shortened his grip on the bat when he had two strikes against him.

"Anybody gets a big kick out of taking a cut at the ball and hitting it on the nose," Ruth explained. "Why, you take a sixty-year-old golfer. Nothing in the world gives him such a thrill as clipping that golf ball on the button with a full swing. They'll tell you the science of fine shots is what counts. But that's all baloney. What counts is socking that ball and giving it a ride."

Even his failures were memorable. A Ruthian pop fly "went out of sight" and settled into the fielder's glove "after a minute or two." Washington second baseman Bucky Harris "used to get nervous watching those skyscrapers come down." Once he saw Ruth get a triple on a pop fly with two outs and the bases loaded. "The wind caught the ball and the infielder misjudged it. I ought to know—I was the infielder. And if I hadn't retrieved it fast, Babe would have scored, too." And when he swung and missed, Ruth often evoked loud laughter, doing a vaudevillian double-take and staring at his bat in disbelief.

In Saint Louis that summer, three cowboys were ushered into the Yankee dressing room to meet Ruth. They told him they had ridden three days on horseback to catch a train in Wyoming. "Baby Ruth," one of them drawled, "I'd have ridden all the way to Saint Louis to see you hit them home runs."

Everyone wanted to meet him, to press the flesh of America's new superman. And the twenty-five-year-old Babe was enjoying every minute of it.

As his fame grew, he demanded special privileges. When the Yankees toured the East he drove from town to town in his new fire-engine-red Packard rather than take the train. This privilege nearly cost him his life on the night of July 6. He was driving from Washington to New York with Helen, coach Charlie O'Leary, catcher Fred Hoffmann, and outfielder Frank Gleich. Aiming for Philadelphia by midnight, they rocketed along the dark road, singing and joking, their spirits lifted by alcohol. When Ruth sped around a curve near tiny Wawa, Pennsylvania, the car skidded and turned over, and bodies flew in every direction. Ruth climbed from the wreckage and began to search for his companions. Except for a few bruises and torn clothing, Helen and two of the Yankees appeared to be unharmed. But Charlie O'Leary lay unconscious in the middle of the dark road.

Ruth knelt beside him, praying tearfully, "Don't let him die, Lord, don't let him die!"

Charlie opened his eyes, sat up groggily and said, "Where the hell is my straw hat?" They found a farmhouse nearby, where they stayed the night, and the next morning they got a ride into Philadelphia, where one newspaper, hearing rumors of the crash, had rushed to the streets with stories that Babe Ruth was dead. He quickly called Ruppert in New York to assure him that stories of his demise were exaggerated. Later that day he arrived in Manhattan, a sprained wrist lightly bandaged, at the wheel of a new car.

At the Polo Grounds two day later, the indefatigable Knights of Columbus gave Ruth a diamond-studded watch fob. He was trying to keep alive a 22-game batting streak when he strode to the plate in the fifth inning and "the multitude implored him to blister the ball." Despite his sprained wrist, he smacked his 25th homer into the seats, and "the whole lower stand became a field of waving straw hats." The next day, said one paper, "that long thunderous rumble which echoed over Harlem is a sure sign that Ruth is at bat. 'Crack it, Babe!' chorused 30,000 throats." And crack it he did, for another homer. Against Detroit the following afternoon, the 35,000 fans jeered when the opposing pitcher walked Ruth three times. "Every last mortal in that gathering," said one paper, "wanted to see Babe hit, and the idea of one man blocking the will of a populace was more than the crowd could bear."

When Ruth broke his own home run record of 29 on July 15, he did so in typically dramatic fashion. It came in the eleventh inning with two men on base to win the game. On the same date the previous season, he had only eleven homers. Now, it was hard to calculate how far he would go in the sixty-one games that remained. Thumbing through their imaginations and thesauruses, the bewitched men of the pressbox hailed "the epoch-making clout" and predicted that "the mauling menace" was bound to set a record that no one could equal!

More than 26,000 people attended the next day's doubleheader against Chicago, eager to witness the record-breaking "detonation." Finally, in the fourth inning of the second game, the Babe "slouched up, swinging an extra bat or two." When the pitcher let loose, Ruth swung and the fans sprang to their feet. The ball floated into the tumultuous right field bleachers as Ruth trotted leisurely around the basepaths, grinning broadly.

He was the king. The boys in the pressbox stepped up their feverish competition to describe the indescribable. He was the Big Bambino, the Mauling Mastodon, the Behemoth of Bust, the Mammoth of Maul, the Colossus of Clout, the Sultan of Swat, a Modern Beowulf, the Prince of Pounders, the Mauling Monarch, the Bulby Bambino, the Blunderbuss, the Mauling Menace, the Rajah of Rap, the Wazir of Wham! One writer, doubtlessly fueled by a flask of bootleg hooch, called him a "dauntless devastating demon" who hit "clangorous clouts"!

Offers poured in from everywhere. A shoe company promised Ruth a pair for every homer. He accepted but told the company to donate the shoes to a Catholic orphanage in New York. Back at Saint Mary's Industrial School in Baltimore, said the *Sun,* "every time the Babe hits another homer, a roar goes up which can be heard all the way to the Wilkens Hair Factory, some eight blocks away."

The press hounded Ruth for "exclusive" stories. Earlier in the season, Fred Ferguson of United News (a subsidiary of United Press) left messages all over New York for Ruth to call him. He wanted to offer the Babe $1,000 for the year with a bonus of $5 per homer, provided Ruth wired him each time he hit one over the fence and briefly described the circumstances. Ferguson finally found him engrossed in a crap game with six teammates at the Aldine Hotel in Philadelphia. Taking a deep breath and wondering what United News might think of "gambling losses" on his expense account, Ferguson got down on his knees and joined in. When Ferguson cleaned everyone out, Ruth at last noticed him, heard his proposition, and signed a contract.

The young Westbrook Pegler was assigned to translate Ruth's wire dispatches into English for the syndicate's national audience. But a dozen homers went by without word from Ruth, until the angry Ferguson wired the Babe, demanding action. Two nights later, hours after Pegler had dreamed up Ruth's account of a home run against the Tigers and sent it on the wire, a telegram arrived from Detroit: "SOCKED ONE TODAY. FAST BALL. HIGH OUTSIDE. SEND CHECK. BABE."

By May, said Pegler, "Babe's public was expanding and I was as-

o interview him exhaustively for his life story and rush back
York to put it into deathless prose."

.....y night, he tried to waylay Ruth in the hotel lobby, but the
Babe, who was always on his way to a date, would bark, "Oh, make
up something! Make up something!" And off he'd go in a cloud of
cigar smoke. Pegler begged Ping Bodie, Ruth's roommate, to alert him
when the Babe got back, but most nights he didn't return. (That was
the season when Bodie, referring to Ruth's bed-hopping, issued the
immortal line: "I room with Babe Ruth's suitcase.") One Saturday
night in Chicago, he played cards all night. The next morning he went
to Mass* and played sandlot ball with a group of children until noon.

Pegler finally got a few minutes alone with Ruth that Sunday afternoon. He rushed back to New York, where George Buchanan Fyfe of
the *Evening World* and he pounded out 80,000 words in four days.

"Peg threw in all kinds of seven-syllable nouns and verbs," recalls
Marshall Hunt. "Some of the sentences he put into the Babe's mouth
were monumental contributions to the history of baseball." They surely
were. Part of the ghostwritten autobiography appeared in *Collier's*
later that summer, under the title "Why I Hate to Walk!" In
that article Ruth-Pegler-Fyfe complains that a pitcher wasn't giving
him a decent pitch to hit: "I might as well have been standing there
with a fathom of garden hose; my old bat was about as useful as
a breeches buoy on the Erie Canal." Later, describing the best
tactic to persuade pitchers to throw strikes, he says: "Hitters
needn't worry so long as the fans are on the job with that humiliating weapon of torture—the razzberry."

That August Ruth was signed to do a film called *Headin'
Home,* which was cranked out in a few weeks in Haverstraw, New
York. Each morning the Babe drove across the Hudson and up to
Rockland County, and returned in time for batting practice, blushing
through his chalky makeup as his fellow Yankees razzed the daylights
out of him. He missed six games that month when, while on location,
he was bitten on the wrist by a wasp and his arm became badly
swollen. The film—a silent with captions by Bugs Baer—had its world
premiere in Madison Square Garden. Ruth played a good-natured,
bumbling young iceman who whittles a bat from a tree limb and
knocks his first home run five blocks out of the local park, through
the stained glass window of the church. From then on, it's a direct

* A Yankee teammate recalled that "often after all night out, Babe would haul
a few of us protesting Protestants to Mass with him. When the collection came,
he would plunk down fifty bucks and figure he'd paid up for the sins of the
week." This was typical of his philosophy. Once at a golf course, he hit a bad
shot and began cursing terribly. He was shocked to see a young boy nearby. He
quickly carried the child to the clubhouse and stuffed him with ice cream.

line to stardom. Later he comes home bearing lavish gifts for his widowed mother and sister, and marries—who else?—his childhood sweetheart. The story skips about aimlessly, with Baer's captions poking good-natured fun at Ruth all the way. One New York film critic said, "Whenever a celebrity of the sports world or divorce courts appears in a picture, the public, as a rule, doesn't expect much in the way of story and acting." But he was pleased to note that Ruth's film tried for "comedy, not heroics," and, if nothing else, a sequence that showed him hitting a long home run in the Polo Grounds was "a genuine thriller."

The producers of the film paid Ruth $15,000 in advance and later gave him a check for $35,000, warning him not to deposit it for "at least a week, when our funds clear." Ruth walked around with the check in his wallet for months and enjoyed flashing it at friends, waiters, hotel clerks, and everyone else he could collar. "I'm a little short, can ya cash this for me? Harh!" Finally, when he went to a bank with that creased, grimy piece of paper, he listened with disbelief as a clerk informed him that the company was no longer in business.

Another film company didn't even offer Ruth a rubber check when it tried to cash in on his blossoming fame. They put together newsreel shots of him in action and made two shorts, *Babe Ruth: How He Makes His Home Runs* and *Over the Fence*. Ruth's lawyers sued for a million dollars and sought an injunction, but the state supreme court decided that the Babe's hits were "news," that he was "a public character," and allowed the pictures to be exhibited.

Despite these setbacks, Ruth's earning prospects were bright. The press was building him into a national hero and polishing the image as it went. *Current Opinion* that October called him a "keen-eyed young man" who had been raised in "a Catholic protectory" and cautioned that no reader "should get the impression that he was an incorrigible or a particularly bad boy." His late father, the article explained, had been "engaged in a business that was abolished by the Eighteenth Amendment." Ruth's "fondness for boys," it went on, was illustrated by the homer that he claimed gave him "more enjoyment than any other." One afternoon, when he smacked a ball out of the Polo Grounds and onto a nearby field, "a group of urchins were having a game there with a tattered string ball, which they were keeping together with much difficulty. The new ball—from Ruth's mighty bat— came like a gift from heaven." And, to illustrate Ruth's strength, the article added, "the legendary batsman has one defective knee that has a tendency to slip out of joint. Such a dislocation recently occurred during . . . a crucial game. The effect on the man suggested that of a wounded bear. He sat down and pounded at the knee with his fists, trying to set it back into place. He put one hand on his thigh and the other on the lower part of the leg, tugging and trying to reset the sliding joint. Then he shouted to a fellow player, 'Bring me a ball bat! Maybe we can hammer this thing back into place!' "

Even without the ballyhoo, Ruth was having a sincere love affair with the fans. "Never has a ballplayer been such a hero outside of his own bailiwick," said one writer in Chicago the day the Babe slammed his 38th homer. The 25,000 Chicagoans "were up on their toes waving their hats and yelling like Old Ned." When Ruth returned to his outfield post, "the bleacherites gave him back the ball he hit . . . and he tossed them a new ball in exchange. The fans are fond of Ruth because the fact that he is a baseball hero hasn't made a larger hat necessary." They were also fond of him because he offered the surest guarantee of thrills in the baseball world. The way he was going —and the way he *kept* going in subsequent years—each time he stepped up to the plate the odds were only 2–1 against his getting on base via either a hit or a walk, only 5–1 against his scoring or knocking in a run, and just 15–1 against his smashing a home run. This meant that if a fan attended only four Yankee games in a season, it was probable that he'd witness four Ruth hits (half of them for extra bases) and at least one home run.*

The writers continued to grope for new words to chronicle the Ruthian saga. They called him "the human howitzer" when he hit his 41st "hurrah slap" over the fence in Detroit on August 6; the ball "went across Trumball Avenue into a garage where a mechanic was talking kindly to a stubborn Ford." The next day, a judge in Cincinnati announced that he and his young son would journey to Cleveland for a vacation and that the length of their trip was indefinite. "It all depends on when the Babe hits a homer. We'll just keep following him from town to town until he does," the judge said. Ruth stopped off again in his home town for an exhibition game and a Baltimore paper advised that "a member of the Knights of Columbus will walk out on the diamond and present the Bulby Bambino with a handsome diamond ring . . . it will force Babe to realize that although a thousand other cities and towns may have jacked him up on the pedestal of glory and honor, there is no place like home." The writer said he hoped the Babe would "sew wings on the ball" and that the Knights of Columbus bauble would "incite the Babe to put a Busy Bertha twang to the old horse pelt when the Oriole pitcher grooves it." Wow!

---

* Discounting bases on balls, Ruth during his career hit a home run for every 11.7 official times at bat, a phenomenal record approached by no other player. By comparison, Henry Aaron's home run ratio is roughly 16–1.

The *Times* exulted on August 20 that "His Royal Nibs, Babe Ruth, the Bazoo of Bang," had hit a "splendiferous spank" over the roof for his 43d homer. So great was the uproar following the homer—"hats went up in the air, cheers echoed over Harlem and there was a riot of noise which lasted several minutes"—that Theodore Sturm of Bellerose, Long Island, "succumbed to heart disease."

The fans around the American League circuit were like addicts, craving more and more long smashes by the "Prince of Pounders." In Washington that month, a full house rooted for the Senators, "but that wasn't essential to their happiness; their real hunger was to see that ball started overland for Peoria by the aerial route." At the Polo Grounds a few days later, fans walked out in the seventh inning, when it appeared that Ruth wouldn't come to bat again. In Boston's Fenway Park on September 4, the Babe hit his 45th and 46th homers and passed all possible challenge (during the season, someone had dug even deeper into baseball's archives and discovered that Perry Werden had hit 45 homers for the minor Western League in 1895). That day Boston's Knights of Columbus, not to be outdone by their fellow Knights in New York and Baltimore, gave Ruth a pair of diamond-studded cufflinks; he had already lost the diamond watch fob given him in New York earlier that season.

On Labor Day, he hit no homers, and in fact was struck out three times by a three-fingered pitcher named Dave Keefe, but he smacked "the longest double ever hit" at the Polo Grounds and was dubbed "the greatest wrecker since Samson pushed over the temple." Ruth was such a hero, declared one writer, "that he blocks the traffic going to and from the club house. Men and boys fought with one another yesterday after the game to reach his side and grasp the mighty hands which clutch the home run bat. Girls and women make him pose for snapshots and proud fathers edge their lads up to him to lay his mammoth paws on their curly heads. At the gates, hawkers sell pictures of the Bazoo of Bang and others are selling the latest popular song, 'Oh You Babe.' Palmists hound Babe to let them read the lines of those million-dollar mitts and autograph hunters armed with .45-calibre fountain pens dog his footsteps. . . . Babe doesn't dare take the main streets homeward, having to sneak through the byways in closed taxicabs to get back to his hotel. His telephone has been tinkled right off the wall and the Post Office Department is getting rich on the stream of mail which flows into Babe's hotel." One can only speculate on how this went over in rural and small-town America, where the daily newspaper, perhaps a weekly magazine, and the Sears, Roebuck catalog represented virtually the sole contact with the outside world.

Ruth's long wallops created such a fuss that he was regarded as somewhat of a physical freak. The great fastball pitcher Walter Johnson (or *his* ghost writer) expressed doubt that the Babe had any real weakness: "I have seen him reach out with those long arms of his, and that big wagon-tongue bat, catch hold of a ball that was at least two feet outside the plate and pull it into the rightfield stands." Wielding a bat so enormous that "most players would find it an impossible burden," Johnson said that even the Babe's groundballs "skip along the turf like a bullet and seldom bound true."

A physicist named Professor A. Hodges told the Cleveland *News-Leader* that Ruth had a near-magical faculty for hitting the ball with the bat's "center of percussion," a point a few inches from the end. All ballplayers, he explained, "are aware when the ball hits this spot on the bat, not only through the absence of jar to the arm, but also through a peculiar satisfaction which is hard to define." Professor Hodges then calculated that Ruth applied "24,000 foot-pounds of energy per second" when he swung his bat, "which is about forty-four horsepower." The medical world then tried to explain what happened to the fans when Ruth connected for a homer. According to "nerve specialists" at a New York hospital, "there arises a tremendous concept of anticipation which is fulfilled when the homer is made; the sympathetic nervous system overstimulates the endocrine substances; the suprarenal gland affects the insoluble glycogen so as to change it to glucose; the thyroid gland affects the body's proteid metabolism so as to supply new proteid substances for those which are broken down, and the crowd, displaying mass emotional instability, acting along the familiar lines of mob psychology, brings about a general demonstration in which individual participation is wholly involuntary." That's exactly what must have happened on September 10 at the Polo Grounds when—in the presence of the visiting boys' band from Saint Mary's Industrial School—the Babe hit the ball into an "adjacent voting precinct" for his 47th homer and "the band almost wrecked their instruments in making a demonstration."

On September 24, the "Mauling Monarch" passed "the half-century mark" during a doubleheader in Washington. A crowd of 25,000 "blazed into hysteria" when he connected for his 51st homer and "gave the slugger a whoop and a hurrah he will never forget" as the Babe "cantered over the plate, smiling a smile as broad as his massive shoulders and raising his cap to the populace." Ruth, said one enthusiastic writer, "has hit as many home runs as Heinz has pickles . . . in fact, he is the greatest pickler the world has ever before known."

Four days later, however, the public was shocked by news of the

"Black Sox" scandal, which caused the game's prestige to sink slowly into the mud. Eight members of the Chicago White Sox had been indicted by a grand jury for conspiring with gamblers to "throw" the 1919 World Series against Cincinnati. White Sox owner Charles Comiskey had denied the charges but was shown irrefutable evidence. Several players confessed and were barred for life, including the great "Shoeless Joe" Jackson, whom Ruth himself had once described as the most natural hitter he'd ever seen.

As is often the case in times of crisis, there was a yearning for a "strong man" of unimpeachable character to come in and clean up the mess. Baseball found him in the person of fifty-four-year-old Federal District Court Judge Kenesaw Mountain Landis, a thin, irascible, craggy-featured man with blazing eyes, a defiant chin, and a shock of disheveled white hair. He was the perfect man for the job. Landis had been appointed to his judgeship in 1905 by Theodore Roosevelt after actively supporting Progressive Republican candidates in Illinois. According to one biographer, he was a "despot" in court; during long cases "he would look bored, or screw up his nose as though smelling something odiferous." He was a super-patriot who, at the outbreak of World War I, said Kaiser Wilhelm "should be lined up against a wall and shot." He had no patience with "radicals." It was Landis who called Big Bill Haywood and other members of the International Workers of the World "scum and filth" when they "tied up the war effort" with their labor organizing activities. He had no patience with "sissies," either. At that time, the wristwatch was considered a foppish affectation, except in the case of officers on the battlefield, who found it to be useful and practical. If a lawyer in Landis's court raised his wrist to check the hour, the judge would snap at him, "What branch of the service were *you* in?" But the judge had also developed a reputation for championing the rights of the little man when, in 1907, he levied a fine of $129 million against Standard Oil in a rebate case; no matter that the case was overruled by the Supreme Court, as happened with several of his controversial decisions.

The baseball club owners knew they had a friend in Landis, who was an avid fan. In 1915, the "outlaw" Federal League filed suit in his court, demanding that baseball's reserve clause (which bound players to one team for life) be declared monopolistic and in violation of antitrust statutes. Landis sat on the case for eleven months, rather than render the inevitable verdict, until the matter was settled out of court, with the Federal League plaintiffs receiving handsome cash sums. Even before the Black Sox scandal broke, his name had been mentioned as a candidate for baseball commissioner, and there had been growing pressure to appoint him earlier in the year, when the club owners were divided in a bitter struggle caused by Boston's sale of Carl Mays.

And so, in November of 1920, Judge Landis was catapulted from his relatively obscure job, with its $7,500 a year judicial salary, to the new $50,000 post as "czar" of baseball; the old three-man commission that ruled the game previously was done away with, and the commissioner was given strong powers. When he accepted their offer, he said, "The only thing in anybody's mind now is to make and keep baseball what the millions of fans throughout the United States want it to be."

Landis's appointment helped to restore faith in baseball, but even more important was Ruth's fantastic batting that fall, which day after day exhilarated fans all over the country.* An elderly man, now retired, recalls growing up in Worcester, Massachusetts, at the time: "There was a store window on the main street downtown that had a big sign designed like a thermometer, measuring Ruth's home runs. It was changed after each day's game. I remember when the Yankees came to Boston, my dad and I would get up as early as six in the morning so that we could make the forty-mile trip to Boston by game time."

When the season was over, Ruth finished with 54 home runs, nearly double his record amount the previous summer. The Babe had out-homered not only every other player, but *fourteen of the other fifteen big league teams.* He had personally accounted for about one of every seven homers in the American League. He was so feared by pitchers that they walked him 150 times (once every four times at bat). He also led the league in runs batted in (137) and had the fourth best batting average, with "only" .376. His slugging average of .847 is a record that remains unbroken today and stands the best chance, perhaps, of surviving his other records. Never before had a single athlete so dominated the national game. Although the Yankees finished third in the league, they were runaway champions at the ticket booths.

The 1920 Yankees became the first team in history to draw 1 million fans and set a record that stood for decades. The attendance of

---

* There has never been any suggestion that Ruth was involved with the base-ball "fixers," but he was such an important element in the game that the gamblers tried to manipulate the odds that September, floating a late-night rumor that the Babe and other players had been seriously injured in an auto accident near Cleveland. The plan, it seems, was to get their bets in early on the Yankees, at higher odds, because of Ruth's expected absence from the lineup, but the rumors were quickly denied.

1,289,422 customers was nearly double that of 1919. The Giants, who finished second in their league, also drew well, but 100,000 less than the American League upstarts with whom they shared the Polo Grounds. This irritated Giant owner Charles A. Stoneham, who wrote to Ruppert and asked him to find a new home for the Yankees. Ruppert suggested that they jointly build a new stadium for both teams, but Stoneham demurred, telling a friend, "let them build a park in Queens or some out of the way place, and wither on the vine." Ruppert then exercised an option to buy ten acres of land in the Bronx between 157th and 161st streets and River Avenue, which was owned by the William Waldorf Astor estate. When the land purchase was announced, it was said that the site was "only sixteen minutes by subway from 42d Street" and that the mammoth new stadium would be "impenetrable to all human eyes . . . save those of aviators." Cap Huston was again angered, because Ruppert bought the land without consulting him, but he marshaled all of his engineering background in helping to design the new Yankee home, which would take about two years to build.

In the meantime, Ruth brushed aside his contract with United News to cover the 1920 World Series between the Dodgers and the Indians, claiming he could earn much more on a barnstorming tour. So the exasperated folks from United News sent a man named Sidney Whipple to follow Babe along the barnstorm route. From such diverse places as Perth Amboy, Camden, and Trenton, Whipple whipped up essays by the Babe on the strategy employed in the World Series, which was taking place in Brooklyn and Cleveland.

The barnstorming tour headed for Rochester a few weeks before the 1920 presidential elections. Franklin Delano Roosevelt, who was campaigning for vice-president on the ticket of James M. Cox, stepped down from the train in Rochester and was surprised to see a large crowd that spilled out to the streets beyond the station. The police struggled to escort FDR and his group through the station, and when they reached their hotel they found another mob, but the crowd was strangely indifferent to their arrival. "When I got to my room," Roosevelt recalled, "I turned to one of my companions and said, 'What an amazing turnout. We may not be as badly off as people think.' "

One of the local democrats replied, "I hate to discourage you, sir, but the crowd didn't turn out for your speech. Babe Ruth and his barnstormers are expected in shortly to play a ball game here."

Ruth earned a fantastic $90,000 during that fall tour. He was accompanied by Fred Hoffman, Wally Schang, and Carl Mays. As the group's business manager and banker, Mays would stuff each day's earnings into a cigar box, tape the box, mark the date, and sit down with Ruth on a Sunday night to settle accounts. The Babe's "cut" was based on guarantees for himself of $3,500 for each weekday game, $5,000 on Saturdays, and $6,500 on Sunday. But he wasn't one to quibble over details, and he wanted his "pals" to be happy, too.

One weekday, for example, attendance had been poor and the other men had to take $600 from their own pockets to make up Ruth's $3,500. When he noticed their glum expressions, he asked, "What's wrong?"

When Mays told him, Ruth said, "Gimme my cigar box. I'll just take the coarse stuff."

"He riffled through the pile for twenties, fifties, and hundreds," Mays recalled. "Then he tossed the box back to us. There was $1,300 left."

The tag end of Ruth's odyssey took him to Cuba, where he received $10,000 to play a dozen games in several cities of the island. Afterward, on December 28, he sat in a Pullman car in the Washington, D.C., train station while en route to New York. He appeared to be "in splendid condition," and told reporters he had "picked up some money and made a host of new friends in the tropics."

But one of those friends, a tourist from Cincinnati, later said that Ruth "couldn't stay away" from the Cuban race tracks. "Babe surely got his, and got it plenty. He thought he had a set of winners, all certain to gallop home. Some of them are still running!" It wasn't all bad luck. Ruth—who in some ways was as ingenuous as the bumpkin he played in the film that summer—was taken in by swindlers who claimed to have "inside information" on the races. He was allowed to win $30,000 on a 3–1 shot the first day, but it was downhill thereafter. He lost those winnings and $100,000 of his own money, including $26,000 on a single race. Twice he telegraphed his bank in New York for additional funds, which were lost.

At one point, with a horde of angry bookmakers on his heels, he escaped in a train from Santiago to Havana. He and Rosy Ryan, another player, stood up all the way in a cramped toilet sharing a gallon bottle of rum.

When he reached his Havana hotel room, he confessed to his wife, "Helen, I'm cleaned out." But she saved the day, miraculously producing a checkbook that contained $30,000 in funds she'd managed to conceal from her wild-spending spouse; she wrote a check that satisfied the creditors and allowed them to leave the island.

It had been quite a year!

*   *   *

Short of cash, Ruth agreed to play a series of exhibition basketball games that winter with the Paterson Big Five against the famous Original Celtics in New York, New Haven, and Waterbury. It was billed as a "showdown" between Ruth and Johnny Beckman, the Celtics star. Ruth arrived for the first game at New York's 71st Regiment Armory in a raccoon coat and quickly slipped into a Paterson uniform, with the big "P" on the shirt distended by his growing belly and his knees protected by leather pads. When he walked onto the court, 7,000 fans cheered him for a full five minutes, and he cracked to a teammate, "Hey, kid, I guess they like me, even in this getup!" He was an aggressive player, jumping about and sometimes wrestling with his opponents, but as one reporter put it: "Ruth's greatest need is said to be the highly essential art of putting the ball in the basket." At one point he missed nine straight shots. But it was all good fun and he was paid handsomely. In fact, he was carrying about such large sums of money that he got a permit to carry a pistol.

"You've Got This Country Goofy"

In early February, 1921, Ruth walked into the Yankee business office at West 42d Street. He weighed 220 pounds. His face, punctuated by a big black cigar, was fast acquiring the famous moon shape, and his belly was already of prodigious size. Breezing past the receptionist, he opened the door to a private office and boomed a cheery "Hiya!" at Ed Barrow, who had also left the Red Sox, to become general manager of the Yankees.

Barrow, recalling the trim young Babe of those early years in Boston, raised his bushy eyebrows and roared back, "My God, you fat slob; off to Hot Springs!"

During the few days prior to leaving for Hot Springs, Ruth kept shooing away a persistent young man who waved a piece of paper at him each time he entered and left his suite at the Ansonia Hotel. It was twenty-nine-year-old Christy Walsh, who had started out as a reporter and cartoonist on the West Coast and later handled a series of ghostwritten articles for the famous auto racer Captain Eddie Rickenbacker. Walsh was convinced that he could strike it rich by signing up other sports celebrities to similar arrangements, but he was flat broke and viewed Ruth as the cornerstone to success. He camped on the doorstep of the Ansonia Hotel for days, but since the hotel had entrances on three streets Ruth kept eluding him. Each time he got close enough to talk, the Babe would yell, "Get an appointment!" and run off. Now Walsh was desperate, because Ruth was scheduled to leave for Arkansas the next morning. That night, he stopped into a delicatessen near the Ansonia for a snack when the phone rang. The owner lamented, *"Oy vei,* Baby Root vants a case of beer, and mine delivery boy ain't here."

"Ten minutes later," Walsh recalled, "I was in the Ruth kitchenette, actually counting bottles with the Babe. I asked him if he recognized me."

"Sure!" said the Babe. "Ain't you been bringing our beer the last two weeks?"

Walsh identified himself, and before Ruth could heave him out the door he asked the Babe how much United News paid him for his ghostwritten home run comments.

"Five bucks each. Why?"

"I'll get you five *hundred* for any article you write," snapped Walsh. With that, they sat down, opened a bottle of freshly delivered beer, and began to talk. Ruth agreed to allow Walsh to be his personal representative. Then Walsh realized with horror that he'd left the contract on the counter of the delicatessen, which was closed. The next day, he rushed over to the Pennsylvania Station, where Ruth stood waiting at the iron gate. He pulled the wrinkled contract from his pocket, Ruth signed it, and Walsh immediately went off in search of a ghost.

"The way he threw money around," says Harry Hooper, "I always thought to myself, 'Someday I'll be playing a benefit for the Babe.' When I joined the White Sox and he was with the Yankees, I saw him one evening in the lobby of the Ansonia Hotel. Over his shoulder, he says to me, "I took 'em for ten grand today.' 'You did what?' I asked. 'Ten grand, I won on the races.' 'You dang fool,' I says to him. 'They'll take you for every cent you've got.' Inside of a few weeks, they did clean him out. But when Christy Walsh became his agent, that saved him from leaving baseball broke."

That first year alone, Ruth's newspaper earnings soared from $500 to $15,000. Over the next two decades, Walsh helped Ruth to become a rich man and became wealthy himself, retiring while in his forties.

*   *   *

Ruth spent several weeks at the Majestic Hotel in Hot Springs, Arkansas, bathing in the spas, playing golf, or hiking in the woods. Close on his trail was Marshall Hunt of the *Daily News,* so close that many people thought he was Ruth's manager and begged him for introductions to the Babe. "The Majestic was a real fleabag," says Hunt, "because Barrow was paying the bills and he wasn't averse to saving a buck." So, after a morning workout, the Babe and Marshall often passed up the hotel's food and set out in a rented car to explore the countryside for farmhouses that advertised "Chicken Dinner." "What the Babe really wanted," says Hunt, "was a good chicken dinner and daughter combination. He usually tried to connect with the daughter, or maybe even the wife, and in those times the husband wouldn't give a damn if the woman picked up a few extra dollars. We made quite a few trips."

After the evening meal at the Majestic, it was the custom for the hotel guests to sit on the veranda in creaky rocking chairs and watch the sunset. Many of the guests were elderly women. The Babe—all spiffed up and marking time for his date—would sit among them and chat, answering their questions about baseball in his most courtly manner. One evening, a white-haired lady seated nearby inquired, "Tell me, Mister Ruth, are you enjoying the baths? I'm seventy-five years old and they do me a great deal of good."

"Well," said the Babe, "I get sent down here, but I go along with it. I lost quite a few pounds already. One thing, though, the water's a bit strange. After I drink a lot, when I go to the john and urinate it foams just like beer! Has that happened to you?"

For a moment, all the creaky rockers on the veranda stopped, as though catching their breath, and then resumed. The Babe got up soon afterward, bowed stiffly and said, "Excuse me, very pleasant chat."

"Gawd, you oughta watch what you say, Babe," hissed one journalist who had overheard the tête-à-tête.

"What the hell's the matter, you bastard?"

"Well, your language in front o' those ladies!"

"Fer chrissakes, I *said* 'urinate,' didn't I?"

*   *   *

On March 4, after Helen came from New York to join him, the Ruths took a train from Hot Springs to the new training camp in Shreveport, Louisiana. Barrow had decided to switch sites after learning of the Yankees' drunken orgies in Florida the previous spring. But Shreveport was in the midst of an oil boom, and Ruth recalled it had "some of the toughest and freest-spending people I've ever met."

It seemed that half the people of Shreveport had been partying for the past few days, and a good number of them were at Union Station to see off a bunch of drunken oil men and welcome the newcomers. The Babe and Helen were mobbed; only his bobbing pole cap could be seen from afar as he elbowed his way through, while small boys "yelped at his heels" and "two Negro porters quarreled for the privilege of carrying his hand baggage to a waiting auto." The next day, at Gasser Park, the Babe was nearly worn out from posing for hordes of amateur photographers before he began practice (little did he know that a Shreveport optician had offered $5 for the

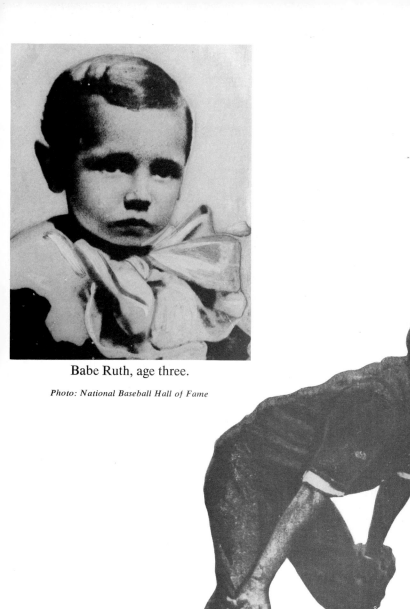

Babe Ruth, age three.

Photo: National Baseball Hall of Fame

Ruth in 1912
playing for
Saint Mary's
orphanage.

*Photo: New York
Daily News*

Babe Ruth signing contract with Baltimore club in 1914.
Jack Dunn, president of the club, is seated next to him.

*Photo: Courtesy
Harry Hooper*

Ruth as a
young slugger
with the
Red Sox.

Photo: Courtesy Harry Hooper

Ruth and
his wife,
the former
Helen Woodford,
after their
wedding
in 1914.

Photo: Wide World Photos

Babe Ruth
at the time
of his sale
by the
Red Sox to
the Yankees
for $125,000
in 1920.

Photo: Culver Pictures

Famed operatic soprano
Amelita Galli-Curci, flanked
by Babe Ruth and
Franklin Delano Roosevelt.

Photo: Culver Pictures

Batting sequence during
Ruth's early years with
the Yankees.

Photo: New York Daily News

Judge Landis shaking hands with Babe Ruth
and Bob Meusel during a visit to the Yankee
training camp in New Orleans in 1922.
Despite the cordial scene, the Commissioner
of Baseball refused to lift the players' suspension.

Photo: Culver Pictures

Babe Ruth and his wife Helen
on their farm at Sudbury, Mass.

Photo: Wide World Photos

Famous photo of Ruth and other glassy-eyed friends taken in an Illinois brewery in 1922 by a private detective hired by the Yankee management to report on the players' extracurricular activities while on the road.

Photo: Culver Pictures

Babe Ruth, Lord and Lady Mountbatten, and Colonel Ruppert, owner of the Yankees.

Photo: Culver Pictures

Ruth at home with his daughter, Dorothy. *Photo: New York Daily News*

The Babe hitting
his 60th home run
of the 1927 season
at Yankee Stadium.

Photo: Wide World Photos

Grantland Rice, Graham McNamee, and Babe Ruth.

Anna Q. Nilsson and Babe Ruth in the 1927 movie *Babe Comes Home*.

best snapshot of the slugger). But when he took his turn at batting practice he slammed nine shots out of the park, including one over the center field wall.

The town couldn't do enough for him. One rainy day, he was invited to Shreveport High School, where the students "almost separated him from his right arm" and then gave him a five-foot-high bat made of violets, pancies, carnations, and lilies of the valley. He had driven to the school in a brilliant green Essex roadster, courtesy of a local auto dealer. The mayor issued a public proclamation that day: "Permission is granted to His Majesty, Babe Ruth, the King of Swat, to operate an automobile without displaying a State license in the City of Shreveport."

* * *

In that age before television and radio, people throughout the South were eager for a firsthand look at the great slugger. When the Yanks played an exhibition game in nearby Lake Charles, says the New York *American,* "promptly at 3 o'clock all the stores and offices and even the railroad station closed and a holiday was declared until 6 P.M. Old folks who had never seen a baseball game were coaxed out, and many infants were carried in on the arms of their mothers." The Babe didn't disappoint the 3,000 fans who flocked to see him. He hit one over the right-center field fence that "cleared the street beyond, and struck the roof of a shed on the opposite side, after missing a knot of colored fans perched on the porch of a house near the shed." In New Orleans a few days later, fans overflowed the playing field, and the next morning's paper noted, with disappointment: "RUTH FAILS 12,000. GETS ONLY TRIPLE."

* * *

Early in the 1921 season, Ruth appeared at an American Legion benefit in New York, where the famed mind-reader Dunninger asked him up on the stage. He was told to jot a question and answer on a piece of paper and hold it in his hand. The answer, said Dunninger, "is sixty." Ruth shook his head in bewilderment and the crowd burst into applause, not only because of Dunninger's skill, but because the Babe was aiming for sixty big ones! The whole nation cheered him on.

In Washington on May 7, former President Wilson attended his first ball game since Harding's inauguration and saw "the Battering

Bambino" hit "a volcanic clout" out of the park. In Saint Louis later that month, he hit one over the fence that landed some 550 feet from the plate.

People had him "nuts," he complained. They camped on the front doorstep of his apartment building, forcing him to sneak in through the janitor's entrance. Two weeks after he installed a private phone, complete strangers had the number and called up at all hours of the night to argue baseball. He was getting about two hundred letters a day from "all kinds of people." One day, he said, "I got eight letters from jailbirds, all askin' me to use my influence to get them out. Great life, isn't it?"

But the great public interest in his slugging was most profitable. Byline articles by Babe Ruth, hastily composed by Christy Walsh's stable of ghosts, were selling to papers all over the country. Soon there would be a $3.95 Babe Ruth Sweater for Boys, a $1 Babe Ruth Cap for Boys, Babe Ruth Home Run Shoes, and school notebooks with Babe's picture on the cover. He even endorsed the All-American brand of cotton underwear, although he refused to wear anything but silk undershorts (to please him, the company supplied several custom-made pairs, in silk, for his personal use). And, although he always smoked big black cigars, his face was soon seen in magazines singing the praises of a certain cigarette. That year the Baby Ruth candy bar came out on the market, and hundreds of children sent him the wrappers, asking for his autograph. Ruth demanded royalties for this apparently blatant use of his name but was turned down in the courts. Years later, when he tried to put his own "Ruth's Home Run Candy" on the market, the Curtiss Candy Company, manufacturers of Baby Ruth, persuaded the patent office to turn him down on the grounds that the new product would cause confusion among candy buyers. In 1973 an inquiry was sent to Curtiss's main office in Chicago and brought this reply:

> Our candy bar made its initial appearance in 1921, some years before Babe Ruth . . . became famous. The similarity of the names, therefore, is purely coincidental. Our candy bar was actually named after President Cleveland's daughter, Baby Ruth Cleveland, who visited the Curtiss Candy Company plant years ago when the company was getting started and this largely influenced the company's founder to name the candy bar "Baby Ruth."

Cleveland hadn't been president for nearly a quarter of a century when his daughter was so honored, and Ruth was clearly famous by 1921; in fact, his exploits dominated the front page of every afternoon daily in New York, even overshadowing President Harding and other nationally important figures.

But the Baby Ruth affair was a mere nuisance to the Babe, who was earning—and spending—money at a record pace. Whenever Christy Walsh scolded him for his expensive life-style or for carelessly leaving his wallet lying around, bulging with hundreds of dollars in greenbacks, Ruth would wave him off with, "Aw, you never have any fun outa life!"

* * *

Now, at twenty-six, he had made the swift transition from Baltimore street tough to wide-eyed Boston recruit to self-assured star. He was granted the privilege, unique among ballplayers of the time, of rooming alone. When he strode into the Yankee clubhouse before a game, he immediately became the center of attention. He wore the finest clothes that money could buy. His nails were freshly trimmed by a manicurist. He would hurry in with a batch of letters and drop them in the lap of some teammate, saying, "Open these for me, will ya, kid? Keep the ones with the checks and the ones from the broads." (That was some improvement over his previous system. Once when he was in a hurry, he tore up most of the envelopes and threw them into a large wastebasket near his locker. Team trainer Doc Woods sifted through the pile and pieced together $6,000 in checks from royalties and endorsements.) The players loved to open the pink and blue envelopes, recalls Waite Hoyt. "It was delightful. The ladies were quite frank in their invitations." Whitey Witt once found a wire from Florenz Ziegfeld. "Hey, Babe, Ziegfeld says he'll give ya fifteen hundred bucks to be in a show next winter." "Aw, I ain't no actor," said Ruth. But Mike McNally, a reserve infielder, said, "Jesus, that's a lotta money. You can *learn* to act for that kinda money."

"Yeah," Ruth grunted as he leaned over and removed his fancy dress shoes.

"If you're in the show," McNally asked, "can you get me a coupla Annie Oakleys?"

"Sure, kid," said Ruth. "I'll getcha alla the broads you want."

* * *

The pay telephone in the clubhouse, installed mainly for Ruth's convenience, rang incessantly. His fame had attracted numerous friends—gamblers, sportsmen, show people, and members of high society who thought it amusing and chic to know a sports idol.

Like a big kid just back from the circus, Ruth loved to tell his teammates of his adventures the night before. One evening, he appeared at a benefit performance sponsored by a woman of New York City's elite. The matron was effusive in expressing her gratitude, and before the blushing Babe knew what he was saying he blurted out, "Aw shit, lady, I'd of done it for anybody!" Another time, he told them of attending a party with friends at a Fifth Avenue mansion. The waiter handed them glasses of champagne, but soon they were drinking it right out of the bottle. As the night wore on, "me and a bunch got out by the fountain; we dove in and dragged each other out by the heels. Whatta time!" When one Yankee asked whose party it was, he answered, "Oh, it was Mrs. ———; she was the hostess and her husband was the hoster."

He was meeting so many people, and his memory was so poor, that he called most men "kid" or "doc," depending upon their age, and addressed a few closer friends as "stud." Any woman under thirty-five was "sister," and someone older "mom." One evening he told a friend that he had to go to dinner with "those movie people." He meant Doug Fairbanks and Mary Pickford. He even found it difficult to recall the names of his fellow players. He never knew "Whitey" was a "Witt." Tony Lazzeri was simply "Wop." Other Yankees were "Flop-Ears," "Chicken Neck" and "Rubber Belly." He called Benny Bengough "Barney Google." During one World Series that Ruth covered for the Christy Walsh newspaper syndicate, he was down on the field and passed catcher Moe Berg.

"Hello, Babe," said Berg.

"Hiya, keed," Ruth replied jauntily.

Berg chuckled at Ruth's inability to remember his name. But the Babe seized him by the arm, thought for a moment, and then broke into a triumphant grin, chanting, "Moe, Moe, he's got the dough!"

*   *   *

Soon after joining the Yankees, Ruth bought a custom-built maroon Packard with a twelve-cylinder engine, which his teammates nicknamed "The Ghost of Riverside Drive." As the Yankees dressed in the clubhouse, they were always warned of Ruth's last-minute arrival by the roar of those twelve cylinders in the distance. They would run to the window and see him come to a jarring, brake-screeching halt in the parking lot. Once a thief stole the ornamental radiator cap from his car, but being in a hurry Ruth drove crosstown without it. When he arrived, his big car was spurting steam and slavering foam like a rabid monster.

There are countless tales of companions who rode with Ruth, sitting frozen and white-knuckled in their seats as he sped about.

"Actually, he wasn't that bad a driver, just a bit reckless," says Marshall Hunt who rode with him often and claims he was "never worried." As a passenger himself, Ruth never displayed fear of speed. Late one night, he, Hunt, and two other companions were returning from Fire Island via the Queensboro Bridge. Hunt was at the wheel, speeding down a slope that was quite slippery because it was paved with wooden blocks. There was a sharp turn at the bottom. One passenger in the rear seat yelled, "Jesus! You're going too fast! There's a curve down there!"

But Ruth calmly cracked, "If he doesn't make it, we'll just have to make a new hole."

* * *

The Babe created a great sensation on June 8 when he was jailed for driving his "maroon, torpedo-shaped machine" over the New York City speed limit. In April he had appeared on a similar charge and got off with a $25 fine. Now, the same judge reminded him of the previous offense and, mumbling something about "famous persons expecting leniency," accused Ruth of "defying the law."

The Babe was apologetic and added, in a very timid voice, "I don't want to go to jail."

Threatening to revoke his license next time and throw him in the jug for six months, the magistrate fined him $100 and sentenced him to a day behind bars. Babe peeled a $100 bill from a roll in his pocket and was taken into the Traffic Court jail at 300 Mulberry Street, where he was fingerprinted and put into a cell with five other speeders. It was 11:30 in the morning. He was sulky. There was a game at 3 P.M. against Cleveland, and his contract provided that he could lose $500 for each game he missed. Then someone advised him that the city jail's official day ended at 4 P.M. A call was put in to the Polo Grounds and his uniform was rushed over. Inside the cell, the Babe put on the uniform beneath his dove-colored business suit. Then he sat and marked time. The news spread quickly all over town that the Babe was in jail. One of his cellmates, described as "a Negro chauffeur, Chester H. Williams," became somewhat of a celebrity after the episode when he told a flock of eager reporters what went on behind bars.

"That was a pretty heavy fine he made you pay, Mr. Ruth," said Williams.

"No, that was nothing," said Ruth.

"A hundred dollars is an awful lot of money to me!" said Williams. "The judge's fine was $25 and I had it here in my hand, but when he said I could serve a day in jail instead, I jumped for the cell!"

When the other four inmates learned of Williams's $25, they suggested a game of craps. "Mr. Ruth didn't answer," said Williams. "They didn't have fifty cents among them and they wanted me to go up against that with my roll of bills. I told 'em nothing doing. Then they abused me something terrible. They pinched me and kicked me and called me names. There were some roughs in that cell, I can tell you. Mr. Ruth was the only gentleman among them."

About 1:30 P.M., the "roughs" were removed to the Tombs, leaving Ruth and Williams alone. "He wasn't very talkative. I had to quit saying things to him because he didn't want to answer, just kept nodding. Once, though, he jumped from the bench, ran to the far end of the room and yelled, 'That fellow's tryin' to take my picture!' "

A news photographer had climbed the fire escape to the third story of a building across the street and was aiming his Graphic at Ruth's cell. A colleague on the sidewalk yelled up, "Do you see anything?"

"I see a shadow," said the photographer.

"Snap the shadow!" the man shouted.

Hiding in the dark corner of the cell, Ruth told Williams he'd have to "run like hell" to make it to the Polo Grounds.

At 4 P.M. the main entrance to the jail was clogged by a thousand fans and about four dozen reporters, news photographers, and movie cameramen. There was a roar when they spotted the Babe—looking a lit lumpy with his baseball uniform under his suit—emerge from a side basement gate and leap into a waiting car. As the crowd stampeded toward him and his car sped from the curb, "several children barely escaped the honor of being knocked down by Ruth." It was later calculated that he made the nine-mile trip to the Polo Grounds in eighteen minutes, reaching speeds faster than the one for which he was fined. At 4:40 P.M., the Babe appeared alone through the center field gate of the Polo Grounds, like a matador entering the arena, and the crowd of 20,000 gave him a standing ovation. He entered the game in the sixth inning. Although he got no hits, everyone was sure that his presence had inspired the Yankees to rally in the final inning and win, climbing to within half a game of first place.

* * *

As the summer of 1921 wore on, the Babe drove relentlessly toward another new record. When he hit his 29th homer on July 2, it gave him a career total of 132 and made him, at twenty-six, the biggest home run producer of all time.* One couldn't pick up a newspaper without finding Ruth's name in the headlines.

"There's always the question comes up," says Marshall Hunt, "did we, at the time, overvalue his worth? Did we overemphasize things? I don't think we did. Every so often, when you got to thinking, 'Maybe I'm wasting my time at the ball park,' along would come a Sunday and thirty or forty thousand paid customers would be having the time of their lives. Then you had to readjust your thinking and say, 'Well, God Almighty, we've got something here!' I mean, it wasn't a great cultural thing, it probably didn't mean much in the way of human advancement, but I also believe that a person needs a little time for enjoyment, and certainly Ruth and the Yankees provided that."

Ruth tied his previous record of 54 home runs on September 9, when he took one of his "spinning swings" and hit "the longest drive ever made in the Philadelphia park." Six days later, against Saint Louis pitcher Bill Bayne, "the Wondrous Walloper" brought 30,000 Polo Grounds spectators to their feet with his 55th homer, a new world's record for the third consecutive year. "The minute Bayne let go of the ball," Ruth remarked after the game, "I said to myself, 'Here comes number 55.' It was the funniest feeling I ever experienced! My arms and legs seemed to sense what was going to happen!"

In 1921, Ruth led the league with 59 home runs (compared with only 23 for George Kelly, the National League champion) and set records that stand today: most long hits in a season (119) and most total bases (457). Miller Huggins called him "the most destructive force ever known in baseball."

There was no doubt that a new era was in the making. As *Spalding's Official Base Ball Guide* noted that fall, "For the first time since Cincinnati has had its new base ball stand, Duncan drove a hit over the left field fence in 1921 . . . in New York, Ruth twice batted a home run into the bleachers in center field; base ball enthusiasts had gone to the Polo Grounds year after year awaiting the day when such a thing might happen." Many explanations were offered. The World War had made Australian wool yarn scarce, requiring the use of "livelier" yarn, and new machines bound the yarn more tightly

* The man with 131 was the long-retired Roger Connor, a burly fellow with a handlebar mustache who in the 1880's played for the Troy, New York, club of the old National League as a left-handed third baseman.

around the baseball's inner core, making it more resilient. Rules changes had outlawed the spitball, emery ball, shine ball, and other forms of doctoring that made pitches dart about in wild directions. Umpires were ordered to put a shiny new ball in play each time one was scuffed or soiled. Everyone was swinging from the heels. But in the midst of this widespread revolution, this accent on brute force, Ruth towered high above the rest.

* * *

By now, most Americans swore that he was super-normal, and science "confirmed" the fact. After a game at the Polo Grounds that September, Ruth went to Columbia University's Psychological Research Laboratory with Hugh S. Fullerton, sports editor of the *Evening Mail*. Two scientists there put him through a three-hour battery of tests. In a syndicated story, America was told "WHY BABE RUTH IS THE GREATEST HOME RUN HITTER: BATTING STAR REAL SUPERMAN." The scientists said his coordination of eye, brain, nerve system, and muscle was "90 per cent efficient, compared with a human average of 60 per cent." His eyes were "about 12 per cent faster," his ears "at least 10 per cent faster," his nerves "steadier than 499 out of 500 persons," his attention and quickness of perception "one and one-half times above average," and in "quickness and accuracy of understanding, about 10 per cent above normal."

The word caught on. "Now and again a superman arises in the domain of politics or finance or science and plays havoc with kingdoms or fortunes or established theories," said F. C. Lane in *Baseball* magazine that season. "Such a superman," he added, "is Babe Ruth." Lane traced the number of big league home runs in previous seasons (they leaped from 235 in 1918 to 445 in 1919, and to 629 in 1920) and said, "Ruth has fired the enthusiasm of the entire country . . . he has not only slugged his way to fame, but he has got everybody doing it! The home run fever is in the air." Not long afterward, Ford Frick published a poem in a New York paper, comparing Ruth to the Colossus of Rhodes, who was admittedly "a big bruiser," but "never hit 59 homers in a single season." Even the hardboiled young Westbrook Pegler found such enthusiasm irresistible. That summer, his sweetheart was in the hospital and he sent her a gift in a large square box. When the nurse opened it, there was, says one of Pegler's biographers, "a pledge of indescribable and eternal love from a sportswriter—a genuine Babe Ruth autographed baseball."

"We are a nation of hero-worshipers," complained Ring Lardner that summer, saying he had lost interest in the game because of the emphasis on slugging. In his humorous column, he put the blame on Babe Ruth's long-distance hitting: "He become a big drawing card and the master minds that control baseball says to themselfs that if it is home runs that the public wants to see, why leave us give them home runs, so they fixed up a ball that if you don't miss it entirely it will clear the fence."

But even Lardner found Ruth's personality irresistible. Later on, for *Collier's*, he wrote a rib-tickling account of "the Rise of a Home Run King" whose boyhood pal in Baltimore was H. L. Mencken:

> They used to take long walks in the woods together, looking for odd Flora. It was an ideal companionship, for both loved to talk and as neither one could understand the other, no law of ethics was broken by their talking simultaneously. I would repeat some of their conversations, but Mencken's words can't be spelled and the Babe's can't be printed.

Some writers were fascinated by the fact that Ruth could violate every training rule in the book and yet perform so superbly. Heywood Broun called the Babe a "liberator who endeavored by personal example to show that no fun can ever hurt you" and a fine advertisement for "gay midnight freedom."

But Miller Huggins tried to persuade Ruth to tone down his lifestyle. "You've got this country goofy, Babe," he said, "but all this success may spoil you, ruin your career." He gently counseled him to go to bed earlier and watch what he ate and drank. If he took off twenty-five pounds and got proper rest, Huggins promised, "you'll hit even *more* home runs." Disarmed by his manager's paternal approach, the Babe promised to give it a try. He went to bed at nine that night and was hitless the next day. He did this three nights running, with the same result. Finally, he exploded. One night in Detroit, Ping Bodie walked up to reporter Arthur Robinson, who traveled with the Yanks at the time, and said, "Come on, we're goin' out. The Babe is in an uproar. The panic's on." They went out, came back and played cards all night. In between, said Robinson, "the Babe ate probably fourteen sirloin and hamburger sandwiches with some odds and ends thrown in." The next day, after only two hours' sleep, he hit two homers, one of them over the center field scoreboard.

The day the Yankees clinched the 1921 pennant, a reporter saw "tears of happiness" in Miller Huggins's eyes; Cap Huston walked tipsily into the clubhouse, grabbed Ruth, and roared, "You big sonofabitch, you're surely worth every nickel we put into you!"

Yankee fans had waited eighteen years for the team's first pennant.

And now they would meet the Giants in the first Series played entirely within the city. The Yankee-Giant Series also represented a head-on clash between the old and new styles of baseball. Giant manager John McGraw was the acknowledged mastermind of the traditional style, chipping away for narrow victories with well-placed singles, stolen bases, hit-and-run plays, and intricate strategies. Ruth and Company personified the wave of the future, the atom bomb that threatened to make guerrilla warfare on the diamond an anachronism.

The night before the Series opener, New York was like a huge cocktail party, despite Prohibition. Fans poured in from all parts of the country. Hotel lobbies and corridors were as "thick with people as mosquitoes on the Hackensack Meadows." Rooms were impossible to find. A strip of four tickets for the Series, normal price $22, was going for up to $60.

On opening day at the Polo Grounds, the field boxes glistened with celebrities. George M. Cohan, the Broadway songwriter, sat near General Douglas MacArthur, Commandant of West Point. President Harding had sent Attorney General Harry M. Daugherty to represent him. There were tycoons, politicians, and big time racketeers, sitting in the close proximity that they usually reserved for backroom deals. Strangely enough, though, about 5,000 of the 38,000 available seats—in the cheaper sections—were empty. Many fans, fearing it would be impossible to find a seat, stayed away. But interest was at an all-time high. An elevated train standing in the yards to the north of the Polo Grounds was "crammed to suffocation" by company employees. "Half a dozen necks craned from every window of the car." The train platforms were more packed than for rush hour. Other fans clung precariously to the bridge tower near the Harlem River and the 'L' signal tower nearby.

Ten thousand fans sat in Madison Square Garden, where a big board had been erected to simulate a baseball diamond. Miniature players were moved about the board as reports came from the Polo Grounds over a special wire. Details of the game were sent to the ships at sea through a wireless setup atop the roof of the Commodore Hotel. And, for the first time in history, the new invention of "radio telephone" was employed to broadcast a World Series. Station WJZ, which had begun broadcasting just a few days before, was transmitting its signal from a shack atop the roof of the Westinghouse plant in Newark. The first announcer, Thomas H. Cowan, sat in the shack and held a telephone receiver to one ear, listening to a reporter from the Newark *Call,* who watched the game in the Polo Grounds. When the reporter yelled "Strike one!" over the phone, Tommy quickly repeated "Strike one!" into his microphone. By the end of that first game, says one historian, Cowan's hand holding the phone receiver "became bloodless, the shell of his ear raw." The next day he switched to a headset.

During batting practice for the first game, a mysterious seaplane flew 2,000 feet over the stadium; Helen Ruth was inside, dropping three "good luck" baseballs to her husband. As the fans "oohed" and "aahed," the white parachute that held the balls floated downward and landed outside the stadium. But the Babe needed no further inspiration. The thrill of his first New York Series, with the whole nation urging him on, was enough. He was so fired up that he couldn't sit still while the Yanks were at bat, and Huggins allowed him to coach at third base, where he was like a one-man band, pacing about, clapping his hands, yelling, whistling.

When he first came to bat, there was a five second hush and then a mighty roar as he whacked a single and drove in what proved to be the winning run. Still revved up, he stole second and third bases in two successive dustclouds. In the meantime, Yank pitcher Carl Mays—a "Brobdingnagian," whose pitches "seemed no bigger than a fleck of shimmering sunlight on a gnat's wing"—was shutting out the Giants.

The Yanks also took the second game before 38,000 fans at the Polo Grounds. But while stealing third base during that game the Babe tore open his right elbow. The next day, as the Giants won, he aggravated the injury with a wild sliding attempt to steal second base and had to leave the game in the eighth inning. Ruth reported to the park for game four with his arm in a sling. Doctors had lanced his elbow, but the wound was still draining pus. Nevertheless, wearing a tight bandage around his elbow he came to bat in the ninth inning and socked a home run, his first of fifteen in World Series competition. But this blow wasn't enough to prevent the Giants from winning.

Ruth "rose to his greatest heights" in the fifth game, which the Yankees rallied to win. He should have been in the hospital. The infection in his left elbow was still open, with a tube there to drain out the pus. His left wrist, battered by so many slides, was tightly bandaged. Both legs were wrapped to the hips in bandages, and a charley horse in one leg made him limp perceptibly. But he was plucky enough to lead the Yanks in their winning rally. With the score tied 1–1, in the fourth, he confounded the Giant defense by dropping a perfect bunt down the third base line and beating the throw. Bob

Meusel hit a long double and Ruth ran all the way home from first to break the tie. Near collapse, he sat in the dugout for several minutes and then walked shakily out to his spot in left field.

That night, two doctors examined Ruth at his suite in the Ansonia and ordered him to stop playing until the wound healed. "Okay," he said, chewing a cigar. "I'll suit up and coach third base." "No," said one doctor, "you stay out of uniform, or you might talk Huggins into letting you play."

Unable even to steer his car, Ruth had a friend drive him to the Stadium the next day, and he watched the game with frustration. When he was shown a column by Joe Vila of the New York *Sun* about his "alleged injuries," he nearly exploded. His eyes blazing with anger, he rushed over to the press box, where Vila held up his type-writer as a shield. "You wrote that I got no guts!" the Babe yelled. Then, pulling off his jacket and rolling up his sleeve, he said, "If *you've* got any guts, print a picture of this hole in my arm!" But no retraction was forthcoming, and the Babe sat glumly through the rest of the Series, which the Giants won. "The Yankees without Ruth," said one paper, "were deflated to just another baseball team."

*   *   *

By mid-October the Babe's arm was well enough for him to lead a group of Yankee players on a barnstorming tour of the country. But commissioner Landis warned them of a rule, dating back to 1911, that forbade all players on championship clubs from taking part in post-season tours. The idea, apparently, was that league champions earned enough from their World Series shares. But Ruth rebelled, saying that players on second-, third-, and fourth-place teams also shared in the Series proceeds but were allowed to barnstorm. "I'm out to earn an honest dollar and Landis isn't going to stop us." Wally Schang and Carl Mays heeded Landis's warning and abandoned the tour, but Ruth was scheduled on October 13 to catch a midnight train for Buffalo, accompanied by star outfielder Bob Meusel and two young pitchers, Bill Piercey and Tom Sheehan. He called Landis at his suite in the Commodore Hotel and advised him of the trip.

"Oh you are, are you?" snapped Landis. "That's just fine. But if you do, it will be the sorriest thing you've ever done in baseball." He hung up the phone violently and began to curse. "Who does that big ——— think he is?"

Newsman Fred Lieb was with Landis when Ruth's phone call came. Noting the judge's anger, Lieb rushed over to the Hotel Martinique to warn Cap Huston of the imminent crisis. Huston, who was snoring off an all-night drinking bout with his friend Harry Frazee, woke up and rushed in a taxi to Grand Central Station, trying to reach Ruth before his train left for Buffalo. But Ruth insisted that "we've got to go through with it" because he'd signed a contract.

The next day, after walloping a homer against a team of Buffalo's Polish Nationals, Ruth repeated to the press, "Landis is wrong." The following afternoon, in Elmira, he insisted that he would play out the exhibition schedule until November 1. But the tour was a fiasco, plagued by cold weather, rain and fearful park owners who, not wanting to offend Landis, canceled some of the games. By October 21 the tour was called off, and Ruth (on the advice of Huston, who caught up with him in Scranton) issued an apology to Landis. It was also rumored that Huston bought off the tour promoter in order to cancel the remaining games. As for Ruth, who claimed he only wanted to earn "an honest dollar," the Yankees agreed to double his salary the next year to $52,000.

The Babe went off on a brief hunting trip with Red Sox pitcher Herb Pennock, but he still had energies—and a yearning for "honest dollars"—to spare. On October 28, it was announced that he would make a twenty-week vaudeville tour for $3,000 per week. Promoter E. F. Albee decided to bill Ruth as "the superman of baseball" and, at the suggestion of his friend, boxing impresario Tex Rickard, tried to drum up publicity by sending a wire to George Bernard Shaw in England: "WOULD IT BE QUITE APPROPRIATE TO BILL BABE RUTH AS 'THE SUPERMAN OF BASEBALL?' " The crusty author of *Man and Superman* wired back across the Atlantic: 'SORRY. NEVER HEARD OF HER. WHOSE BABY IS RUTH?"

Undaunted, the Babe worked hard to learn his lines with straight man Wellington Cross and after some out-of-town warmups opened at New York's Palace on November 14. His dressing room table was stacked high with telegrams from Buster Keaton, Helen Keller, John Ringling North, from dozens of baseball stars, and from a curvy dancer friend in Chicago who wired: "KNOCK 'EM DEAD, BABE. THE PERFECT 36 GIRL." That night, Ed Wynn was in the musical comedy *Perfect Fool* at the George M. Cohan Theatre; Marilyn Miller and Leon Erroll were in a Ziegfeld triumph called *Sally* at the New Amsterdam; and Billie Burke starred in Booth Tarkington's latest comedy, *The Intimate Strangers,* at the new Henry Miller. But Ruth's debut drew such a crowd that the fire department refused to admit any more standees.

Coming on with a grin so wide that it "almost hid his baseball uniform," the "chubby, naïvely attractive" Babe drew warm reviews from the critics—and howls of laughter from his Yankee teammates in the front row when they noticed that his fly was open. With that *faux pas* hastily corrected offstage, he lumbered through his paces. Said the critic of the *World*:

> That vivacious Babe Ruth, you must see him! All lip-rouged up like a tight-wire lady, with a voice as sweet as a furnace shaker in action. Hands that can't find a place on that whole stage to rest comfortably. A grace of carriage somewhere between John Barrymoreish and Elephantish. He came out yesterday at the Palace while the gallery boomed and the flappers flapped and the standees whooped 'er up til the poor chap stood on one foot, then the other, hoping they'd hurry and subside so he wouldn't forget his lines.

After a song or two, several spicy jokes, and references to Judge Landis and a certain traffic court magistrate, Cross and Ruth drew guffaws with their burlesque of a mind-reading act. The Babe sat blindfolded on the stage as Cross circulated in the crowd.

"See if you can strike this!" Cross shouted, holding up a tiny article.

"A match," said the Babe after only a moment's hesitation.

"Don't puff so hard!" said Cross. "What's this?"

"A cigar!" replied the seer.

"How many articles have I in my hand?" When the Babe's brow furrowed, Cross yelled, "Come, come, madam, you make me sick!"

"Oh yes," said the mind-reader. "Six."

That winter, about the same time that young Ernest Hemingway made his first postwar visit to Paris, two European war heroes came to America and, during a tour of New York's marvels, saw Babe Ruth. General Alphonse Jacques, commander of the Belgian Army, met the Babe outside the Palace for a quick batting demonstration. Christy Walsh had made sure that the press photographers were alerted. The Babe held up his bat, pointed to the end, and said a word which he had rehearsed for the past few minutes: *"Voilà!"* He drew it back for a full swing and the General said, *"Ah, oui."* Whereupon Ruth swung hard and someone cried to the Belgian visitor, "Look out for your nose!" Later that day, Babe appeared at a ceremony honoring Ferdinand Foch, Marshal of France and Generalissimo of the Allied and Associated Powers on the Western Front. They met at Saint Patrick's Cathedral to publicize a fund-raising drive for a new Knights of Columbus building in Manhattan. The Babe was to hand the Marshal a painted brick, symbolic of the beginning of the project. Posing awkwardly in front of the cameras, Ruth thrust the brick so quickly towards Foch's bemedaled chest that the military man jumped back as if he'd been shot. Someone hastily explained the purpose of the brick and Foch smiled and nodded.

With the ceremony over, Ruth, knowing no French, gripped Foch's hand, noted his dazzling array of medals, and asked politely, "You were in the war, weren't you?"

"Oui, oui," said Foch.

* * *

After New York, the vaudeville act set off on a national tour. While in Washington on December 5, Ruth heard the news that Judge Landis had fined and suspended him and the three other Yankees who went with him on the trip in October. Landis called their decision to ignore the rules "a mutinous defiance" and fined them their World Series share of $3,362. He also suspended them until May 20 of the 1922 season, meaning that Ruth would miss a month's action. Ruth appeared to take it calmly. In his hotel room, said one reporter, "he disposed his bulky form on a delicate pink chaise longue and carefully smoothed the sleeves of his variegated silk shirt." "Leave Judge Landis make the next move," he said, and then digressed, reminding the room service waiter to "bring lotsa potatoes with the steak."

There was a national uproar over Ruth's punishment. Fans sent petitions with thousands of signatures asking Landis to pardon the Babe. Ruppert and Huston, worrying about the financial consequences of Ruth's absence from the lineup for a month, send Ed Barrow to Chicago to convince Landis that the Yankees, not Ruth, would suffer the brunt of the penalty.

When Barrow reached Landis's office, the judge yelled: "I suppose you want to see me about that big baboon." Despite the criticism of the fans, Landis vowed not "to ease up on that big ape."

Ruth continued westward with the vaudeville tour, enjoying life as always. In Chicago's Congress Hotel, recalls Marshall Hunt, "the wine agent came by. Babe was leaving for the theater and said, 'Joe, fill up the closet.' Joe filled it up with cases of booze and the Babe did a double take at the bill when he got back. It was $4,000. The closet was as big as an ordinary sleeping room! Well, an adjustment was made there."

Another day, National League batting champion Rogers Hornsby hosted a party for Ruth at the Congress. Hornsby, it was said, was so fanatical about preserving his keen vision that he refused to go to the movies. He also proved to have a good eye for attractive women and a bizarre sense of humor. Somehow he secured a large galvanized metal tub, the kind used by farmers to feed animals. He also brought along a group of girls. Midway in the party, he told them, "Everybody into the other room and put on their party dresses!" Giggling, the girls changed into scanty costumes made of paper. Hornsby then herded them into the big tub, which was about two feet deep with luke-warm water. They squatted down and stood back up, and the soaked paper slid off, leaving them nude. "It was kind of pointless," recalls one party guest, "but that was Rogers's idea of a joke, and the Babe got a tremendous kick out of it."

En route to the West Coast, the Ruth tour stopped in a small town in Minnesota, at a three-story brick hotel facing the square. Ruth and he were looking out the window, says Marshall Hunt, when the town band arrived to serenade the visiting hero. "It was hailing as hard as I ever saw. The tuba player lost his hat somewhere along the line and the hailstones were beating down on his bald head and filling up his tuba, too. So every once in a while he'd have to turn the tuba up-side down and get the ice out. Then right back at it. He was a very dedicated tuba player. 'Goddammit, Babe,' I said, 'give this thing a thought, will you? This is certainly indicative of the great esteem that these people hold you in. This is really a serious thing!' I went on and on, laying it on thick. The words were coming pretty easy. But the Babe kept looking out the window and finally turned to me and said, 'C'mon, kiddo, let's eat.' "

FOURTH INNING

R is for Ruth.
To tell you the truth,
There's no more to be said,
Just R is for Ruth.
      OGDEN NASH, *ABC of Baseball Immortals*

"Are Tonsils but Useless Appendages?"

Ruth's boisterous personality sometimes frightened more timid souls from sharing his dinner table. He yelled for his food, told off-color stories in the same booming voice, and, says Robert Smith, grabbed "a drink, a doughnut, or a passing waitress with the uninhibited egoism of a man whose heart was pure."

But with time, as his fame grew, he acquired a thin veneer of social graces, a sense of *noblesse oblige,* if you will. In February of 1922 he was heading for a stopover in Saint Louis while en route to Hot Springs, where he would "boil out" the winter's accumulation of fat. The train was filled with a convention's worth of attractive college girls. They crowded around the Babe in the club car, where he puffed a cigar, sipped at a highball, and politely answered their questions.

"You know," said one girl to a passenger, "Mister Ruth is such a perfect gentleman! He talks so nicely. He's almost chivalrous!"

His instincts usually warned him when to rise to such occasions, but sometimes there were comic results.

One spring in Florida, he steered his car into a gas station. On the other side of the pump an elderly woman sat behind her chauffeur in another fine vehicle.

"Pardon me, Mister Ruth," she said, "I see you have a new car. Are the brakes on it hydraulic or mechanical?"

Ruth, who simply drove cars and knew only where the gas tank was located, slipped into his oiliest voice and replied, "Really, madam, I haven't the faintest consumption."

"*Conception,* Babe," whispered Marshall Hunt, who sat next to him. Ruth, who never was sure when his friend was kidding, looked sideways at him with an arched eyebrow. (He had a talent for malapropisms that delighted the press corps. Some years later, he lay in bed with an injured leg when Dan Daniel visited him and commented,

103

"You sure appear to be in great agony. What are you doing for it?" "Oh," said Ruth, "applying hot and cold complications.")

When the train carrying Ruth and the college girls arrived in Saint Louis, he got off to relax for a few hours before catching the 9 P.M. Missouri Pacific for Hot Springs. The station was crowded, and Ruth—smiling and doffing his camel's hair cap—pushed his way through, followed by Hunt and a porter with their suitcases and golf bags. As Ruth ducked into the waiting cab, fans demanded his autograph. By now he was accustomed to signing virtually anything that would take ink—baseballs, snips of paper, caps, sweaters. Finally, the driver turned around and asked, "Where to, Mister Ruth?"

"To the House of the Good Shepherd," said the Babe, referring to Saint Louis's most luxurious brothel.

Turning to the starter, the cab driver yelled, very loudly, "To the House of the Good Shepherd!"

Everyone in the station knew the place, and they were delighted. Several people applauded. As the cab pulled away, a knot of kids ran along behind yelling, "To the House of the Good Shepherd!"

The place was run by an immense, friendly madam named Sally who served exquisite aged steaks, along with massive helpings of mashed potatoes, gravy, home-made biscuits, and pie. "That night," says Hunt, "we had dinner there and the Babe accommodated a couple of them. I think he got one on the house."

On another occasion, the Babe's regular stopover in Saint Louis was less tranquil. He stomped down the steps yelling at the madam, "God *damn* you, Sally!"

"What's the matter, Babe?"

"That was the *awfulest* screw I ever had in my . . . god-*damn*, get *rid* of that one, she is . . . *jeez!*"

At this point, a histrionic woman wearing a robe descended the stairs and, in a high-pitched Southern accent, said, "Mistah Ruth, Mistah *Ruth!* Ah've had *several* travelin' salesman friends who say ah am the *best* on this earth, absolutely the best!"

"Like *hell* you are!"

Sally tried to calm the Babe, seating him upon a plush chair in the parlor and serving him a drink. Then she waved the woman back to her room, as she ascended the stairs she insisted, "I *sweah,* Mistah Ruth, they tell me, and they are *good* salesman, they make lots of money."

Ruth became the highest-paid player in baseball in 1922, when he signed a three-year contract for $52,000 per season. He and the Yankees were a few thousand apart when Cap Huston came down to Hot Springs to smooth out the difference. Ruth and Hunt sat boiling out in adjacent tubs when Huston shed his clothes and made it a threesome. As the pounds dripped away and Hunt gave good-natured advice to both sides, they began to haggle. Huston swore he could go no higher than $50,000, and the Babe held firm at $52,000 but agreed to settle by flipping a coin. Huston phoned Barrow in New York, who put in a call to Ruppert in Tarrytown, and the coin toss was approved. Shortly before midnight, up in Huston's room, Cap flipped a half dollar into the air, the Babe yelled "Tails!" and so it was. Ruth's new contract contained a clause stipulating that

> . . . he will refrain and abstain entirely from the use of intoxicating liquors and that he shall not during the training and playing season each year stay up later than one A.M. on any day without the permission and consent of the club's manager.

The three men stayed up much later than that, drinking toasts to the new contract.

The next morning, Huston proudly announced that Ruth now earned a salary "worthy of a railroad president." It was a lot of money in those times. A story in *Collier's* that spring estimated the total overhead of the Yankee team at approximately $600,000 a year. Of this amount, $120,000 represented player salaries, and Ruth earned about 40 per cent of the total!

That year, 5 million of the 6.7 million persons who filed a tax return reported an income of under $4,000; most of the millions who didn't bother to file earned even less. Ruth's salary was minuscule, of course, compared with the sixty-seven persons who reported incomes of $1 million or more that year (John D. Rockefeller, Jr., paid *taxes* of $7.4 million that year). It was far less than the income of Mary Pickford, who earned $1 million, or even Jack Dempsey, who raked in $300,000 for his bout in 1921 with Georges Carpentier. But it was far more than the $15,000 salary of the Chief Justice of the United States and equivalent to the combined salaries of five members of the President's Cabinet.

The *Times,* on its editorial page, noted: "Babe Ruth with his bat attracts more American citizens than Toscanini ever did with his baton . . . there are millions of American urchins who would rather be Ruth than Warren G. Harding . . . a democracy is willing to pay high for its amusements."

*   *   *

The old families of New Orleans, where the Yanks trained in 1921, could sometimes be "frosty" to a stranger, says Hunt, but the Babe's peculiar charm opened many doors.

Judges, politicians, and businessmen often made special trips to the

New Orleans park to meet the Babe and ask him to attend "a function" at their old estates, where he could enjoy "a real Southern
dinner." They often sent their cars to the Grunewald Hotel to pick
him up.

Hunt recalls accompanying the Babe on several of those "motion
picture evenings," with Negro waiters in silk hose, dozens of attend-
ants, and even a small orchestra playing behind the potted palms.
Ruth behaved very well at these "functions."

The host, says Hunt, "would offer him some dish with a French
name, and the Babe would say, 'I can't pronounce that, but I'll certainly take seconds!' Then the host would tell a story—it was usually
a simple thing—and the Babe could understand and laugh at the
right time. He would hold out his little pinkie, and bow, and say,
'Charmed to meet you.' He was civil, polite, even gallant at times."

Ruth particularly enjoyed weekend excursions into the bayou country, hosted by some New Orleans businessmen. "We'd spend the night,"
says Hunt, "in the natives' houses, where they cooked fish with wonderful sauces, and special breads, on old three-legged wood-burning
ranges. "We'd sleep in the launch with bedrolls. We met fishermen,
poachers, black market operators. Babe loved to camp out; things like
that he never forgot."

He also found time to play baseball, and the fans adored him.
As the Yankees worked their way north in late March, a reporter in
Galveston, Texas, said, "A week ago, the Saint Louis Cardinals came
here on a bright sunny day and took away $67 as their share of an
exhibition game. Today, a cloudy, windy one not suited for baseball,
Galveston Park was jammed . . . the share of the Yankees and the
[Brooklyn] Robins runs up to the 3,000 dollar mark. It was all due
to Ruth." He didn't disappoint the crowd. A sign on the right field
fence offered a box of cigars to the man who hit one over that spot.
Ruth leaned into a low curve and "laced one of his famous sailers
right over the target; the ball sailed and sailed until it seemed as
though it would drop into the gulf."

Since Judge Landis's ban prevented the Babe from playing until
May 20, he took advantage of the time to have his tonsils removed at
Saint Vincent's Hospital in New York on May 4. This minor operation got top-of-the-page treatment, especially when it was reported that
Mrs. Ruth, in the same hospital, at almost the same hour, "underwent
a major operation, similar to several she has had performed in the last
two years." Curiously little is known of Helen during that period.
She was apparently quite ill, and she and the Babe made virtually no
public appearances together. There were rumors of marital problems,
and his wild life was an open secret, but there were no public rifts.

Ruth's return to action on May 20 drew "the biggest throng of the year" to the Polo Grounds. Eighty police officers were assigned to control the crowd of 38,000, and one paper noted with relief that "none of the hundreds of women fainted in spite of the great jam inside the stands." Before the game, Ruth was given a floral wreath, a silver bat, and a large silver loving cup that contained dirt scooped from around the home plate of Saint Mary's School. To celebrate the Babe's return, said Bozeman Bulger, "a political news correspondent of worldwide acquaintance" brought along a quart of scotch carefully wrapped in a newspaper. He planned to offer a toast when the first Ruthian homer of 1922 cleared the fence. But during one exciting play, the man jumped to his feet and dropped the bottle. There was a loud pop, like a gunshot. Heads turned, and the fumes of the "joyful elixir" spread. "Even the ballplayers crouched in dugouts nearby stuck out their heads and sniffed, and Ruth turned around and grinned."

Despite the absence of Ruth and Meusel, New York was in first place, three games ahead of Saint Louis. Knowing that their star outfielders would miss the first month's play, the Yankee owners purchased Whitey Witt from the last-place Philadelphia club just before opening day.

"That's the good break I got," says Witt, who is now retired and lives in the same farmhouse in Woodstown, New Jersey. When he joined the Yankees, Witt recalls, "I told the guys, 'Look, I come from South Jersey and I grow tomatoes; when it don't rain I have to go out in the fields and blow 'em up with bicycle pumps!'

Witt had hit .316 for Philadelphia in 1921. He was fleet-footed, a fine bunter, and a sure fielder. While Ruth and Meusel were out, "I hit like hell; some of the writers were sayin' I was carryin' the club." He hit so well that he stayed in the lineup when they returned. "Ruth played right, Meusel played left, and I played center," he says. "I could run, see? I covered all the ground between those two big guys. They both had great arms, so I'd throw the ball to them. Every time the ball came out, the Babe'd yell, 'Laddie! Go get it, you little bow-legged sonofabitch or I'll kick the hell outa ya! Heh-heh."

One day, says Joe Dugan, who joined the Yanks later that season, "there was a long hit between Whitey and Ruth. 'Go grab it, Whitey!' Next one goes between Whitey and Meusel. 'Go get it, Whitey!' Next one's hit right over Whitey's head. He comes in, puffin', and Huggins calls him over. 'Whitey,' he says, 'I'm watchin' those two big stiffs. Keep chasin' 'em and I'll see that Colonel Ruppert gets you a bonus.' 'To hell with the bonus,' says Whitey. 'Tell him to buy me a bicycle!'"

The Yankees were a wild, hard-drinking bunch that year, and

Huggins's protests were ineffectual, because the team was winning. New York City was booming. Prohibition was just two years old and doing well, thank you. The city had thousands of speakeasies. It was said that you could buy a drink, for example, in any building on 52d Street between Fifth and Sixth avenues. New Yorkers danced to the music of Paul Whiteman, a young man from Colorado who came east the same year Ruth joined the Yankees and was now earning up to $25,000 for a six-night engagement. Filmgoers flocked to see Charlie Chaplin, Theda Bara, Doug Fairbanks, and Mary Pickford at the movie theaters. *Abie's Irish Rose* began the first of 2,327 performances on Broadway. A musical called *Shuffle Along,* written, produced and performed by blacks, had caught the fancy of white theatergoers, who now drove up to Harlem to enjoy such stars as Ethel Waters, Bill "Bojangles" Robinson, and Duke Ellington and chorus lines of "hi yaller" girls. The Babe partook of the city's delights, but he was pestered for snapshots, autographs, and handshakes. More often, he and a few cronies took the ferry across at 125th Street and drove to some speakeasy on a dark New Jersey highway. One of his favorites was Jimmy Donoghue's place in Garfield, where the owner even built a private entrance to a back room where the Babe, together with a small group of friends, could enjoy a night of serious drinking and card-playing. There were other places in New Jersey— Weehawken, Hoboken, Union City—that also offered good liquor and privacy.

"Babe didn't have one set group of pals," says Ford Frick. "He was pretty much of a loner, with lots of friends in and out of baseball. He never lacked for places to go and things to do." But when he went on the town with his teammates, his inner circle almost invariably included tall, taciturn Bob Meusel, Joe Dugan, Benny Bengough, Freddy Hoffmann, Waite Hoyt for a time, and Whitey Witt.

"The Babe loved Whitey," says Dugan. The feeling was mutual, says Witt. "Life was worth livin' with that guy. He was our star, our meal ticket. Some of the guys may have been jealous, but not me! I had enough brains to know that he was makin' money for me!" As a schoolboy in New England, Witt had known a young man named George, who was called "Jidge" by his friends. So he began to call Ruth "Jidge," and it soon became his special nickname on the Yankee club.

But for Ruth life on the road was the best of all. Each city offered different adventures and delights. Everyone wanted to be around him: politicians, businessmen, gamblers. After the games, Ruth would retire to his hotel suite, change to a silk dressing gown and slippers, pop

a big black cigar in his mouth, and receive a long line of visitors—
unless he had a date in some other part of town.

"One of our favorite sports as soon as we hit town," says one
teammate, "was to call up every slut in town that we could locate.
'Hello! Babe here! Listen, kiddo, I'll see ya in front of the hotel t'nite
at eight.' Jesus, I wonder what all those broads thought, standing out
there, lookin' at each other!"

He often paid for his pleasure, directly or indirectly, and not all
of his dates were that alluring. "I never saw him on an expedition with
anybody who was very attractive," says one acquaintance, "and he
had some awful horses up there in Boston." In fact, says Marshall
Hunt, "some of the Babe's paramours for a day would appeal only
to a man who was just stepping out of prison after serving a fifteen-
year sentence."

But the sheer logistics of Ruth's love life were amazing. His friends
could never understand how he went from one town to another and
made so many connections. Even when the Yankees traveled through
the South in the spring, the train would pull in to a town like Vicks-
burg and there on the platform would be a woman waiting to welcome him with a kiss. They never saw him phoning ahead and
could only speculate that the girls knew the team's itinerary and got
in touch with him. One man used to wonder, "Did he have a booking
agent all the way north? God almighty, the thing worked like clock-
work!"

The Yankees traveled in two Pullman cars, one for the team and a
"slop-over" for the writers and a few excess players. Early in the season, the Yanks and other Eastern teams—Boston, Washington, and
Philadelphia—competed among themselves for a few weeks. They
boarded an 11 P.M. train in New York and were in Boston the next
morning. They stayed at the Brunswick, where Leo Reisman and his
Orchestra offered "syncopating sounds" in the basement supper club.
Ruth had spent six years with the Red Sox and never lacked for com-
panionship in Boston. In Washington, it was the old Raleigh Hotel,
and from there he ventured into Baltimore to carouse with another
bunch of pals. During the Harding Administration, Ruth was also a
frequent guest at the White House, which, despite Prohibition, had
a private bar on the second floor, where Harding and his Ohio Gang
held late-night poker sessions. In Philadelphia they stayed at the old
Aldine Hotel, whose one redeeming feature was food served on the
American Plan by a faithful old waiter named Charlie, who wore
striped pants and had holes cut all around his shoes to relieve his
bunions. Camden, New Jersey, was only a cab ride away, however,
and had a good assortment of speakeasies.

Everyone looked forward to the first swing west. After they left New York aboard the deluxe Twentieth Century Limited, they got their huge $1.50 steaks as they passed by Poughkeepsie, and the setting sun gave a lovely glow to the banks of the Hudson. The next morning, as they ate breakfast and flipped through the newspaper, they looked out the window and watched farmers plowing the fields of Indiana. It was a time for reading, writing letters, or playing cards. One season, the Yanks developed such a passion for bridge that the minute they got off the train they rushed to their hotel rooms to complete a game and had to be reminded to report to the ball park on time (the same happened with the Philadelphia Athletics one season, when they discovered mah jongg). Ruth played bridge, but he preferred hearts or poker. When the Yankees played stud poker with a fifteen-dollar limit, recalls one teammate, "the Babe had all the money and we were scared t'death to bet against him!"

Whitey Witt liked to kibbitz while the Babe played cards. Witt and Dugan had a long-running joke about the cavernous size of Ruth's nostrils. Standing next to him, Witt would say, "Boy, if I had your nose fulla nickels!"

"Get away from me, you little sonofabitch," Ruth would growl.

"I start walkin' away," says Witt, and "first thing I know his highball glass comes sailin' right over my head! I think he finished the drink first, though."

The Babe was not always on the receiving end of the gag. He had a penchant for practical jokes. He often dropped lighted cigarettes into his teammates' uniform pants, just as they were pulling them up. He loved to stuff one small member of the Yankees into his locker and leave him in there just as the team ran onto the field. He smashed straw hats, nailed pipes to walls and shoes to the floor. He once planted a small bomb in a friend's car and then got in with his friend to personally enjoy his prank. When the bomb went off and destroyed part of the car, he said, "Gee, I didn't know it was that strong." While returning from a fishing trip to Long Island, he passed by the Park Avenue apartment building of his doctor. A doorman stood out front with a uniform that had so much gold braid he looked like an admiral. Ruth told his friend to stop the car. He jumped out, dropped one of the big smelly fish in the surprised doorman's arms, yelled, "Deliver this to Doctor ———— on the top floor!" and jumped back into the car.

One time, he bought a little item that resembled a hot water bottle. On the train, in hotel rooms or lobbies, he would slip it upon the seat as someone was about to sit down, and it sounded like a terrific passing of wind. He would howl. His funny stories were in the same earthy vein. One of his favorites was about the German restaurant where the customer finished his lunch and the waiter took out his pad and pencil to total up the bill: "Beef zandwich, vifty zents . . . vun cup of coffee, ten zents . . . vun apple pie, vifteen zents . . . Dot's zeventy-five zents." Then, the Babe would add, "the guy belches, and the waiter sez, 'and vun coocomber, eighty-five zents!' "

Sometimes, when the Babe tired of playing cars or gabbing, he snuck off to his berth. During one long train trip, a group of players and writers were playing bridge when they heard the strains of a popular waltz. Bozeman Bulger pulled open the green curtains of the berth and "there sat Ruth, completely undressed, absorbed in the operation of a phonograph. 'Wanna hear *I Kiss Your Hand,* Madam?' he asked. 'Great thing t'have good music along.' "

Chicago, one of the stops on the Yankees' Western trip, was a crude, noisy town. Even Lucky Luciano once called it "a god-damn crazy place; nobody's safe in the streets." The "black-and-tan" spots, with their fantastic dance acts, held a great fascination for some Yankee players and writers, but the Babe sought more private pleasures. To avoid celebrity hounds, he ate most of his meals in the Cooper-Carlton Hotel; he entertained there or went to private parties, some of them hosted by the mobsters who ran Chicago. In Cleveland the Yankees stayed at the Hollenden House, and in Detroit at the elegant Book-Cadillac. The Yankees sometimes took the ferry from Detroit to Windsor, Ontario, and sipped fine Canadian whisky. There was gunfire virtually every night along the Detroit River; the Internal Revenue Service and the Purple Gang were engaged in a constant game of cat-and-mouse, as the mobsters hauled huge kegs of liquor into the country.

In Detroit one night, Dugan, Witt, and Pipp dropped in at Ruth's hotel room and found him with three girls. The phone rang, and Ruth, after answering it, said, 'C'mere, Whitey. Now look. There's some bottles o' booze there in the closet. You entertain these three; I wanna go out and see this other one that called."

"They didn't want to have much to do with us," says Witt. "Babe was the one with the big roll o' dough that could've choked a horse. But we stayed around, wound up breakin' a few glasses on the floor, and we left."

At 2 A.M., Ruth returned to his empty room, undressed for bed, and cut his bare foot on a shard of glass. The next day, he came limping into the clubhouse. He couldn't say much, because Huggins was there, but he glared at Witt, Dugan, and Pipp and yelled, "Lookit 'em! You treat 'em good and this is what I get!"

Saint Louis was their favorite town. They stayed at the Chase, just across the street from Forest Park. On hot summer nights, since air conditioning was a thing of the future, they sat out in the hotel's big patio exchanging tall stories. "The Yankees were full of guys who were out for conquests," says one writer, "but it was a subject never mentioned. They loved to talk about hunting and fishing, and, surprisingly, 90 per cent of their conversation was about baseball. Huggins used to say that's why the team did so well, because they were always discussing the strengths and weaknesses of the other teams." On very hot nights, some of the men even took a blanket and slept in the park. Ruth perspired heavily and didn't like the confines of his room. In addition to the pleasures of the House of the Good Shepherd, there were some fine places to eat. Busch's Grove served wonderful fried chicken and beer. There was another place in a tough part of town run by a heavy German woman, who reputedly cooked the best spareribs on earth. Many times, when the Yanks left Saint Louis, Ruth had two dozen racks of ribs delivered to the train. He would set up shop in the ladies' room of the Pullman car and sell them to the boys at a quarter a rack, plus all the home brew they could drink. Like a good German burgher, the Babe served the food and beer, chewing ferociously at his own barbecued rib, his face smeared with sauce, enjoying a record on his little portable phonograph. One of his favorites, recalls Red Smith, was Moran and Mack's recorded comedy routine about "Two Black Crows." He'd hear it "one hundred times and howl at the hundredth repetition: 'How come the black horses ate more'n the white horses?' 'Search me, 'cept we had more black horses than white horses!' " There was another time that Hunt whipped up a private wingding in Saint Louis and phoned Barrow in New York, asking if he and Ruth could miss the train and fly back east later that evening. Barrow assented reluctantly, saying, "Goddamn you. You're gonna kill that bastard yet!"

After the wingding, about 11 P.M., Babe and Hunt got to the plane and delayed the takeoff, waiting for a messenger. He finally arrived with a huge bundle. "What's that?" asked the pilot.

"Spareribs," said the Babe. "I'm gonna open 'em up right now, 'cause I'm hungry."

Ruth and Hunt were the plane's only passengers. A few minutes after they were in the air, they were surprised to see the pilot walking back toward them. "I think he put it on automatic," says Hunt. The pilot asked Hunt to go forward and watch the controls, whereupon he sat down and joined the Babe in chewing away at the ribs. He made several trips back and forth. "By the time we landed in Newark," says Hunt, "I think the three of us ate damn near thirty pounds of ribs!"

Ruth's life was becoming as turbulent on the field as off. He had hit only one homer his first week back, and the fans were impatient. In Washington, on May 25, 1922, just six days after Judge Landis's suspension was lifted, he singled and ran for second when the out-fielder fumbled the ball. He slid and umpire Hildebrand called him out. Enraged, Ruth leaped to his feet, brought up with him a handful of dirt, and heaved it at the umpire. Wiping his eyes with one hand, Hildebrand waved Ruth out of the game with the other. The Babe walked to the dugout and acknowledged the fans' jeering with a good-natured tip of his cap. But one fan seated near the dugout let loose with a few choice words, and the Babe vaulted the dugout roof, clambered through a box full of people, and started up the aisle toward his tormentor, who beat a quick retreat. Ruth stood there, hands on hips, cursing and bellowing. He then went back onto the grass and walked across the field to the clubhouse in center field. As the fans jeered, he shook his fist, but then a cheer rose somewhere, and, as he disappeared through the clubhouse gate, he lifted his cap and waved.

Ruth got off lightly with this offense. He was fined $200 and removed from the captaincy of the club, a sinecure that gave him prestige and a few hundred dollars per season. His hitting was off, and the fans didn't let up on him. He became edgy and irritable. One day, Wally Pipp was having a bad time at first base, and Ruth complained loudly from the outfield. Pipp made another error and after the third out came into the dugout, trembling with anger. "If that big monkey says anything to me, I'll punch him right in his big nose." Sure enough, the moment Babe reached the dugout he barked, "For God sakes, Pipp . . ." That was the last word. Pipp bopped him, and soon they were rolling about on the dugout floor. Frank Baker tried to separate them and was rewarded with a punch in the eye by Ruth and one in the back of the neck by Pipp. The Babe was so angry that his next time at bat he smashed a homer; Pipp, still boiling, hit one over the fence also.

Ruth was in a fighting mood that season. On June 19, with the front-running Yankees in the midst of a losing streak, he was ejected from a game in Cleveland by umpire Bill Dineen. The next day, after batting practice, Ruth walked up to Dineen and yelled, "If you ever put me out of a game again I'll fix you so you never umpire again, even if they put me out of baseball for life!" More harsh words were exchanged, Ruth called the umpire "yellow," and the Cleveland players had to separate them. League president Ban Johnson suspended Ruth for three days when he heard of the fracas, but when he received umpire Dineen's report, detailing the Babe's language, he boosted the suspension to five days without pay, announcing that the salary loss amounted to $1,500. At $300 per day, this put the Babe's base salary at $46,200—not the $52,000 reported in the spring—but it was hastily explained that the larger sum included certain bonus arrangements for home runs. In announcing the suspension, Johnson made public his letter to Ruth, berating him for his "shameful language" and saying that his mind "has plainly been warped." The next day, with Babe out of uniform, the papers announced that "the Ruthless Yankees" beat Cleveland 7 to 3. The team continued to win, but the Babe was having one of his worst years. He was doing so badly that Bugs Baer wrote: "Last year Ruth stuck out like a battlefield at a peace conference; this year he has more competition than a beard in Moscow." Searching for answers, a Baltimore writer wondered aloud: "Are our tonsils but useless appendages? Did the removal of the King of Swat's tonsils influence that marvelous coordination of nerve and muscle that enable him to hang up incredible home run records? Has it influenced that cool nervous system which was indifferent to the jeers of fandom, so as to make him as temperamental as a prima donna? Who knows?"

The Babe's sagging performance on the field seemed to have no impact upon his popularity. On July 17, it was announced that he and Bob Meusel would appear at the George M. Cohan Theater at Broadway and 43d Street to publicize the film *In the Name of the Law*. Meusel was to stand atop the theater building and drop a ball down to Ruth on the sidewalk. About 15,000 fans jammed Times Square to watch the great feat. Traffic in the area was held up for forty-five minutes. Several spectators were trampled upon, and one was knocked down by a mounted policeman's horse. At half past noon, the Babe emerged from the theater lobby in shirtsleeves. From atop the roof, Meusel dropped one ball that fell into the crowd, Ruth muffed a second and finally caught the third, sparking a loud cheer.

Because of the tight pennant race, the Yankee management tried to limit the players' extracurricular activities. They hired a private detective named Kelly to trail them, and the man ingeniously passed himself off as a wealthy traveling salesman who enjoyed following the club around the circuit. He made his first appearance at the Hotel Ansonia in New York, rented a suite, and invited several of the players up for drinks. Gradually he gained their confidence. One time he even suggested to them that one young sports writer "may be a spy, hired by Ruppert," and they avoided the poor fellow as though he were a leper. On road trips, Kelly magically gained access to the team car and joined the players in card games. He offered them inside tips on the horses. "He'd buy us neckties, shirts," said Whitey

Witt. "We figured, what the hell, the guy enjoys spendin' his money, let's help him out! Heh-heh." One evening in Chicago, the Babe came over and said, "Look, Whitey, a friend of mine is havin' a ham 'n cabbage dinner out at his brewery tonight." Pointing to Kelly, who stood nearby, he said, "Bring him along too if ya want." The brewery was about thirty miles out, in Joliet, Illinois. About a dozen Yankees made the trip and returned to their hotel after 3 A.M. During their fiesta at the brewery, while everyone was in a jovial mood, Kelly appeared with a camera and asked them to pose. Some days later the Yankees were in Washington, sitting in their hotel lobby. "The bell-hop came along and says, to one of us at a time, 'Huggins wants to see you up in his room,'" Witt remembers. "I was one of the first to go up there. They had everything. Photos, reports on what we were doin', all the details. Huggins is laughin' like hell, and says to me, 'Too bad I wasn't with you!' He claimed he didn't know a thing about it, that Huston and Ruppert had hired this detective." So I come back to the lobby and tell the other guys, 'Kelly's the guy that sent in all those reports. He squealed on us. Kelly's the guy.' They called seven or eight of us up there, Meusel, Lefty O'Doul, Freddy Hoffman, Carl Mays, a whole bunch. Babe was the last to be called, and he couldn't believe it. Finally, he goes up and comes back to the lobby. "If I get my hands on that sonofabitch, I'll kill him!' he says. 'I'll kill him just as sure as you're born.'"

As the Yankees clung to their league lead, Ruth suffered one disaster after another. On August 13, he had to have an operation for an abcess on the calf of his left leg, which had been injured while he slid into a base. The Babe loathed sliding pads, which most players tied around the waist and strapped around the legs under their uniforms. He often "ripped patches of skin from the sides of his thighs," a teammate recalls. "Every year he had two or three such strawberries, which he washed in alcohol and covered with gauze and adhesive tape." On August 30, he was ejected from another game after umpire Connelly called him out on a third strike. Says one account, "The Babe's fiery Peruvian blood boiled in his veins with an audible hissing sound." This time, Ban Johnson suspended him for three days for using "vulgar and vicious language." When reporters tried to reach Ruth for comment at the Hotel Ansonia, his wife said he was "out fishing." But a Baltimore paper suggested he spent part of his enforced holiday in his home town, where he barely escaped a police raid on a speakeasy called Bowley's Quarters.

In late September, when the Babe was playing in Cleveland, his wife inexplicably turned up at a Giants game in the Polo Grounds, accompanied by a nurse who held a sixteen-month-old baby girl. The

reporters were flabbergasted. They followed so closely in Ruth's footsteps, they couldn't believe he'd fathered a child without their knowledge. Was the child recently adopted? one reporter asked. Mrs. Ruth
nearly flew into a rage. "Adopted? I should say not. The baby's mine,
mine, *mine!*" She claimed the child was born on June 7, 1921, at
Saint Vincent's Hospital in New York. A reporter in Baltimore
checked with a family friend who said that the child had been
born shortly after Ruth and his wife narrowly escaped injury in an
auto collision, that the child weighed only 2½ pounds at birth and
had to be placed in an incubator. Mrs. Ruth added that two girls and a
boy had been born to her and died in infancy. "I didn't want to say
anything until I was sure that little Dorothy was healthy," she added.
When the news was transmitted by the wire services, a reporter asked
Ruth at Dunn Field in Cleveland for details of the baby's birth. He
said she was born at Presbyterian Hospital on February 2. The press
rushed back to Mrs. Ruth with the discrepancy. "The Babe's always
been careless about dates," she said. Some of his Yankee teammates
agreed about his poor memory but found it "incredible" that he
couldn't recall if Dorothy was born during the winter or during
the baseball season. Reporters rushed back to Ruth once more. He
shrugged and said, "I guess Helen knows." Employees at the Hotel
Ansonia said they had only seen Mrs. Ruth with the baby a month
before. The child's origin remained a mystery that would not be resolved until years later.

If the Babe seemed foolish in answering reporters' questions about
his daughter, he was even more foolish during the 1922 World Series,
which the Giants swept in four games. It was the first time that a series
was broadcast directly from the ball park. Grantland Rice "related
his story of the game directly to an invisible audience of five million
along the Eastern Seaboard . . . not only could the voice of the radio
observer be heard . . . but also the clamor of 40,000 fans inside the
Polo Grounds made listeners feel as if they were in the grandstand."
Ruth batted a measly .118, getting only two weak hits. His performance upset him, and the jeers of the fans and Giant players were
like salt on his wounds. Every day the Giants in the dugout yelled at
him: "Nigger! Nigger!" After the third game, accompanied by Bob
Meusel, Ruth burst angrily into the Giants' dressing room. He went
up to Johnny Rawlings, one of the loudest bench jockeys, and said,
"You call me that again and I'll choke ya to death!"

"'What's the matter, Babe, cantcha take it?'" said Jesse Barnes.
"What about all the stuff you said to *me* yesterday?"

The argument grew more heated, and they seemed to be near
blows when one Giant player yelled, "Ah, Ruth's just tryin' to get his

name in the paper. He knows the reporters are here, and he's gotta do *somethin'*, the way he's hittin'."

Suddenly aware that half a dozen reporters were present Ruth backed toward the exit. "Look, guys, please don't write anything about this!" Just before he left, though, he poked his head back into the Giant clubhouse and yelled, "I'm sorry this happened. I don't mind being called a ———, or a ——— [he used hair-curling examples that no magazine or newspaper ever dared to preserve], but lay off the personal stuff!" As he left, half the Giant team was on the clubhouse floor, roaring with laughter.

The Series loss ended the season on a bitter note for the Yankees. The owners argued, and Huston sold out his half interest in the club to Ruppert. Ruth's batting average had dropped by 63 points, and his home run production fell from 59 to 35. It was widely felt that Ruth's poor showing, due to his carousing, was the key to the team's misfortune. There were rumors that he would be "severely disciplined" and that some of the other Yankees might be traded away. Bad luck continued to plague the Babe. On October 12, he had an auto collision at Broadway and 86th Street and had to pay $600 in damages. Finally, he left on a barnstorming tour of several Western states after securing Judge Landis's permission.

After the tour, on the night of November 15, Ruth attended a baseball writers' dinner at the New York Elks Club. His manager, Christy Walsh, told the reporters it was a "back to the farm" party and even had a large papier-mâché cow placed atop the main table. Walsh wanted to convince the public that Ruth would spend the winter at his Sudbury farm, far from Broadway's temptations, and would be in fine shape for the coming year. The speaker of honor was State Senator James "Jimmy" Walker, who enjoyed a good drink, a shapely calf, and other fine things of life, and who later became New York's most flamboyant mayor.

Walker shocked his audience when he rose and immediately said, "Babe Ruth is not only a great athlete, but also a fool!"

Ruth, says Gene Fowler, "sat back like a stunned hippopotamus."

"His employer, Colonel Jacob Ruppert," Walker said, "makes millions of gallons of beer and Ruth is of the opinion that he can drink it faster than the Colonel can make it." Pointing his finger at the Babe, Walker yelled, "You can't! *Nobody* can! Here sit some forty sportswriters and big officials of baseball, our national sport. These men, your friends, know what you have done, even if you don't. They are sad and dejected. Why? I'll tell you. You have let them down!"

Ruth appeared a bit angry, and began to squirm in his seat as Walker said, "But worst of all, worst of *all,* you have let down the kids of America. Everywhere in America, on every vacant lot where the kids play baseball, and in the *hospital,* too, where crippled children dream of the movement forever denied their thin and warped little bodies, they think of you, their hero, they look up to you, *worship* you! And then what happens? You carouse and abuse your great body, and it is exactly as though Santa Claus *himself* suddenly were to take off his beard to reveal the features of a villain. The kids have seen their idol shattered and their dream broken."

The Babe was moved to tears. As he wept, Walker reached over, placed a hand gently on his shoulder and said, "Listen, Babe, the other day a ragged, dirty-faced little kid on the street asked me for a dime to make up a quarter he was trying to get together.

" 'And what will you do with a quarter?' I asked him.

" 'I wanna get me a cap with Babe Ruth on it, like the rest of the gang.'

"If we did not love you, Babe, and if I myself did not love you sincerely, I would not tell you these things." More sobs. Then, like a skilled country preacher, Walker intoned, "Will you solemnly promise, for the dirty-faced kids of America, to mend your ways? Will you not give back to those kids their great idol?"

"So help me, Jim, I will," said the Babe, tears streaming down his face. "I'll take just one little drink tonight, but I give you my word of honor that it's the last until next October. I'm going back to the farm and get in shape!"

Daubing at his eyes with a handkerchief, Ruth shook hands with the writers as Christy Walsh patted his back. They went down the elevator and in the lobby a process server handed Ruth a summons, notifying him that he was the defendant in a paternity suit.

Ruth made an earnest, if bumbling, attempt at farming that winter. Friends who went to visit him in Sudbury were amazed. He'd spent a good amount of cash on concrete floors in the sheds and on other facilities for raising livestock. He chopped wood, repaired the roof of his house, cared for the turkeys and the cows, and sat at the fireplace smoking an exotic meerschaum pipe. He saw a big future in building a "fur farm," hoping someday to raise fur-bearing animals for the market on a large scale. He also bought hundreds of chickens, but each morning he'd go out to count them and find a dozen or so dead, victims of disease. It was estimated that each egg produced on the Ruth farm that year cost roughly two dollars.

Missing Ruth's bulky presence in New York, Marshall Hunt went to Sudbury that winter. When he got off at the deserted train station there was about two feet of snow. Unable to locate a cab, he trudged over to a service station and spotted the driver of a hearse, who wasn't busy at the moment and consented to drive him out to Ruth's place.

"Oh, it's you," said the Babe, looking a bit sleepy. He was alone. Ruth prepared a big breakfast of scrambled eggs. Afterward, Hunt noticed a grand piano in the living room. He struck a few chords and said, "The top's pretty badly scratched, Babe."

"Oh yeah, that's from one of my best tricks. It always worked when we had company this winter. I'll show ya in a minute."

Ruth disappeared and soon returned with a cat. He put the animal on a rocking chair and waited until it fell asleep. Then he quietly opened the window a few inches, went into another room and came back with a shotgun.

"My God," Hunt thought to himself, "the sonofabitch is gonna shoot a cat for my benefit."

Ruth stuck the gun out the window and fired.

"The cat made a magnificent leap," says Hunt. "Jesus, what a trajectory! It hit the floor once, and landed atop the piano, where it put out its landing gear and added a few more scratches."

"Babe," Hunt asked, "what kind of cat is this that you can keep playing the same miserable trick on him?"

"I dunno, but he does it every time!"

"He thought that was his greatest parlor trick," Hunt recalled. *"Slayed* the people, he said."

Ruth was too accustomed to Broadway's bright lights to stay away for long. In mid-January, he decided that an infected finger needed a doctor's care and went all the way from Sudbury to Saint Vincent's Hospital in New York. The next week he was back in town for another look at the finger. He planned to attend a dinner in New York that night but assured reporters, "Nothing but ice water for me; I haven't had a drink all winter."

"The House That Ruth Built"

New York was ankle-deep in snow in February, 1923, when the Babe boarded a train at Penn Station for his annual "tubbing" ritual in Hot Springs. Mrs. Ruth was there to kiss him goodbye; she and little Dorothy would join him in a few weeks at the Yankees' spring camp in New Orleans. Sitting in his Pullman compartment, "Farmer Ruth" told reporters that country life during the winter had agreed with him. He'd made "many foolish mistakes last season," but now he said he was brimming with health. After a week of hiking and "tubbing" at Hot Springs, he dropped from 215 to 209 pounds, his lowest weight since he was a pitcher for Boston. He trained hard; so hard, in fact, that after a strenuous 36 holes of golf his lingering cold escalated to a 104-degree fever; he suffered a night of delirium and required a nurse at his bedside. By mid-March he was in New Orleans, and a reporter found him in his room at the Grunewald, soaking his "barking dogs" in a giant pan of water.

The Ruth's apparent domestic tranquility received a sharp blow a few days later when headlines all over the country revealed that he was the defendant in a $50,000 breach of promise suit. Dolores Dixon, a "chestnut-haired" girl with "cherubic" features who worked at a telephone switchboard in a Manhattan department store, claimed that she was also carrying his unborn child. The papers had been served on Ruth after the Elks Club dinner the past November. Miss Dixon's lawyer tried for an out-of-court settlement, but Ruth reportedly told him, "Go to hell! I wouldn't give you fifty *cents* for this!"

"It's blackmail!" roared Ruth from his New Orleans hotel, with little Dorothy and Helen at his side. "Look, I'm no angel," he admitted, "but ever since I made my home run record I've been hounded by con men, gamblers and scheming women."

The next day, Miss Dixon's attorney released more details. He said that she was an orphan and had lived at 583 Riverside Drive (not far from Ruth's residence) with her "guardian," Barbara Escoe. They were introduced by "mutual friends" in the spring of 1922, and Ruth "used to be with her four to five times a week, taking her out frequently in his car." Ruth, the lawyer said, was stopped twice for speeding violations while Miss Dixon was in the car. In July, he claimed, Ruth took her aboard a boat in Freeport Harbor, Long Island, and "sexually assaulted her." Ruth had, indeed, made a publicity appearance at a circus in Freeport that month. But his lawyer denied the charges. Miss Dixon's lawyer released more details, which were eagerly lapped up by the nation's readers. Ruth called her "my little watch charm," because she was barely five feet tall. He also called her "my little golf girl," because he said he was going to play golf on the afternoons that he allegedly saw her. He gave her money and gifts "several times." Miss Escoe's brother, who lived in an East 8th Street tenement, told a story that made Miss Dixon sound more like Candy than an ingenuous orphan. "Oh, Babe Ruth knows her. She has it on him and several others. Ruth isn't the only ballplayer who's going to be brought into this case." But inconsistencies in the Dixon story were published by a not-too-friendly New York press. Her age was first given as fifteen, then seventeen, then nineteen. She appeared to be in hiding. Where was Dolores Dixon? Ruth's lawyer produced a witness who would "prove" it was all "a blackmail plot." The account of Ruth's formal court reply was buried in a one-paragraph item in the *Times;* it did not deny that he knew Miss Dixon but rejected allegations that he promised to marry her, or had engaged in improper conduct. At a press conference one month later, Ruth's lawyer waved a signed agreement, saying that Miss Dixon had withdrawn the suit "without cost to either party." He claimed to possess her "signed confession" to the blackmail scheme but refused to show it to reporters; he would deliver it to the district attorney for possible legal action, he said. The case dropped from sight. Whether it was blackmail, or whether the complaint was artfully hushed with a payoff, is anyone's guess.

* * *

On April 18, 1923, more than 74,000 people—the largest crowd ever to witness a baseball game—crowded into the new $2.5 million Yankee Stadium, and 25,000 more were turned away. Viewing the crowd, Damon Runyon said, "The heads were packed in so closely that Al Goullet, the six-day bicycle rider, could have ridden his bike around the stadium on the track of their hats."

It was a great day. Governor Al Smith was there to heave out the first ball. Celebrities were all over the place. The Seventh Regiment

Band walked onto the field, "looking like the guardesmen of Napoleon, with their long gray coats, shakoes, white trousers and white belts." Then "a familiar figure in dark blue military uniform stepped briskly across the field to take command of the musicians. There was a whoop from the crowd." It was John Philip Sousa!

Up in the pressbox, nearly 150 writers from all over the country were there to chronicle the historic day. One of them was Fred Lieb of the *World,* who decided to call the stadium "The House That Ruth Built," a term that lives today.

Bob Shawkey made the first official pitch in the Stadium, and Chick Fewster of the Red Sox hit a grounder to the shortstop who threw him out. In the Yankee half of the first, Whitey Witt led off and was also put out. The Yankees erupted in the third inning. With Shawkey and Witt on base, Dugan drove in a run with a single. Up came the Babe, who had flied out in his first try. The 74,000 fans screamed for a homer. What, after all, could be more appropriate than for the mighty Babe to slam the first one out of the "house" that he had built? With the count two balls and two strikes, Boston pitcher Howard Ehmke threw and Ruth swung. The ball soared gracefully into the right field seats, which forever after would be called "Ruthville." The fans, according to popular historian Hendrik Willem Van Loon (who was covering the series for the Christy Walsh Syndicate), "were on their feet yelling and waving and throwing scorecards and half-consumed frankfurters, bellowing unto high heaven that the Babe was the greatest man on earth, that they loved the Babe, that the Babe was some kid, and that the Babe could have their last and bottom dollar, together with the mortgage on their house, their wives and furniture." Well before the game ended in a Yankee victory, Van Loon retired to the Harvard Club to type his essay. He left, he said, because "long experience has taught us to leave well enough alone . . . to see the immortal George Herman Ruth make a home run is the ultimate hope and desire of all normal Americans."

The next day, Ruth hit a 450-foot triple into the spacious center field area of the new stadium. By now, the New York *American* featured a daily box on the sports page called "The Truth on Ruth," which carried details of his homers and his times at bat in each game. A week later, President Harding came to see his Washington Senators play the Yankees in the new stadium, and Ruth again rose to the occasion. Wearing his brown slouch hat and puffing one cigarette after another, Harding leaped to his feet with everyone else when the Babe connected for his second home run of the season. After crossing home plate, Ruth jogged over to Harding's box seat and doffed his cap.

*   *   *

One warm afternoon in Washington that May, the Babe, sweaty from practice, trotted over and said "hello" to Jimmy Barton, the star of a variety show called *Dew Drop Inn* that was about to open at the National Theater. Barton had invited two pretty showgirls to the game, Claire Merritt Hodgson and Bobbie Kane, saying that he wanted to introduce them to his friend the Babe.

It was a brief, uneventful meeting. But the next afternoon Eddie Bennett, the Yankees' little hunchbacked batboy, appeared at the door of Claire's dressing room with a note in Ruth's flowing hand: "I don't know what hotel you're at, so I'm sending this note. Will you have dinner with me this evening? Babe Ruth."

On the telephone, Claire asked Ruth why the invitation was for his hotel suite. "Lord, Miss Hodgson," he boomed, "I can't go into any restaurant; I get mobbed every time." When she agreed to go, on the condition that she could bring her friend Bobbie, he laughed and said, "Don't worry. My suite'll be *lousy* with people. It always is." He was right. There were a lot of people, and it was more a party than a dinner. All evening Ruth held a whisky glass in his hand, and there was always some sycophant to keep it filled, whereupon he would growl, "Thanks, keed."

"You know," Claire said, "you drink too much."

Smiling, the Babe replied, "You sound just like Miller Huggins, but you're the first *dame* who ever told me."

Claire had come to New York three years before "for whatever reasons there are that make small towns small and unhappy marriages unhappy." Her father, Colonel James Monroe Merritt of Athens, Georgia, taught at the University of Georgia and had a law practice. Just before her fifteenth birthday, Claire, a vivacious, dark-haired girl, eloped with a thirty-three-year-old widower named Frank Bishop Hodgson. A child, Julia, was born, but the marriage failed. In November, 1920, accompanied by little Julia and her Negro maid, Marie Martin, Claire checked into the Waldorf-Astoria, carrying with her a letter of introduction to Howard Chandler Christie, the well-known portrait painter. After securing a few modeling jobs and bit parts in silent films, she moved into a four-room apartment on West 70th Street between Broadway and Columbus. In 1922, her former husband died. The next year her father died, and her mother came to live with her in Manhattan. By 1923 she was, as she later described herself "a good-looking young woman and a mediocre actress who had a baby." Christie had introduced her to Sigmund Romberg, the composer, who recommended her for the part in *Dew Drop Inn*.

After her introduction to Ruth in Washington, the show took her to New Haven, and the Yankees continued around the league circuit.

But they spent hours on the telephone. When the show opened in New York and the Yankees returned home, Ruth met Claire's mother and her two brothers, Eugene and Herbert, who soon became frequent hunting and fishing companions. He was crazy about her daughter, Julia. Gradually, what may have begun as one of Ruth's many short-term romances turned deep, serious, and irreversible. "My home became his, my mother his, my daughter his," said Claire. But each time they talked of the next step, came the lament, "I'm a Catholic, I'm married, and I got a kid." As the relationship continued, Ruth's wife, Helen, grew suspicious and felt more threatened than if her husband were merely toying with a series of mistresses. "Ours was a long courtship," said Claire. "More than five years, filled with frustration, not a little humiliation, and an uncommon amount of terror . . . we had to hide."

*   *   *

But the romance didn't hinder Ruth's baseball performance. That August, a *Daily News* editorial said that he was "in his greatest year." His home run total had slipped, but he was hitting sensationally. Even before the season ended, as the Yankees led the pack by 17 games, Ruth was unanimously selected as the most valuable player in the American League. He finished with 41 home runs, enough to lead the league, and a .393 batting average, the best of his career. Cautious pitchers granted him 170 walks, a record that stands today.

The first of the fabled "subway series" between two New York ball clubs was played that October. Ruth was limping from a slight leg injury, but in a practice session before the series, a reporter said, he was "brimming over with the joy of living and playing the game . . . and the other Yankees followed his example, like sheep following their leader." Each day, newspapers would run a special box on the sports page detailing Ruth's fortunes every time he came to bat.

More than 58,000 fans turned out for the first game of the Series at the new Yankee Stadium, surpassing the previous World Series attendance record of 46,620, set in 1916. Clowns Nick Altrock and Al Schacht made them roar with their burlesque of the Dempsey-Firpo fight on the infield grass.

Casey Stengel, then an aging outfielder, won the game for the Giants in the last inning with an inside-the-park homer. Ruth hit a triple in the fifth but was thrown out at home when he tried to score on a short fly ball; he rammed into Snyder, the burly Giant catcher, who stood firm, and "caromed off, shot through the air, and landed squarely on his side several feet away."

Ruth squared things the next day at the Polo Grounds when he hit two homers in consecutive innings and led the Yankees to a 4–2 victory. Afterward, there were "howls of jubilation" in the clubhouse, and Ruth, with an "ear to ear grin," yelled, "This is a cinch park to hit homers in; I could get eighty a year here!" The action returned to Yankee Stadium for the third game, where 66,000 fans wedged their way inside and 25,000 more were left on the sidewalk. Fifteen minutes before game time, cars stretched far across the bridge leading to the park, up the 155th Street viaduct and west as far as Saint Nicholas Avenue in Manhattan. Casey Stengel was again the Giants' hero as he wafted a homer barely over Ruth's head into the seats, beating the Yankees 1 to 0. The Yankees liked to ride the daffy Stengel just to hear his comebacks, and when he hit that homer he ran around the bases with his thumb to his nose and his hand pointed toward the Yankee bench. The Babe was angry after the game. "They wouldn't give me a good one to hit!" he yelled in the clubhouse. "I was all set to break up the game in the eighth, but Nehf wouldn't get one close enough for me to reach with a broom!"

But the Yankees swept the next three games and won their first World Series title. In the final game, Ruth got them off to a quick advantage in the first inning with a long home run, his third of the series. The lead seesawed until Bob Meusel hit a bases-loaded single in the eighth to clinch the victory. After two humiliating series defeats to McGraw's Giants in 1921 and 1922, the Yanks were ecstatic over their first world's championship. In the locker room, Ruth wrapped his big arms around Meusel in a giant bear hug. Then he shook little Miller Huggins's hand so hard that the manager winced. In the midst of the shouts and laughter, Ruth climbed up on the rubbing table and, "embarrassed and bashful even among his own teammates," offered a little speech. He took a diamond ring from a jeweler's case and held it up. "Boys, we owe a lot to Hug here." The tiny manager "blushed beneath his weatherbeaten tan." "Hug," said Ruth, "we want to present you with this ring as a token . . . Oh, hell, here!"

"This is the happiest day of my life!" said the acquisitive Jacob Ruppert. "Now I have baseball's greatest park and baseball's greatest team!" Ruppert gave a boisterous victory party at the Hotel Commodore, and, Ruth recalled, "a few of the boys got kind of dizzy before a happy night was over." They had many reasons to rejoice. More than 300,000 people had paid $1,063,815 to see the six games, making it the first "million dollar" Series. Each Yankee received a record $6,160 as his winning share. The next day, league batting champion Harry Heilmann, who doubled as an insurance agent in the off-season, talked Ruth out of a good portion of that check. He sold him a $50,000

annuity policy that would begin to pay off in twenty years; it was
the first time that the Babe had soundly invested any of his cash. After a bit of big-game hunting in New Brunswick, the press reported,
he would spend the winter at his Sudbury farm "to milk the cows
and swing the axe and feed the chickens, and spend the long eve-
nings in sweet memories of an illustrious campaign." But before that,
he was off on a brief barnstorming tour. On October 24, at a benefit
dinner in Scranton, he made a plea for lifting the ban on Sunday baseball in order to "keep young men away from crap games, card
parties, and other forms of gambling" on the sabbath. The next afternoon more than 6,000 children were at the Scranton park, where
Ruth's "All-Stars" beat a group of local talents. There was an almost
magical affinity between Ruth and young boys. "They happen to like
me," he once said, "and I've always felt cleaner after a session with
kids." He planned to put on a postgame hitting exhibition for the
Scranton youngsters, but they stormed past the police and mobbed him.
The Babe, trying to avoid spiking one of the half-pints, tripped and fell
to the ground. "The boys," said one witness, "thought it was a joke
and piled on top of him. Four husky policemen spent several minutes
in removing the lads from their idol." Ruth wanted to continue, but
police escorted him to his car, where he yelled, "Sorry, kids!" doffing
his cap and waving farewell.

*   *   *

Ruth spent an uneventful winter, except for a minor brush with the
law. He was arrested in January for speeding near his Sudbury home,
and the judge found that he had been driving without a state registra-
tion since 1914, when it was revoked after his involvement in an auto
crash. He got off with a $70 fine. (Ironically, that spring Ruth, wear-
ing a Yankee uniform, was driven around New York in an open tour-
ing car as part of a driver safety campaign. A large sign on the
vehicle said: "You can bat 100% for safety by being careful.")

At Hot Springs in March, the Babe returned from a long morning
walk, staggered into the lobby of the Hotel Majestic, and collapsed.
It seemed like a repeat of the previous spring. Team doctors issued
a bulletin that he was again a victim of influenza and was running
a mild fever. But Will Wedge of the *Times* recalled a few months later
that "down south this spring, the Babe was stricken with colic one
morning after a midnight orgy of eskimo pie, apple pie, pigs trotters,
beans, and beefsteak pie." Whatever the cause, he was indeed ill
and stayed in bed for a week. A constant diet of chicken broth did
the trick; one morning he was seen promenading about the Majestic's

halls in his bathrobe, puffing furiously on a cigar and bellowing for solid food. The illness had cost him eight pounds, dropping him to a svelte 218.

The Babe got off to a strong start in 1924 and won both the batting title (.378) and the home run championship (46), although Washington beat New York in the pennant race. The Prince of Wales visited America that year, and writers began to call Ruth "The Prince of Whalers." A nationwide poll showed that Ruth and Charlie Chaplin were America's two most widely known celebrities. His legend continued to grow, as one national magazine after another offered "intimate details" of the Babe's life.

"Did you know," wrote Arthur Robinson in *Collier's,* "that Babe Ruth does not wear any underwear, winter or summer?" He is superstitious, said Robinson, and the sight of a white butterfly on the playing field would either "terrify" or "exalt" him. If the Yankees won, he made sure to enter through the same hotel door as he exited. "Like many players," he believed that seeing a truckload of empty barrels on the way to the ball park was a sure sign of victory. There were many other tidbits: Ruth's love for his portable phonograph; his "special fondness' for the ukulele; his favorite song, "My Darling Lou," which he sang in a bass voice; his love for food and chewing tobacco; and the fact that he devoured "huge quantities" of bicarbonate of soda to relieve his stomach trouble.

Will Wedge explained that Ruth had become "addicted" to the "bicarb" that spring, when it gave him some relief after his "midnight orgy." After taking the bicarb, one man recalled, "he would belch and all the loose water in the showers would fall down." Ruth had also gone through a "boracic acid craze," said Wedge. He'd gotten something in his eye the previous season, and trainer Al Woods removed it with an eyewash, after which Ruth hit a homer. For about a month thereafter, he "religiously rinsed his peepers" with an eyecup. But the novelty of the cure soon faded, and he "parked his eyecup and gallon of boracic acid on the shelf, alongside of his discarded rubber reducing belt."

He was besieged with thousands of requests for autographed bats and balls, some of which were auctioned off for charity, others to inspire young players, and others—if one believes some of the publicity—to revive moribund children from their sickbeds. Such requests were so frequent that Robinson estimated the Babe had signed "eleven hundred bats and about three times that number of balls" by the first half of 1924.

He often had help. According to Westbrook Pegler, Marshall Hunt was Ruth's "master forger." Hunt soon learned to imitate the Ruthian scrawl with such accuracy that once, as a gag, he wrote out a check to cash for $2,000 and left it on the Babe's hotel room bureau. Ruth came in, looked at it, and said, "By God, they'd cash it!" From then on, says Hunt, "I think he always had a lingering doubt as to what I was doing with his signature."

Ruth was exceedingly careless about money. That spring he entered a New Orleans bank intending to convert four $1,000 bills into a draft and send it to New York. He fished into his pocket and discovered that one bill was missing. After a search of his other suits and laundry in the hotel, he shrugged his shoulders, and not another word was said. The Yankees and Dodgers traveled north together on their barnstorming tour that April and spent much of their train time playing poker. Brooklyn had a catcher named Miguel Angel "Mike" Gonzalez, whose smile revealed a dazzling platinum tooth. Late one night, Gonzalez returned to his Pullman berth, which was opposite that of sportswriter Tom Meany. He pulled a wad of bills from his pocket, stuffed it inside his wallet, the wallet inside one of his socks, and the sock beneath the pillowcase. Turning to Meany, and flashing his platinum smile, he said, "Thot Babe Root, I hope she play beisbol long time, keepa maka lotsa money!" Once, at the Hollenden Hotel in Cleveland, the Babe was talking with a friend in the lobby when Joe Dugan came up behind him and whispered, "Jidge, your pal is empty." Without looking, Ruth reached into his pocket and slipped Dugan a bill. Dugan didn't look at it until he paid the restaurant tab that night and saw it was $500. "They had to get the owner out of bed to change it," says Dugan. Joe returned five $100 bills to Ruth a few days later, and the Babe said, "What's this for?" "The money you lent me in Cleveland." "Thanks, kid, I was afraid I blew it."

He wasn't always so forgetful. One spring a Yankee exhibition game was canceled by rain. Ruth walked into the clubhouse the next day with $8,000 in race track winnings and dumped the whole amount on an equipment trunk, telling his teammates, who received no salary during the spring, to "grab whatever you need." A few weeks later, when the men got their first paychecks in New York, he strode from one locker to another, holding a bat, demanding with a smile, "Awright, how much did ya take? Get it up."

Sometimes he had to borrow money to make ends meet. He burst into the clubhouse one day, claiming to have a "hot tip" on the races. "You guys wanna make some money today? Get on this horse!" He was betting $18,000 on the race, he said. A few Yankees made wagers of $25 or $50. Every time the Yankees came off the field in the game, Ruth dashed into the clubhouse to find out if the race had been run. About the sixth inning he came back to the dugout, his chin down to his chest. The horse had run third. That spring he borrowed money from Hoyt and Dugan to pay his income tax. When his teammates didn't have the kind of cash he needed, he went elsewhere. Mob leader Frank Costello recalled once allowing Ruth to beat him for $5,000 in a golf match on Long Island when the Babe complained he was short of cash. "I didn't want to lend it to him, because I wasn't sure he'd be able to pay back, and then I'd have to be collecting from him," Costello said. But Ruth's friends claim that he scrupulously repaid his loans, ofter with 6 per cent interest, because he'd heard it was the proper thing to do.

Not all of Ruth's money was spent on the horses. Most of it went to support a way of life that would blot out the penury that he knew as a child. Although it appears impossible, friends swear that he once wore twenty-two expensive silk shirts during a sweltering three-day stand in Saint Louis, then left them all behind for the hotel chambermaid. His suite at the Ansonia was always crowded with visitors. Little Dorothy barely slept, and a bewildered Helen knew only a fraction of the guests. Room service waiters padded in and out with trays of food and drinks, with the Babe paying the tab. All the while, Ruth paced about, slapping backs, roaring at jokes, and approving vague business proposals that were forgotten before the night was over. He was the king, he was having one hell of a time, and he didn't give a damn about what he said or did. Once, a young journalist, who was preparing a series on the opinions of celebrities about pressing world issues, cornered him and asked, "Mister Ruth, what do you think of the Chinese situation?"

Mister Ruth took a big gulp from his highball and replied, "The hell with it."

He was no more inhibited on the field. In April, 1924, when an umpire called him out on strikes and the Babe's argument was to no avail, he hurled his bat high in the air, and it landed perilously close to the pitcher. Ruth was thumbed out of the game. That June, when a fight broke out during a game in Detroit and the 18,000 fans stormed onto Navin Field and turned it into a full-scale riot, Ruth rushed out of the dugout and floored Detroit's playing manager Ty Cobb with a wild football body block. He lost his fielder's glove during the melee and was fined $50 for what league president Ban Johnson called "his frenzied effort to participate in the trouble."

Despite Ruth's indifference to "the Chinese situation" and other public issues, his fame attracted politicians, who sought his support. That summer, as the Democrats prepared to celebrate their national convention in New York, it was trumpeted that "Babe Ruth, King of Swat, came out strongly for Governor Al Smith," who was seeking the party's Presidential nomination. Ruth knew nothing about politics, but he was told by friends that Smith was a "good guy" who "came up the hard way, just like you."

A few days later, a letter was drafted for Ruth's signature and sent to Franklin D. Roosevelt, chairman of the Smith campaign committee:

"Sure—I'm for Al Smith. . . . Maybe you know I wasn't fed with a gold spoon when I was a kid. No poor boy can go any too high in this world to suit me."

That summer, Ruth was asked to help publicize the work of the country's Citizens' Military Training Camps. He was enlisted as a private in the 104th Field Artillery of the New York National Guard, but they couldn't find a uniform to fit him. On his next trip to Washington he dropped by the Quartermaster Depot and was fitted out with a khaki suit, after which he was photographed exchanging salutes with General Pershing at the State, War, and Navy Building.

During that visit to Washington, Yankee pitcher Herb Pennock was asked by a prominent Delaware family ("off the record, it was the Duponts," said one source) to attend a lawn party with a few teammates and to bring along two dozen autographed baseballs. They hinted quite strongly that Ruth would be most welcome. Manager Huggins approved the excursion but reminded the men that they had a game in Philadelphia the next day. It was a lovely afternoon. The young heirs and heiresses of the prominent family were enchanted by Ruth, who demonstrated his famous home run swing with a stick of celery. He bowed, and kept his pinkie raised, and said "charmed," but as the hours went by and the drinks went down, his eye wandered toward a shapely brunette maid who was serving the canapes. Soon, while everyone else tried to avert their eyes and sustain polite conversation, Ruth was on the fringe of the crowd, chasing her around. "We gotta get this bastard outa here!" said one Yankee to a boxing promoter from Philadelphia, who had come to the party with the players.

"Babe," said the promoter, "we gotta go."

"I want that broad," said Ruth.

"I'll getcha alla broads you want in Philly. Come on!"

They reached Philadelphia about 1 A.M. and went up to Rose Hicks's place on Broad Street (an apt address for that type of establishment). Four hours later, one Yankee said to another, "I've had enough of this, let's get the Babe and head back to the Aldine." By now Ruth had been upstairs "at least five times," and they found him sitting in a big chair, a brunette on one knee and a blonde on the other. As he poured a bottle of champagne onto his head and the girls playfully shampooed his hair with the bubbly, he smiled and exclaimed, "Anybody who doesn't like this life is crazy!"

The next afternoon at Shibe Park, one of Ruth's companions looked so wobbly that Huggins removed him from the game. Another appeared to be fast asleep on his feet in the outfield. Ruth, with barely two hours sleep, hit a pair of home runs. "That's the way he lived all the years I knew him," says Joe Dugan. "Like I said, he was an animal!"

By year's end, it was announced that Ruth was the not only the league batting champion but also led in homers, runs scored, total bases, bases on balls . . . and strikeouts. After going to see the World Series, he embarked in mid-October on a cross-country barnstorming tour, accompanied by Bob Meusel and Christy Walsh. They covered 8,500 miles, played in fifteen cities in six states, and drew 125,000 fans.

In a small California town (pop. 3,500), more than 15,000 customers paid to see him pitch against Walter Johnson. The local Elks had printed up placards that were placed in every store window: "This store closed Friday afternoon on account of Walter Johnson–Babe Ruth ball game." He hit seventeen homers during the tour; he also made twenty-two speeches at breakfasts, luncheons, and dinners and seven from Pullman platforms. He was guest of honor at four parades, wore his dinner coat nineteen times, wore a silk hat once (under protest), refereed a four-round boxing match in Hollywood, and in Los Angeles was the guest of Jack Dempsey. At Grauman's "Million Dollar Theater" he appeared in person on the same bill with Ben Turpin in the Mack Sennett film, *Romeo and Juliet*. He also took a spin with Doug Fairbanks in his jaunting car on the lot where Fairbanks was filming *The Thief of Baghdad*. He batted a thousand autographed baseballs to ten thousand Los Angeles schoolboys from a stadium grandstand roof, and nearly fell off the roof. He visited eighteen hospitals and orphanages, posed for about 3,800 photos, ate four buffalo steaks at one sitting, refused to wear a nightgown or pajamas at any time, and was later presented with a big red flannel nightgown by the Lions Club of Dunsmuir, California, which also made him a life member. In Kansas City, Seattle, Spokane, San Francisco—newspapers devoted huge amounts of space to his coming. When he hit a homer in Seattle, the local paper swore "the ball hit Mount Rainier on the first bounce!" Even on the train, when he tried to pay his dining room bill a steward said, "You're the guest of the Northern Pacific." Ruth smiled and said, "Well, in that case, how about another order of ham and eggs?"

In early December, before heading back to Sudbury, the Babe, ten pounds heavier after his tour, was invited to a dinner of the New York Baseball Writers Association. As a gag, the writers hired an actor named Vince Barnett to play the part of a tough waiter. He insulted everyone, including Jake Ruppert and Judge Landis, spilling soup, elbowing them aside to serve their dishes. Then he got on Ruth, poking him in the chest and yelling, "Who ever told you you're a ballplayer?"

"He had me crazy," said Ruth. The Babe and Rosy Ryan of the Giants chased him all over the room. Ryan finally brought him down with a flying tackle. The writers rushed over to explain it was all a joke. "Just when I had him by the neck!" said the Babe.

FIFTH INNING

Philadelphia—Two shining faced negro boys, each about eight years old, were brought to the Athletics bench today as mascots [and] were credited by the players with breaking their losing jinx. The youths, beaming at the distinction thrust upon them, kept the players in good spirits with their songs and dances before the game. As a good luck token, the players rubbed the heads of their little mascots before going to bat and base hits began to ring out when they were needed. After the game the youths were showered with coins and promised each would be bought a new suit of clothes.

New York *World,*
September 9, 1925

"The Bellyache Heard Round the World"

As the economy spiraled upward in 1925, President Coolidge proclaimed that "the business of America is business." The year's best-selling nonfiction book was *The Man Nobody Knows,* by advertising executive Bruce Barton, which depicted Jesus Christ as a whiz of a businessman who had "picked up twelve men from the bottom ranks . . . and forged them into an organization that conquered the world." Grantland Rice had immortalized Illinois football star Harold "Red" Grange as "a streak of fire, a breath of flame . . . a gray ghost thrown into the game." An enterprising ad man called his product, the Wills Saint Claire automobile, the "Red Grange of Traffic," because it had "such suppleness, such dash, such unbelievable change of pace." In 1925, Noël Coward appeared on Broadway in *Vortex;* Clarence Darrow and William Jennings Bryan appeared in Dayton, Tennessee, in the Scopes Monkey Trial; Fifth Avenue matrons fought over Negro maids who could teach them the Charleston; Harold Ross founded *The New Yorker;* F. Scott Fitzgerald published *The Great Gatsby;* and Babe Ruth suffered a bellyache that was nearly his undoing.

He started the year in typically Ruthian style. On February 1, before taking the train to Hot Springs, "like a harbinger of spring" he stopped in to see Ruppert and Barrow dressed in a "gaudy overcoat of startling hue" and looking bulkier than ever. He weighed about 230 pounds.

He didn't take his training at Hot Springs too seriously, although he did dunk himself in the hotel mineral baths. Dan Parker, a tall string-bean in his rookie year as a sports reporter, had brought along a big Graphlex news camera and timidly asked Ruth if he'd mind jogging up a steep country road toward the hills outside of town. "Sure, let's go, kid," said Ruth, who started off briskly as Parker staggered behind with the camera. Halfway up the road was a souvenir photo shop with roaring broncos, the wooden kind. The Babe, says Parker, "donned a cowboy hat and chaps, mounted one of the critters, grabbed a rope, and gave out with some blood-curdling yippee-yah-yohs," while the neophyte journalist "blundered through a series of double exposures, slide-covered shots, and other such crimes." Resuming his roadwork, the Babe neared the top of the hill—and suddenly collapsed to the ground. As Parker frantically focused his camera, "Babe turned around as he lay there, panting with a 'when are you going to take it?' expression." Parker nervously tripped the lever before pulling out the slide, but the Babe got up, brushed himself off and kept jogging. Parker was dumfounded. Had the great man suffered a dizzy spell? He consulted with veteran Ruthophile Marshall Hunt, who "took the cynical view" that Babe was thinking of Ed Barrow, the only man in baseball whom he feared. "He wants to show Cousin Ed he's training hard down here, instead of carousing." Whatever the motive, Parker felt Ruth was "the kindest-hearted guy in the world, who toppled over just to provide a rookie writer with a good picture and something to write about."

The Yankees forsook New Orleans that year and set up their spring camp in Saint Petersburg, Florida, which was then a village of 15,000 residents in the midst of a land boom; homesites in snake-infested swamps were changing ownership four and five times a day at spectacular leaps in price. When Ruth left Hot Springs in early March, he took with him a little Boston Bull Terrier, a going-away gift from a friend. He bedded the pup down in a vacant drawing room on the train, but the next morning a porter opened the door and found puddles all over the floor. "It's against the rules to carry an animal like that, Mister Ruth."

"It's all right; I know the owner, forget it!"

"But there'll be an inspector on board along the way and he'll fire me."

"If the inspector fires you, I'll beat the crap outa him. Forget it!"

The train stopped briefly in a small town, and Ruth decided to take his pup for a stroll. The dog had a collar but no leash. Babe spotted the porter's big feet and asked to borrow his laces, which he knotted together into a leash. Moments later, residents of that tranquil community were startled to see the Sultan of Swat walking about with a tiny dog on a shoestring, doffing his cap and booming out, "Good morning!" Suddenly, the laces parted and the dog scampered beneath a house—it was flood country, and many of the homes were raised from the ground. Nearly half the town joined in a madcap chase after the pup. As the train whistle blew, the Babe came puffing back with the dog in his arms—and no laces.

"Mister Ruth!" said the distraught porter. "How can I go about my duties without any shoelaces?"

He kept on and on and seemed close to tears, when Ruth said, "God Almighty, George (he called all porters George), I can't give ya *mine!*"

When the train reached Saint Petersburg, Ruth handed the man ten dollars. "First thing you do, George, is buy some new laces."

"Yessir!"

"My address is Yankee Stadium . . ."

"I know, I know."

". . . and if anybody threatens to fire you, just let me know; I'll beat the livin' jesus outa him!"

"Oh, yes, I'm sure you will!"

Ruth managed to trim away ten pounds of fat during the first few weeks at Saint Petersburg. Trying to slim down even more, he sometimes passed up lunch and stayed behind in the clubhouse to do calisthenics. One afternoon Whitey Witt, Benny Bengough, and Wally Schang returned from lunch at the hotel and found Ruth lying naked on a bench in the clubhouse, bicycling his legs up in the air. At the door of the clubhouse, the trainer always left a box of grapefruit halves for the players to suck on. The temptation was too great for Witt as he saw the Babe "kicking away, his heinie stickin' out." He took one of the grapefruits and flipped it at him. "Oh, he was howlin'! Damn thing hit him right in the . . . well, it nearly killed him. I didn't mean to hit him *there.*" Witt hid in the toilet until Ruth quieted down, but when he came out the Babe was still white-faced. The Babe said angrily, "I *do* know the guy who threw that grapefruit had a dark suit—saw him outa the corner of my eye—and if I find out who, I'm gonna *kill* him!" All three men had dark suits on, but a few weeks later Witt confessed, "Babe, I'm the guy who did it." By then he'd forgotten all about it.

The Babe's bookies had longer memories. That first week in camp, a New York City bookmaker claimed in court that Ruth had "dealings" with him more than a year before and still owed $7,700. Ruth had quit betting around that time, shortly after the Yankees played an exhibition game in Canada and stories of their flamboyant wagers got back to Judge Landis, who issued an order forbidding players from betting on the horses. They were up in Boston one day, says Witt, "sittin' around like a bunch o' quail on the clubhouse stools, when in comes old Judge Landis. He goes right over to the Babe, sticks his finger under his chin, and says, 'If I ever hear of you bettin' another hoss, I'm gonna put you out of baseball.' That was it right there." In

Saint Petersburg, Ruth was nursing a fractured finger when the news of his alleged gambling debt broke. "I used to lose and I used to win," he said, "but I never kept track of things. I took for granted what Callahan [the bookie] told me. When I quit betting, I didn't owe him anything." The matter was settled out of court, but stories the next day asserted that Ruth was "broke," that he was "growing old and fat."

They seemed credible. At 3 A.M. on April 5, the Babe was under a doctor's care in Atlanta, suffering chills and fever. Moments before the Yankees departed for Chattanooga, he appeared at the station heavily muffled in sweaters, his face pale. He slept all the way and took no part in practice, but when the exhibition game between New York and Brooklyn began he peeled off four or five sweaters and thrilled 8,000 spectators at Andrews Field with a pair of home runs, one of them clearing the center field fence at the 400-foot mark. The Yanks lost, but, said one writer, "the fans came to see Ruth hit homers, and he hit them." He was reported "back to normal" the next day in Knoxville, when he hit another; the ball cleared the left-center field wall by thirty feet and severed a limb from a large tree where a dozen boys were perched watching the game. A few years later, Bozeman Bulger called it Ruth's "funniest" home run:

> Outside the park of Knoxville was a venerable oak tree . . . its great spreading limbs were crowded with little darkies perilously perched for a view of the hero. The picture from a distance was that of a tree full of blackbirds . . . even before the ball struck, darkies began dropping from the limbs. The game was interrupted while the crowd roared with laughter. . . . "Boy, I'm tellin' you," exclaimed one of the Brooklyn players a Southerner, "that tree fairly rained pickannies for the next half hour."

The hundred-mile trip to Asheville, North Carolina (the next stop on the northward tour), wound its way through a mountain range, much of it along the swift currents of a river. Several players suffered mild attacks of train sickness as the cars swished around the sudden bends. When Ruth stepped off the train in Asheville on April 7, he keeled over face forward toward the marble station floor, but Steve O'Neill, a brawny catcher, stopped his fall. The Babe was suffering from a combined attack of "grippe and nerves," said one doctor, and he was ordered to stay behind with Yankee coach Paul Krichell while the rest of the team continued its tour. Half the New York press corps stayed with him, too. "If Ruth had a hangnail," said Tom Meany, "writers covering the Yankees rushed to the wires with at least a one-column box on the agonies and travails of the great man. If he was observed taking an aspirin, it was practically a scoop for the writer who saw him reach for the sedative."

The next day it was announced that Ruth would take an 8 P.M. train for New York to be examined by his own doctors. Krichell searched around all afternoon in local stores for a pair of pajamas, since the Babe never wore them. He finally found a "passionate pink" outfit and told the knot of writers in the lobby, "I went everywhere looking for a size 48, but the best I could get was a 42—we'll have to slit the back of the shirt and do the best we can." Ruth looked quite ill that evening when Krichell helped him out of the hotel. "Every bone in my body aches," he groaned as he got into a lower berth, while Krichell dickered with the occupants of the train's only drawing room in a vain attempt to secure it for his sick star. He slept during much of the trip north, and the reporters aboard sent bulletins at every telegraph stop.

When the train pulled into Washington the next morning, more reporters jumped aboard and said that newspapers in England claimed Ruth was dead (although baseball aroused little interest in England, the British were always amazed by the Babe's gigantic salary). Krichell quickly squelched the rumor and told them the Babe had eaten breakfast and was resting comfortably. However, when the train neared New York and was leaving the Manhattan Transfer, the Babe's forehead glistened with perspiration, and he said he felt faint; he walked back to the washroom, where he fell to the floor and banged his head against a radiator. Krichell and a few writers rushed to his aid, carried him back to the berth, and revived him by splashing his face with cold water. But shortly after the train entered the tunnel beneath the Hudson River, Ruth fainted dead away once more. The moment the train reached Pennsylvania Station, messengers were dispatched to find the staff surgeon of the railroad, who rushed over. Mrs. Ruth, unaware of her husband's relapse on the train, chatted calmly with reporters on the platform.

Long minutes passed, and the Babe failed to emerge from the Pullman car, whose shutters were drawn. Finally, his unconscious form was lifted through a window and rested on a stretcher, a blanket covering all but his shoes and the ubiquitous cap. Mrs. Ruth, Krichell, and Barrow formed a solemn escort as the stretcher was lifted to the baggage room on a freight elevator. They waited impatiently for an ambulance from Saint Vincent's Hospital, but word came that the vehicle's steering apparatus had broken down en route and another ambulance was being summoned. "I feel rotten, Helen," Ruth whispered to his wife, who had tears in her eyes. Suddenly he was seized by a violent convulsion, and it took six men to hold him still as his arms flew wide and his legs kicked out, jerking him up almost to a sitting position. Ten minutes later he was gripped by another convulsion. By then the ambulance arrived and an attendant gave him a hypodermic injection. But, as he was being lifted into the ambulance, he had a third seizure, nearly leaping off the stretcher, and a second needle was administered. Twice more his body shook violently as the ambulance—its siren damaged—sped silently to the hospital. "The big fellow doesn't take care of himself, he leads an active life and eats heartily," said a doctor who had attended Ruth for several years. When a reporter asked whether the Babe's late hours or dissipation had anything to do with it, the doctor laughed and said, "He's very careless."

Soon, it was billed as "the bellyache heard round the world." Shortly after his illness, the New York *Evening Journal* showed a photo of Ruth with twelve numbered hotdogs superimposed on his stomach. The caption said: "Notice how snugly they nestle in the vast cavern of his interior." Despite the fact that Ruth's breakfast the day he arrived in New York consisted of soft-boiled eggs, orange juice, and toast, writers even today perpetuate the myth that he had "gorged twelve hotdogs and eight bottles of soda pop."

"It wasn't a bellyache, it was something a bit lower," said one oldtime Yankee. The baseball writers, says Quentin Reynolds, "invented the fiction of the 'stomach ache' . . . to protect Ruth." While recovering from his illness, Ruth told reporters that part of the problem was "influenza" and then rubbed his "equatorial region" and said "damned if I know myself what the rest was." Years later, he admitted, "It was what the reporters called a 'stomach ache,' but I was sicker than that." The year 1925, said his second wife, Claire, in her book, "was a long time ago in our mores." Babe told her, she said, that he'd slid heavily into first base during a game in Atlanta and suffered a painful groin injury, but "it was simpler to let the public think that the great star was just a hog." Quentin Reynolds, however, called the groin trouble a "disease" that was checked by "the brilliant work" of doctors at Saint Vincent's. The doctors, however, told the press that Ruth's miseries were due to "a slight attack of influenza, a cold, a run-down condition, a bump on the head, and indigestion" brought on by overloading his stomach with "steaks and potatoes in the early morning hours." An April 12 editorial in the *Times* wished him well, saying that "it involves no disrespect to Calvin Coolidge or to Charles W. Eliot to suggest that . . . the Home Run King is the first citizen of the land."

Ruth's "influenza and indigestion" two days later developed into an "abcess" requiring an operation. The papers continued to mention his "indiscreet eating." After a twenty-minute operation the night of April

17, it was reported that he was resting well but would be out of action for at least two weeks.

A few days later, Mrs. Ruth was admitted to the same hospital, and their daughter, Dot, was sent to stay with friends in Sudbury. Helen had a "nervous condition" reportedly brought on by worry over her husband's illness. "She was so far behind the parade," says one friend. "She was just a little waitress and could never keep up with the Babe's pace once he hit New York; eventually, she broke down."

By the end of April, Ruth's hospital stay was extended "two or three weeks more." Finally, on May 2, the "stricken king," flanked by huge bouquets of roses and wearing white pajamas, held his first press conference. He looked pale and felt "weak as a kitten" but said cheerfully that at least his hospital stay had carved away thirty unwanted pounds. In mid-May a chauffeur, Tom Harvey, took Ruth for his first auto ride; Helen remained in the hospital. A few days later—his Yankee uniform hanging loosely around his waist—the Babe worked out at the Stadium, slamming line drives far back into the seats. Slowly he gained back some of those lost pounds. He continued to sleep at the hospital, where he received treatment for his mysterious malady. Helen was said not to have progressed so rapidly, and her hospital stay was prolonged.

Baseball's "greatest invalid" returned to action on June 1 and received a riotous welcome from the fans. Playing six innings, he hit a single, missed a home run by inches, and made a heroic catch, jumping against the fence for a long fly ball and rolling on the ground "like a tumbler." That afternoon, veteran first baseman Wally Pipp complained of a headache and was replaced by Henry Louis Gehrig, a shy twenty-two-year-old dropout from Columbia University. Gehrig remained in the lineup for a record-breaking 2,130 consecutive games and became known as "the Iron Horse."* For the next eight years, the shy, methodical Gehrig and the flamboyant Ruth would be known as "the greatest one-two punch in baseball." The son of German-Americans who worked as janitors in a New York apartment house, Gehrig was a frugal, obedient boy who married late in life, after he bought his parents a house in the suburbs. He was at first awed by Ruth. The Babe paternally lectured him on the virtues of thrift and warned him of the dangers of accepting phone calls from strange women on the road.

Ruth suffered another setback in June of that disastrous 1925 season. A ball glanced off his ankle during batting practice, and he hobbled about for several days with a brace. "It's just one thing after another," he said gloomily. "The way my leg feels now, I won't be

---

* Gehrig actually started his 2,130-game streak the previous day when he appeared as a pinch-hitter.

playing much the rest of the year." That same week, it was revealed that he'd offered to sell his Sudbury farm for $50,000. Rumors said he was "broke," but Ruth claimed the farm had become "a nuisance" because he couldn't find a dependable caretaker to watch the place during the many months that he and Helen were away.

Referring to his illnesses, he complained that he felt "fifty years old," but he wasn't acting that old off the field. He took it easy for a few weeks after leaving the hospital, but then, says Quentin Reynolds, "he tried a few tentative advances into what the doctors said was forbidden territory to a convalescing patient." By the time the Yankees were off on another Western trip, he was his old swinging self. During one westward train ride, Huggins called Ruth and Meusel out to the platform and scolded them for their carousing. Winking at Meusel, Ruth lifted the tiny manager into the air and dangled him over the rail of the speeding train, just a few feet above the blur of the tracks. In Chicago a few days later, it was fifteen minutes before game time and still no Ruth. Huggins paced back and forth, asking road secretary Mark Roth, "Seen him yet?"

"Nope, not yet."

After batting practice, Huggins yelled, "This is the end! I'm going to talk to that big ape when I catch up with him!" Just then a sweaty Ruth rushed in from a taxi and bellowed, "Hiya, keed!" As the game began and the first batter was out, the Babe ran from the dugout and kneeled in the on deck circle. The second batter walked, and Ruth stepped up and smacked a home run. Later, with two men on base, he hit another. The Yanks won, and Ruth had knocked in all five runs. After the game Ruth took a quick shower, didn't even bother to comb his hair, threw his clothes on, and headed for the door.

"There he goes now, Hug," said Roth. "Aren't you going to say anything to him?"

"What the hell can you say to a guy like that?"

But finally, Huggins reached his bursting point. As the New York *Telegram* noted that season: "It's an open secret that Ruth has for years been treating Huggins as a joke, and constantly flouting his authority." Earlier in the year, Huggins had fined him $1,000 for some hijinks in Cleveland, but Ruppert had allowed the fine to be rescinded. In 1922, when a private detective reported that Ruth was "the leading spirit at a wet Broadway party," Huggins also had slapped a fine on his wayward star. But Ruth was hitting, the Yanks were winning, fans crowded the ballpark, and—above all—Colonel Rupert was raking in a bumper crop of dollars. Now, however, the team languished in seventh place, and the Babe's batting average was more than one hundred points below the previous season's. Huggins consulted with Barrow and Ruppert and warned them that the team's fortunes would never improve unless he could impose discipline. For the first time, he was given carte blanche.

In Saint Louis on August 28, the Yanks were already out on the field and the game was about to start when Ruth rushed into the clubhouse, tearing off his shirt and tie.

"Sorry, Hug," he said airily. "Had some personal business to take care of."

"You've had too much personal business lately," Huggins snapped. "Don't bother to suit up; you're suspended and I'm fining you." He ordered Ruth to get back to New York "immediately," even though the rest of the team would not depart until the following night.

Ruth exploded with a flood of curse words, but Huggins responded in kind, and the Babe stormed out of the clubhouse.

There was a stir in the press box when Ruth failed to bat in the first inning, and a mad rush to the telephones when the reporters found out why. He was suspended and fined $5,000, the largest sum in baseball history. After the game, a confident Huggins, surrounded by reporters, said Ruth was guilty of "misconduct off the field," which included "drinking and a lot of other things besides." The Babe still didn't believe it. He was seen "relaxed and smiling" at his room in the Buckingham Hotel that afternoon. Despite Huggins's orders, he canceled his 6 P.M. berth on the New York train (standing up a small army of reporters at the station) and visited "a friend" on the other side of town.

Meanwhile, reporters in New York rushed over to see Mrs. Ruth at her suite in the Concourse Plaza. For the first time, questions were raised publicly about her husband's "friendship with a New York widow." What about rumors that she would sue the Babe for $100,000 and separate maintenance?

"My husband and I are the same old pals we were when we married," she insisted. After she had seen them out, Helen's frayed nerves gave way, and she locked herself in her bedroom. Soon she was under a nurse's care.

The press continued to focus upon Ruth's marital problems. The *Daily News* spoke of "little birdies chirping about his friendship with Claire Hodgson, "a widow who lives with her mother and two brothers in a seven-room apartment on West 79th Street." Ruth's big figure "looming through the doorway" had been a "familiar sight" to employees at the building during Mrs. Hodgson's tenancy, said the *News*, which added that she had visited Hot Springs earlier in the year and "spent much time with Ruth."

The Babe was less jovial the next day when he reached Chicago and sought an audience with Judge Landis to plead his case. "If Huggins is manager," he said angrily, "I'm through with the Yankees. Either he quits or I quit! Huggins is making me the goat for the team's rotten showing. He's been laying for a chance to get me, and I gave it to him by staying out until 2:30 Saturday morning in Saint Louis." Ruth denied that he'd been "dissipating," and said he'd merely been visiting the home of friends until midnight. Then "we took an auto ride because it was so warm." As for the fine, he snorted, "Hell, they don't fine bootleggers $5,000 and men get out of murder charges for less!"

But in New York Ruppert said, "Whatever Huggins says, goes." In Chicago league president Ban Johnson said, "Ruth has the mind of a fifteen-year-old." It sounded a bit comical coming from good old boozy Ban, but he harumphed and added, "Misconduct, drinking, and staying out all night cannot be tolerated." Huggins also took the offensive. Stories leaked from "unimpeachable sources" that the manager had compiled a chart embracing "four years of insubordination," which would be submitted to Judge Landis to justify Ruth's punishment. The Saint Louis incident was "merely the blow-off for nearly four years" that Ruth had been "the ringleader among the prima donna members of the Yankees."

The sources spoke of Ruth's "extravagances and drinking episodes," his "growling insults" when Huggins urged temperance, and the way he'd changed for the worse "since he got into the big money." He was linked with several women, including Bea Palmer, described as a girl "who had been snatched from Chicago's back-of-the-yard district to attain fame as Queen of the Shimmy Dance." The New York *American* claimed that Mrs. Ruth once slapped the face of her drunken husband when he bet $1,000 on a dog race in Saint Petersburg and added that "the wife of a famous golf player slapped his face at a country club dance."

The next day Ruth learned that league rules prohibited him from appealing to Judge Landis for at least ten days. He left orders at his Chicago hotel not to be disturbed before 10 A.M. At the appointed hour, a platoon of reporters stood outside his room. The first in line knocked and was handed a suit of clothes through a slight opening in the door, with the instructions to "get it back in an hour." There was a burst of laughter. Ruth peeked out and exclaimed, "Holy smoke! I thought you was the bellboy!" His room was too small to accommodate all the newsmen, so he phoned downstairs and reserved a larger suite. During the press conference, he denied stories of his misconduct but was greatly subdued when he spoke of Huggins and made no threats to quit baseball. "Guess I said enough about that yesterday," he said. That afternoon, Ruth boarded the Twentieth Century Limited for New York, accompanied by "his pet portable Victrola and his huge suitcase that contained, among other things, nine pairs of white flannel trousers, for which he has a failing." A cheering crowd of 3,000 at the station in New York saw him "come lumbering up the incline, lugging his famous black enamel grip." He was met there by Father Edward Quinn, who had been stationed at Saint Mary's Industrial School some years before. The two men jumped into a cab, and the reporters gave chase in cabs of their own. A smaller but no less vociferous crowd greeted Ruth when his cab reached the Concourse Plaza; the reporters followed him upstairs, and he agreed to a press conference in the living room. His wife lay in an adjoining bedroom under a nurse's care. Her nerves were shot, and she also had a nasty finger infection. Angered by reports of her husband's scandalous conduct, she had tried to yank the wedding band and diamond engagement ring from her finger, but the finger swelled abnormally and the rings had to be filed off.

Ruth said he was "sore" about the stories of his extramarital affairs because "these things have put Mrs. Ruth on her sickbed." There was "nothing wrong" with his friendship with Mrs. Hodgson "or any other woman," he said, adding, "I'd be very much obliged if the boys stuck to my baseball troubles and let my other affairs alone."

When he saw Colonel Ruppert a few minutes later, the Yankee owner greeted him jovially, but Ruth emerged unsmiling from the private meeting. That afternoon he went to Yankee Stadium and saw Huggins in the clubhouse.

"Hello, Miller," he said contritely.

"Hello."

Ruth broke the awkward silence, asking, "Well, what do I do?"

"Babe, I can't see you today. I can't see you tomorrow. I'll call you when I want to see you."

"Can I put on a uniform and practice, just to stay in shape?"

"I'll let you know when I'm ready to see you."

And so it went for a week. The Babe paced around like a caged lion. Without baseball, he felt useless; it was his life. Several times he called Huggins, asking whether he might "get in some batting practice, to stay in shape." Each time the manager drily told him, "I'll let you know when." One afternoon, an off-day for the Yanks, Ruth drove to the Stadium, stared out at the field and vacant seats for a few minutes, and went sadly back home. In a penitent tone, he told reporters, "What I said in Saint Louis about Huggins is the kind of thing a fellow would say when he's sore. I'm sorry. I want to make peace." A swarm of photographers came to his apartment that week, asking that he pose with his wife to discount stories of their estrangement. The Babe obligingly went to her bed and, following their stage directions, laid his head upon her breast as the room was made brilliant by flashbulbs. Tears filled Helen's eyes, and the Babe turned away, as his own eyes brimmed over. Blushing, he went to the window and gazed outside for several minutes before facing them again.

The next day he received word from Sudbury that his pet terrier had broken loose and taken a vicious bite at the udder of a neighbor's prize cow. The cow died, and the neighbor threatened to sue. "They come in bunches, like bananas," sighed the Babe, adding, hopefully, "Well, this luck can't last forever."

In the meantime, a battle royal raged among the nation's newspapers, most of which declared that Ruth had "let down America's kids." The New York *Telegram* was among the mildest critics, saying Ruth couldn't mend his "erring ways" because he was "practically illiterate."

One of his few defenders was New York *World* columnist Heywood Broun, who claimed: "You can't make a Spartan out of an ancient Goth." It would take "a great deal more than a $5,000 fine and a short suspension," he said, "to whittle Ruth down to the stature of Calvin Coolidge in the eyes of young America." Calling Ruth "magnificent in his way as Paul Bunyan," Broun ripped into baseball writers "who complain that Babe has shattered the ideals of millions of youngsters . . . Ruth never pretended to be the perfect ideal . . . this figure was wholly the creation of the writers. They set up a character which was not true and now blame the man who posed for the picture."

Ruth was finally allowed to return to the lineup, and he celebrated a day later by slamming his 300th career home run. But when the season ended a few weeks later, the Yankees were still in next-to-last place; the Babe had appeared in only 98 games, hit a mere 25 home runs, and—despite a last-minute hot streak—batted less than .300 for the first time in nine years. Was he through? A story in the New York *Telegram* asked: "What has the future in store for Babe Ruth? It is doubtful that Ruth again will be the super-star that he was from 1919 to 1924. By next year he will be 32 and the Babe at 32 will be older than Eddie Collins, Walter Johnson, or Ty Cobb were at that age . . . he has lived a much more strenuous life."

It was a grim time, but it also marked a turning point in Ruth's career. His manager, Christy Walsh, had often expressed fear that Ruth might be injured on or off the field and urged him, to no avail, to invest in annuities. This crisis offered Walsh his "first real break" in persuading Ruth to salt away money for the future. The Babe needed cash in a hurry and promised that if Walsh would lend him the money he would give him permission to hold aside a portion of his earnings and invest it.

Also following Walsh's advice in the area of public relations, Ruth embarked upon a campaign of "repentance." Walsh arranged a spot for him as a member of the New York City Police Reserve. At a ceremony in police headquarters, Ruth looked proud when he was given a shiny nickel shield, but he balked when he was asked to be fingerprinted for police records. "Do I have to do that? I thought it was the *other* fellas that got fingerprinted." Finally, he allowed them to ink his big fingers.

Brother Matthias had called him from Saint Mary's several times during the crisis to soothe his troubled spirit and see whether he could salvage Ruth's marriage. Out of gratitude, he invited Matthias to New York, and as the two big men pigeon-toed their way along Manhattan's sidewalks the Babe pointed to a gorgeous Cadillac in an auto showroom and asked, "Do you think I ought to buy that car?"

"If you think you can afford it, George," said Matthias.

The next day the car was delivered to Matthias's hotel, with a note of thanks "for what you and Saint Mary's have done for me." Some time later, Ruth recalled, Matthias "stalled the car on some train tracks and a freight train came along and smacked it lopsided; so I gave him another one."

That fall, in a "confession" published in *Collier's,* Ruth admitted that he'd been "a Babe and a Boob" and promised that he was "through" with "the pests and the good-time guys." He admitted to having thrown away more than $250,000 on gambling, high living, ill-starred business ventures, and legal fees to fight suits and attempted blackmail. He said he had been "taken" by women for amounts ranging from "a few hundred to thousands of dollars." Between 1921 and 1925 he had owned nine cars "of the most expensive American make." He didn't regret all of his extravagances, he said, because he was merely living up to his title of Home Run King, but he did lament "the messes" he'd gotten into through bad judgment.

Although he stood to lose "thirty or forty thousand dollars," he would make no exhibition tour that winter. Instead, he would retire to the woods and get back in shape. Nor would he return to Hot Springs, because he was convinced that the sudden change in climate brought on his attacks of influenza and grippe.

In early November the public learned that Ruth was "a new man" after a three-week hunting trip in the wilds of New Brunswick, Canada. Yankee pitcher Bob Shawkey, who had been with him, came to New York with the "glad tidings" that Ruth had hiked forty miles from the hunting camp to the nearest railroad station, "without so much as a word of protest."

Either the curative effect of this hunting trip was vastly exaggerated or Ruth abused himself terribly in the next few weeks, because when he walked into Artie McGovern's gymnasium in mid-December he was pronounced "a physical wreck." McGovern, the owner of a gym in New York, was hired by the Yankees to whip their star into condition for the 1926 season. "He weighed 254 pounds," said McGovern. "His blood pressure was low and his pulse was high. He was as near to being a total loss as any patient I have ever had under my care. . . . His stomach had gone back on him completely. His waist was 4½ inches larger than his expanded chest. He suffered from indigestion. His eyes had been affected. The slightest exercise left him short of breath. His muscles were soft and flabby." Based on an average weight loss of three pounds during each game, McGovern estimated that the Babe had lost "about two and a half tons" in the past decade, but "he can also gain ten pounds in a day."

McGovern put Ruth on a rigid program of rest, diet, and exercise. Between-meal snacks were prohibited, and he drank glasses of warm water instead. He spent four hours each day taking brisk walks, sweltering in steambaths, lunging about on a handball court, catching medicine balls in his big gut, and lying on his back and lifting his legs to strengthen his flabby middle. By mid-January, an apparent miracle had been wrought. He walked into the Yankee office, and Ed Barrow "dug his knuckles into Ruth's abdomen, played a tattoo on his chest, and investigated the condition of the Ruthian legs." Afterward, Barrow "wore a broad smile" of complaisance." McGovern, proudly displaying a large measurement chart, announced that Ruth had lost twenty-three pounds, his waist had "wilted" from 48½ to 39¾ inches, his hips were down from 46 to 40 inches, and even his neck was reduced from 17 to 16 inches. As a reward, he was given a weekend "furlough" at his Sudbury farm, with a warning to report for more workouts on Monday. He continued to exercise with such zeal that he won permission from Barrow to travel to Saint Petersburg on February 3 and spend the few weeks before spring training on the golf course. While in Florida, the Babe ran into none other than Miller Huggins; it was their first meeting in months. It was a new year and, apparently, a new Babe; he offered his hand in a cordial gesture, mumbling something about burying the hatchet, and Huggins responded likewise.

"Keep Cool with Cabbage"

Rud Rennie, a faithful member of the pressbox clan, stood up at the New York Baseball Writers Dinner in late February of 1926 and, in a tremulous tenor voice, warbled a parody of little Miller Huggins (lyrics by Bill Slocum) that had the boys dripping tears of laughter into their fruit salad:

> I wonder where my Babe Ruth is tonight?
> He grabbed his hat and coat and ducked from sight.
> He may be at some cozy roadside inn,
> Drinking tea—or maybe gin.
> He may be at a dance, or may be in a fight.
> I know he's with a dame,
> I wonder what's her name?
> I wonder where my Babe Ruth is tonight?

Ruth was there, and he laughed louder and clapped harder than anyone else at the table. This was the year of Ruth's much-heralded reform, but the boys knew that good old Babe hadn't surrendered completely to the gray forces of virtue. In a few days he would report to Saint Petersburg for spring training, and, perhaps to justify their faith in him, he attended a little "function." A traveling road show had come to Saint Pete's, complete with chorus line. To advertise their debut at the local theater, the manager of the troupe hosted a picnic on a small, palm-fringed islet, just off the mainland. The cast, members of the Saint Petersburg Chamber of Commerce and their wives, the mayor and his wife, and perhaps a few local clergymen, made the short trip in small boats. The Babe was in town, enjoying golf and other delights; as he was one of Saint Pete's most illustrious winter denizens, his presence was considered *de rigueur*. One of the picnickers recalled: "Right in the middle of the party,

149

the Babe took the hand of a very shapely red-haired chorus girl and they just wandered off over a dune and into the palms for about twenty minutes. Right in front of everybody. Well, they came back hand-in-hand, smiling, and just sat down with the rest of us. God, it was funny. Some people were giggling inside. Others were too shocked to talk."

If nothing else, he had learned to be a *bit* more discreet, and there was visible evidence that he'd toiled all winter to get into shape. On the first day of spring practice, he appeared in a heavy rubber sweat shirt and a Helen Wills eyeshade* that made him resemble "above the neck a cross between a tennis star and a bookkeeper." He had learned that life was still tolerable with perhaps two fewer potatoes on the dinner plate, a glass or three less of liquor at party time, an hour or so of extra rest each evening, and an extra wind sprint on the field each afternoon. Even Miller Huggins (crossing his fingers and wondering how long it would last) complimented him on his behavior. The Babe's compromise with reason and advancing age (he was now thirty-one years old) paid off. He astounded everyone by hitting 47 home runs and making 1926 one of his finest seasons.† One of those shots, against Bert Cole in Detroit, sailed so far that writer H. G. Salsinger measured the blast and signed an affidavit swearing that it landed 602 feet from home plate. The Babe's remarkable comeback was the extra spark that helped the Yankees bounce from seventh to first place in the league. (Ruth enjoyed spectacular success in the six years following his 1925 illness, averaging 50 home runs, 147 runs, and 156 runs batted in per season.)

As Americans followed the 1926 pennant race, they were also fascinated by the scandals and "firsts" that gave The Roaring Twenties their dizzy character. In June, millionaire Evangelist Aimee Semple McPherson emerged after a month-long vanishing act (she was first feared drowned, then said she was kidnapped) and stiffly denied stories that she'd been on a hotel-hopping jaunt, under various aliases, with her handsome radio operator. July was the start of a four-week trial in Somerville, New Jersey, for the killing of a Reverend Hall and a Mrs. Mills (both married to other spouses), who were murdered beneath a country crabapple tree. The press ground out 12 million words of copy about the trial (even the *Times* had four stenographers on hand), including the texts of several torrid love notes. In August, a giant tickertape parade down Broadway welcomed young Gertrude

* Young tennis star Helen Wills, whose manner was so regal that she was dubbed "Queen Helen," had made the visorshaped sun shade fashionable when she participated in European tournaments a few months before.

† Batting .373 and leading the league in runs batted in with 155.

Ederle, the daughter of a New York delicatessen owner, who became the first woman to swim the English Channel. Later that month, 30,000 people mobbed Frank Campbell's Funeral Home on Broadway to glimpse the body of screen idol Rudolph Valentino; movie publicists, trying to drum up interest in his yet unreleased films, kept the body on view for so many days that the Health Department finally ordered the coffin shut. In September, more than 120,000 boxing fanatics in Philadelphia paid $1.9 million to see Gene Tunney defeat Jack Dempsey in "The Battle of the Century." The next month, the public was amused by the divorce trial of fifteen-year-old "Peaches" Browning, who fled the bed and board of her wealthy fifty-one-year-old husband, "Daddy" Browning, after a brief marriage. Peaches claimed that Daddy spent most of the time romping about the house in the nude, while her husband complained the marriage was never consummated because Peaches kept crying for "Mama" in the marital chamber. The New York *Evening Graphic* caused a sensation with its "composographs"—faked photo composites with cartoon "speech balloons"—showing the pair in hilarious poses.

By contrast, the Babe's few mishaps that year were quite mild. The State of Massachusetts threatened to arrest him in April for nonpayment of tax arrears, and when he went to the State House to inquire, thinking he'd be gone "just five minutes," he parked his car and locked it right in front of the building; he told a policeman he was "sore" when he came back two hours later and found a ticket on the windshield, while angry drivers—their cars backed up for a few blocks—honked their horns. At a lake near Detroit that June, he pulled in a few scrawny bluegills and was pinched for fishing out of season. The next month he was arrested for speeding along Riverside Drive but got off with a $25 fine since it was his first offense in the city in two years. He was, for the most part, a model citizen. And Christy Walsh nurtured that image by booking him for countless appearances at children's hospitals, orphanages, schools, and charity affairs.

That May he spoke to three hundred boys, members of the Fordham Juvenile League, in the school hall of a church. They listened gravely as he warned them that "no boy who wants to be a big leaguer should smoke," and they cheered wildly when he explained his secret of home run hitting: "The pitcher puts the ball over the plate and I swing at it!" Another time he visited Mount Saint Mary's School in Maryland. Journalist-screenwriter William Laidlaw, then a young student, recalls that classes usually stopped only when the bishop came, "but this time it was Babe Ruth." The kids filed into the chapel, and the headmaster sermonized, "Here is a man who, as a boy, was practically an orphan, poor and homeless, but with Catholic teaching, look at what he's made of himself! He can hit a baseball farther than *any* man! And what gives the ball that extra distance? The power of faith in our Holy God, that's what!" The Babe, beaming at his young audience, made a short speech, and, says Laidlaw, "we weren't allowed to applaud in the chapel, so we all stood up." Later, they all went to the playground and Ruth—wearing a white shirt, tie, and cap—whacked out fungo fly balls. Whoever caught one could run in and get Ruth's autograph on the ball. There was a wild scramble for each ball. Laidlaw calls it "probably the greatest thrill of my life" when Ruth hit one that plopped into his glove; but a bigger classmate grabbed the ball away from him. "I nearly cried!" he recalls.

Under Walsh's guidance, Ruth lent his name to a number of worthwhile causes. In the summer of 1926 he offered to join the Reverend E. J. Flanagan, founder of Father Flanagan's Boys' Home in Omaha, in a campaign to "halt profiteering in homeless boys." Flanagan had charged in the press that some persons adopted boys during the summer to work on farms or in the cities and then returned them to orphanages without pay for their labor. Recalling his own youth, the Babe wired Father Flanagan, "I'm all for the boys," and promised to fight such abuses. When Patrick Cardinal O'Donnell, Primate of Ireland, came to America and saw a ball game in Chicago, the first player to greet him was the Babe, who walked over to his field box, knelt, and kissed the ring on his right hand.

To help publicize the summer activities of the Citizens' Military Training Camps, he appeared at Long Island's Mitchel Field on a 100-degree July afternoon, wearing his National Guard uniform and his fielder's mitt. The announced purpose: to set "a new world's record" by catching a baseball dropped from an airplane. Perspiring heavily, his face flushed shrimp-pink, the Babe removed his military coat and exposed a shirt so tight that the buttons threatened to pop off, *a la* Wimpy. Captain McClelland, the post adjutant, flew up to 1,000 feet in a Sepwith pursuit plane and dropped the first ball; zigzagging wildly in the wind, it fell far from the Babe and nearly beaned a photographer. The pilot landed while the Babe gulped three glasses of ice water. After a brief conference, Captain McClelland took off and dropped another ball from 700 feet up. This one also danced about crazily in the air and landed with a dull thud, far from Ruth's outstretched mitt. After another conference, the pilot took off and dropped a third ball from about 250 feet. Ruth chased it for about fifteen yards, caught up with it, and it struck his chest, knocking him to the ground. By now, he was sweating profusely and his round face looked like a tomato. A fourth ball hit him on the shoulder, again knocking him down; he rose quite slowly and growled a curse. On the fifth try he got his hands on the ball, but it caromed against his chest. The wind carried the sixth ball out of reach. Finally, on "the lucky seventh," he caught the ball, staggered, and held on. The small group of onlookers gave him a cheer. While Ruth showered and changed in the officer's club, one man told him, "If there's another war and New York is attacked, we'll assign you to defense work, catching bombs."

Not all of Ruth's appearances were for charity. Aided by Walsh, he had become acutely aware of the commercial value of his name. A teammate recalls an incident in the Babe's Chicago hotel room that season. He had endorsed a brand of men's underwear; the advertising director of a Chicago department store called and asked Ruth to appear at the counter display each morning while the Yankees were in town. At first, Ruth tried to put the man off, but when he insisted the Babe said, "I can tell you right now it's gonna cost you a thousand dollars," and hung up. Twenty minutes later the man called back and accepted. "Imagine," said his teammate, "he was going to collect a thousand dollars an hour for standing next to a pile of underwear!"

On the field, however, he was still the same, a cross between Hercules and a circus clown. John Kieran, the *Times* columnist, announced that Ruth had introduced the slogan "keep cool with cabbage" to the Yankee dugout. It seems that the Babe had improvised a primitive form of air conditioning to resist the broiling summer sun while he stood in the outfield. "A succulent head of cabbage is dissected and the leaves are spread upon the ice in the water cooler," explained Kieran. Then, Ruth "showed the boys how to take an iced cabbage leaf out of the cooler, trim it so that it wouldn't fall down over the man's shoulders, place it on the head and conceal the whole plot from the general public by pulling the cap down over the cabbage." It was estimated that one medium leaf kept the top of the head cool for approximately three innings, but the Babe's big head required two at a time. There had been an "accident" during the summer of 1926, however. Babe hit a homer, and as the crowd cheered "in his usual courtly way Signor Ruth took off his cap with a sweeping gesture of thanks—and two large greenish-white leaves of cabbage were exposed to view." The enemy dugout, of course, immediately called attention to the connection between "ham" and "cabbage." Was Ruth nonplused? Not much, says Kieran. "He went to the cooler, took out two fresh leaves, put one under his cap, ate the other, and sat down on the bench with a grunt of relief."

* * *

The 1926 World Series, which the Yankees lost to the Saint Louis Cardinals, provided the stage for one of Ruth's greatest personal triumphs. It also provoked an incident that lent credence to the Babe's magical ability to hit a home run upon request—a triumph of American press agentry. But more about that later.

The Yankees won the first game of the series, but Saint Louis took the next two. In game four, played on October 6 at Saint Louis, Ruth provided the most awesome display of power ever seen in a World Series. He smashed home runs his first two times at bat and walked the next time. No man had ever hit three home runs in a single Series game. This was still the dawn of radio, and most announcers were anonymous voices heard over the airwaves. Graham McNamee was broadcasting the series on a national hookup. McNamee, who a short time before had earned $30 a week as a baritone radio singer, became one of the first persons to announce under his own name the previous year, and he had evoked a tremendous response. He became such a celebrity that, during the 1925 World Series alone, he drew an avalanche of 50,000 letters. Here is what McNamee told America of the Babe's fourth trip to the plate in the sixth inning:

> The Babe is up. Two home runs today. One ball, far outside. Babe's shoulders look as if there is murder in them down there; the way he is swinging that bat down there. A high foul into the left field stands. That great big bat of Babe's looks like a toothpick down there, he is so big himself. Here it is. Babe shot at a bad one and fouled it. Two strikes and one ball. The outfield have all moved very far towards right. . . . Two strikes and two balls. He has got two home runs and a base on balls so far today. Here it is, and a ball. Three and two. The Babe is waving that wand of his over the plate. Bell is loosening up his arm. The Babe hits it clear into the center-field bleachers for a home run! For a home run! Did you hear what I said? Oh, what a shot! Directly over second. The boys are all over him over there. One of the boys is riding on Ruth's back. Oh, what a shot! Directly over second base far into the bleachers, out in center field, and almost on a line. . . . Oh, boy! Wow! That is a World Series record, three home runs in one series game, and what a home run! . . . They tell me this is the first ball ever hit in the center field stand. That is a mile and a half from here!

The 40,000 fans at Sportsman's Park went wild. Ruth was the enemy, but he was making history before their eyes. When he trotted to his position in left field, the usually hostile bleacher occupants gave him a standing ovation. The Yankees won that game, and the next, pulling ahead three games to two. In the fifth game, Ruth was credited with the finest defensive play of the series when he rushed after a foul fly close to the left field stands, "risking painful injury," bounced violently against the fence, and held the ball. "It took nerve of the rarest sort to make a play like that," said one correspondent. The remainder of the series would be played in New York, and the Yanks were confident. The teams headed east, with the Cardinals aboard a crack train that made the jaunt from Saint Louis to New York in the "record time" of 21 hours, 20 minutes. They beat the Yankees the next day to even the series at three games apiece. Game seven, played on a damp, cold Sunday, is one of the most famous in series history. Ruth put New York ahead 1 to 0 in the third inning with his fourth homer of the Series, but the Cardinals rallied for three runs in their next chance at bat. In the seventh, Saint Louis pitcher Jesse Haines was defending a 3-to-2 lead but was bothered by a painful blister on his finger and walked three men. Although there were two outs, manager Hornsby waved to the bullpen for Grover Cleveland Alexander. "Old Pete" as he was known (he was forty years old at the time) had pitched a nine-inning victory the day before, and, as Ruth recalled, he was "red-eyed" because "he had celebrated as only he could celebrate." Everyone knew of Alexander's binge the night before, Ruth added, "but not many knew that some of our own fellows had been out the same night, celebrating a series victory that never came to us; we had licked ourselves." "Old Pete" walked to the mound, and, as the legend goes, Hornsby peered into his crimson eyes, sniffed, and decided that if all else failed he could retire the next batter by breathing on him. On Alexander's third pitch to Lazzeri, a tough hitter in the clutch, the Yankee slammed a line drive to left that appeared to be a home run but curved foul. Finally, with the count two strikes and one ball, "Old Pete" whipped it in and Lazzeri swung and missed. End of rally. The oldtimer kept the Yankees at bay for the next two innings, and Saint Louis took the world title. Despite New York's loss, however, Ruth was clearly the giant of the contest; in twenty trips to the plate he had made six hits, including four home runs.

One of those home runs allegedly saved a life, which brings us to the case of Johnny D. Sylvester of Essex Falls, New Jersey, the eleven-year-old son of Horace C. Sylvester, Jr., vice-president of the National City Bank of New York. On October 6, the same day that Ruth hit his three homers in Saint Louis, a small item appeared in the New York press that Johnny, suffering from an "infection," had been "cheered" by the receipt of autographed baseballs from members of the New York and Saint Louis teams. His father had telegraphed the request to Saint Louis, and the balls arrived by air mail; one of them was signed by Babe Ruth, with the added comment, "I'll try to hit a homer for you." The next day, the story ballooned in importance. Now it transpired that physicians had "allotted thirty minutes of life" to Johnny when he was stricken with "blood poisoning," but he was pronounced "on the road to recovery" after hearing the radio broadcast of the Yankee victory over Saint Louis. The doctors were quoted as saying, "The boy's return to health began when he learned the news of Babe Ruth's three home runs." He way lying in bed at the time, "clutching the autographed baseballs," and his fever "began to abate at once." That same day, a *Times* editorial commented that Ruth's home run hitting had "cheered up" a "desperately sick boy in New Jersey." Concluding that baseball was "universal" and its influence "beneficent," the *Times* said that "to make a hero out of a player like Ruth is well worth while."

Immediately after the Series, Ruth and Gehrig formed a team called "The Busting Babes" and left on a barnstorming tour. On October 11 they were to play the Brooklyn Royal Colored Giants in Bradley Beach, New Jersey, but prior to the game a reception was given in their honor by the mayor and leading citizens of the town. They were kept waiting for two hours while—according to news headlines—Ruth called on Johnny Sylvester, who was in bed "sighing deeply and clasping his cherished baseballs."

"How're you feeling, Johnny?" said a big figure in the doorway.

"F-fine," he said, then blurted out, "I'm sorry the Yanks lost the Series." His five-year-old sister came into the room, her hair cut in a boyish bob. "Nice looking brother you have there," said Ruth.

The meeting was interrupted by a phone call from Bradley Beach, asking when in hell the Babe would arrive. When Ruth left, Johnny was "on the verge of both laughter and tears." When Ruth arrived at Bradley Beach "from the bedside of Johnny Sylvester," he said, "He's some kid. . . . I'm glad that my hits helped him." (Early the next season, a middle-aged man walked up to Ruth in Philadelphia and said he was Johnny Sylvester's uncle. "I thought you'd like to know that Johnny is making a remarkable recovery, and I want to thank you on behalf of the family." Ruth would likely have recalled the incident, but the name drew a blank. "Gee, that's fine," he said. "You tell Johnny I was askin' for him." They shook hands, and when the man left Babe scratched his head and asked aloud, "Now who the hell is Johnny Sylvester?")

Ruth continued on his merry way. In Montreal a few days later his two home runs, together with all the shots he and Gehrig hit over the fence in batting practice, forced a cancelation after eight innings; they had run out of baseballs. He later signed a $100,000 contract for a twelve-week vaudeville tour. Somehow, none of the Babe's activities ever proved wholly uneventful. He had to pay $500 bail that January in San Diego after an arrest warrant was issued, charging that he'd violated the state labor law by inviting children from the audience to come up on stage and chat with him. The reward of an autographed ball was not deemed adequate compensation.

Undaunted by such minor reverses, the Babe signed to make a movie in Hollywood, where he remained for most of the winter. Just about then, Greta Garbo and John Gilbert were working on *Flesh and the Devil,* and Ruth's favorite actress, Janet Gaynor, was costarring with Charles Farrell in filming the "four-handkerchief" love story *Seventh Heaven.* The movie industry had awakened to the box office clout of sports idols such as Jack Dempsey, Red Grange, and Bill Tilden, whose films were lambasted by the critics and adored by their fans. Ruth got the full treatment, including publicity shots of Gloria Swanson applying makeup to his big moon face and of Bill Tilden meeting him in a tennis match. For his Hollywood debut (his first film in 1920 was made on the East Coast), Ruth was starred opposite Anna Q. Nilsson,* an attractive Swedish-born blonde who had appeared previously with such notables as Wallace Beery and William S. Hart. Miss Nilsson was miffed at having to work with "an athlete," and the two stars saw little of each other. In fact, the film was virtually made in two pieces, and they appeared together in only a few scenes.

Ed Barrow was worried about Ruth running hog wild in naughty Hollywood, so he sent trainer Art McGovern out to watch over him and keep the Babe on a rigid schedule of proper food, rest, and exercise. Shooting of the film began early in the morning, and McGovern instituted a strict bedtime curfew of 9 P.M. It was "cruel treatment," says Marshall Hunt, who also visited with Ruth during the making of the picture. "Hollywood was at its peak then," he says, "and, Jesus, the Babe would see all this luscious stuff on the streets, in the hotel lobbies, and out on the movie lots, but none of it was for him."

The film was called *The Babe Comes Home* and was adapted from a Gerald Beaumont story titled "Said with Soap." It is a classic of its genre. The hero, Babe Dugan (guess who) is a star with the Angels baseball team. He chews tobacco and dirties his uniform more than any other player. Vernie, a laundress (played by Miss Nilsson) is the girl who cleans his uniform every week. When Vernie attends a ball game one afternoon she is hit by one of the Babe's line drives into the stands. He calls her that evening to apologize. They meet. Babe's pal "Peewee" falls in love with Vernie's friend Georgia. They

---

* Miss Nilsson died in a California convalescent home in February, 1974, at the age of eighty-five.

all go to an amusement park, and while on the roller coaster Vernie is thrown into Babe's arms. Fluttering of lashes, flushing of cheeks, thumping of hearts! They are practically engaged. Vernie sets out to reform the untidy Babe. Scores of tobacco spittoons arrive as pre-wedding gifts. This causes a lovers' quarrel, but the Babe relents and decides to eschew his tobacco (pun intended). Vernie is happy, but the Babe finds that without his chaw, like Samson without his locks, he can't sock a baseball worth a darn. Finally, during a crucial game, Vernie shows to what heights true love can soar. From her field box she heaves a plug of tobacco to the slump-shouldered Babe, who stuffs it into his mouth à la Popeye, strides up to the plate, and bashes the ball out of sight.

During the next few years, Ruth would see the picture ten times. "Every time I hit a town where it's playing," he said, "I go down and look at myself again!"

SIXTH INNING

When the Model A Ford was brought out in December 1927 . . . one million people—so the *Herald Tribune* figured— tried to get into Ford headquarters in New York to catch a glimpse of it; as Charles Merz later reported . . . "one hundred thousand people flocked into the showrooms of the Ford Company in Detroit; mounted police were called out to patrol the crowds in Cleveland; in Kansas City so great a mob stormed Convention Hall that platforms had to be built to lift the new car high enough for everyone to see it."

FREDERICK LEWIS ALLEN,
Only Yesterday

"Hey, Kiddo, a Little Bi"

"Solomon in all his glory was never arrayed in such a vivid suit of pajamas as the Babe sported" when he was routed out of bed at sunrise. The Twentieth Century Limited, en route from California to New York, had stopped in Albany, and a group of newsmen hopped aboard to inquire about his cinema career.

"They tell me I screen great!" he said. "You oughta see me with Anna Q. Nilsson in the bedroom love scene. All okay, you understand, but funny."

"Gee, it's great to be back," he said, describing Hollywood as "dead." All the talk about Hollywood's wild life was "bunk." Working ten hours a day before the camera, he explained, "you ain't got much time for hell-raising; I had to run the bases a million times for retakes!"

He looked as fit as a bass fiddle. Out in Hollywood, Artie McGovern had him up every day at 6 A.M., and he walked and ran five miles to the studio. His diet emphasized fruit juice, toast, lean meats, and vegetables, with "snacks" of glasses of warm water. As his train rolled eastward, Ruth's manager gave the press a "measurement chart," which was displayed in sports pages across the country, showing that his weight was down to 224 pounds and giving dimensions for the Babe's neck, chest, waist, hips, thigh, calf, biceps, and forearms.

Over the years, these preseason announcements of Ruth's physical condition became as regular as Ground Hog day. And news of his contract, said one writer, was awaited by the public "as eagerly as intelligence pertaining to corn crops, stocks, bonds, and rates of exchange."

When the Yankees had mailed him a $52,000 contract, he sent it back, saying that rather than accept such an amount he would open a string of gymnasiums with Art McGovern and start correspondence courses on "how to keep fit and play baseball." In New York, Colonel

Ruppert explained that the $52,000 contract was a "mere formality"; league rules required that a club send every player a contract on or before February 15. If the deadline was missed, the player became a free agent. The Yankees were embarrassed by stories that the Philadelphia Athletics had offered $75,000 to Detroit's aging Ty Cobb. On that basis, it was widely commented, Ruth deserved $100,000. That's exactly what he asked for. In a long letter to Ruppert, he demanded $200,000 paid over two seasons and the refund of $7,700 in fines deducted from his past salaries.

When the train pulled into Grand Central Station on the morning of March 2, 1927, half a dozen gate tenders and a squad of private police had to clear Ruth's way through a crowd at the platform. Outside, an even larger throng cheered him as he walked the halfblock to Artie McGovern's gym, where he posed for photographers. After calling Ruppert at the brewery to set up a meeting later in the day, he sped over to Saint Vincent's Hospital to visit his wife, Helen, who was confined there with an unspecified illness. He hadn't seen her in a few months.

Shortly before 2 P.M., the Babe "with the blush of Hollywood still upon his smile-creased cheeks" emerged from Colonel Ruppert's office after a fifty-five-minute conference, "where they sat behind cigars with the pleasant odor of hops permeating the atmosphere." Ed Barrow herded the four dozen photographers and writers present into the Colonel's office to hear that Ruth had agreed to a three-year contract at $70,000 per season, making him the highest-paid player in baseball (it was learned that Cobb's contract guaranteed only $50,000 per year, with possible bonuses of $25,000). Regarding the refund of $7,700 in fines, Ruppert would only say, "Babe and I have fixed that up all right."

The story made front-page news, rivaling accounts of turbulence in Shanghai, which was described as "the Moscow of China," with "the conservative Northern war lords possessing and the radical Southerners aspiring to capture it." It made the front page again two days later, when Ruth signed the contract, and reporters professed "amazement" that he wielded the pen with his right hand. "I'm a lefthanded hitter and a right-handed signer," Ruth explained amiably. His rise from rags to riches was discussed for a week in the nation's press. One paper had an illustrated chart showing that "every day Ruth earns $457.79, a trip to Europe; every week $3,304.53, a new auto; every month $11,666, a new home; and every season $70,000, enough to support twenty families like this (the photo showed a man and wife with twelve children)." His annual salary was "just a trifle more than seven times" the entire yearly wage of the original Cincinnati club of the 1870's. His three-year guarantee of $210,000 was only $50,000 less than what Ruppert and Huston paid for the entire Yankee franchise in 1915. The Albany *Knickerbocker Press* said that Ruth's salary was "not extravagant," since it amounted to less than $500 per game, while Enrico Caruso drew from $3,000 to $5,000 per performance. "The Babe will bring infinitely more business to the stadium than Caruso brought to the Metropolitan," it said. The Springfield *Republican* said Ruth's money was "honestly earned" but cautioned, "We make a mockery of the system of private profit . . . when the home-run king pockets his $70,000 a year, while the man who finally discovers a cure for cancer may be rewarded by having his picture printed badly in the newspapers."

To put things in even sharper perspective, it should be noted that the Yankee team's median salary that year was $7,000 per player, with Ruth's windfall driving the arithmetical average up to $10,-000. Lou Gehrig was earning only $8,000 and would never go higher than $39,000 during his career. The salaries of men like Joe Dugan, Bob Meusel, Tony Lazzeri, Whitey Witt and Earle Combs ranged from $8,000 to $13,000 that season.

* * *

Eager to demonstrate his marvelous physique, the Babe challenged a reporter in Saint Petersburg to "hit me, hit me as hard as you can." The man doubled up his fist and "let go with a terrific haymaker" that caught Ruth "squarely amidships and almost sank from sight." Smiling, the Babe said, "Feel those arms and shoulders; never been tougher in my life!" He was bursting with energy. In the mornings he played golf and even toured the course with his old nemesis, Judge Landis. In batting practice he lined shots out of the park, dashed around the bases, and yelled, "I wanna get hot! Catch me, Barney!" Benny Bengough put on his catcher's mitt and the Babe turned pitcher, firing them in at "midsummer speed." He was looking forward to a great year.

And it was a great year—a year of fantastic events that still stand out in the nation's history. That August, two Italian immigrants, Nicola Sacco and Bartolomeo Vanzetti, died in the electric chair after seven years of appeals. The two self-professed anarchists were found guilty of killing two men in a 1920 payroll robbery, but many felt they were victims of prejudice against foreigners. Their deaths sparked riots in numerous European cities. In May, 1927, young Charles A.

Lindbergh astounded the world when he flew nonstop in his *Spirit of St. Louis* from Long Island to an airport near Paris, where 100,000 Frenchmen staged the wildest demonstration of glee since the Armistice; that was nothing compared to the welcome along Broadway, where more than 1,800 tons of paper were showered upon Lindbergh's motorcade. In September, 104,000 fans paid $2.6 million to see Jack Dempsey fight Gene Tunney in the "Battle of the Ages" at Soldiers Field, Chicago; Dempsey floored Tunney for the famous "long count" but lost in his bid to regain the heavyweight championship. Talking pictures burst upon the scene in October, when Al Jolson starred in *The Jazz Singer*. And a new gadget called "television" was demonstrated when AT&T president Walter S. Gifford in New York and Secretary of Commerce Herbert Hoover in Washington talked on the phone and saw each other on a 2½-inch screen. It was a miracle.

It was also the year that Babe Ruth, striving to scale his own personal Everest, smashed 60 home runs, a mark that has never been equaled.* The 1927 Yankee team is widely credited with being the greatest in the game's history. Four Yankees that year batted in 100 or more runs, and their lineup became known as "Murderers' Row." The fence-busting Yanks had a .307 team batting average, stole 80 bases, were demons on defense, and had fine pitching. They won 110 of the season's 154 games and romped through the World Series in four straight games.

The season began on a depressing note for Ruth. At the opener in Yankee Stadium, 65,000 fans watched Ruppert's club beat Lefty Grove, but Ruth struck out twice and popped up. He was so disgusted that he told Huggins, "Get me outa here," and Ben Paschal, a righthanded batter, was sent in to pinch-hit for him.

But the Babe soon caught fire and began hitting home runs. He got his tenth in late May during a game in Cleveland. It was described as a 600-foot blast that went "300 feet up and 300 feet down," barely clearing the nearby right field screen at Dunn Field. The crowd was so large that many fans were allowed to sit on the grass in the right field area. A group of Indians from a visiting rodeo sat among the spectators. When Ruth took his outfield position in the fifth inning, an Indian girl ran over and decorated him with a huge headdress of feathers. The crowd roared with delight as the

---

* Ruth hit 60 in a 154-game season. In 1961, Roger Maris of the Yankees hit 61 in 161 games, but here the comparison ends. In 1927, Ruth out-homered all American League teams and five of the eight National League teams. His 60 homers represented about one-seventh of the league's total of 439 that year, while Maris's 61 were about one-twenty-fifth of the league's output of 1,534. The Babe batted .356, compared with Maris's .269.

Babe stalked around for the rest of the inning wearing the brilliant plumage.

* * *

It was a great club that won games with almost monotonous regularity. Joe Dugan told a reporter that year, "I don't know why you bother to come up here every day, you could do it just as well sitting at home. Combs walks, Koenig singles, Ruth hits one out of the park, Gehrig doubles, Meusel singles, Lazzeri triples, then Dugan goes to the dirt on his can!"

It was also a "great gang of friends," said Ruth. On those long train trips, recalled pitcher Oscar Roettger, "when the candy butcher came through the cars, Babe wouldn't ask how many do you have or how much did it cost. He'd wave his hand and buy the kid out, then spread the stuff around."

Ruth had special routines with many of the players. He kidded center fielder Earle Combs, the team's champion "barber," for his nonstop chatter. He kidded Meusel and Lazzeri for their long silences, swearing once that they spent days without saying a word, except for "pass the bread" at the dinner table. One of his favorites was pitcher Wilcy Moore, a big, bald Oklahoman who won 19 games for the Yankees that year. Moore may have been the worst batter of all time and didn't get his first base hit until June. Ruth then bet him $300 that he wouldn't make three hits all season. He got five, and that fall, from his farm, Moore wrote to the Babe, "I've been thinking of you. I bought two mules with the $300 I won from you. I call one Babe and the other one Ruth." In a hearts game, said Ruth, "Moore yells and shrieks and you can't stay in the same room with him. Once he got so bad we ganged up on him and put him back in the car with the newspaper boys until he promised to keep quiet."

But the funniest character of all was Ruth, says Pete Sheehy, who joined the club that year as a seventeen-year-old clubhouse assistant and is now the Yankees' equipment manager.

"You'd be on the bench," says Sheehy, "and Ford Frick, the writer, a good friend of his, would come by and he'd yell, 'Hello prick! Ah, I mean Frick!'"

Often, Sheehy would be watching batting practice when the Babe yelled, "Hey kiddo, a little bi!" That meant bicarbonate of soda. One time Sheehy made a mistake and brought him a glass of epsom salts instead of the "bi," and Ruth boomed out, "Jesus Christ, kid, you're in a transom!"

"He was always kiddin' around like that," says Sheehy. "If a guy was daydreamin', if he was like in a trance, the Babe'd say, 'Jesus Christ, you're in a transom!' "

Above all, Sheehy recalls Ruth's warm rapport with the fans. "You never hadda ask him to autograph a ball. And out on the field, he always gave it that, you know, that little tip o' the cap, in other words, 'thank you.' "

* * *

The Yanks wrapped up the 1927 pennant race a month before the season ended, and all eyes now focused on Ruth's and Gehrig's neck-and-neck race for home run supremacy. Many papers featured a "home run barometer" to measure their duel.

Before a Labor Day doubleheader in Boston, Ruth and Gehrig were tied with 44 homers apiece (that year the third highest man in the American League was Tony Lazzeri with 18 homers, and the National League champion finished with 30). The fans sent up a chant that was heard in ball parks all over the country that summer:

> Go to it, Babe,
> Go to it, Lou,
> Hit the ball
> To Kalamazoo!

Early in the game Gehrig hit his 45th, but the Babe hammered *three* homers that afternoon and surged ahead for good.

There had been so much excitement over the Ruth-Gehrig duel that Ruth's 400th career home run went virtually unnoticed that season. It happened in Chicago. Richards Vidmer of the *Herald Tribune* arrived late, in the sixth inning, and learned that Ruth had hit a homer three innings before. The night before he'd been out on the town with the Babe, and Ruth had made a casual remark about his next homer being an even 400. But none of the men in the press box that afternoon seemed to take notice. During the game, Vidmer wrote a "tear jerker" about a little boy in the bleachers who was playing hooky from school and caught the Babe's 400th home run ball. The usher tried to wrest it away from him, but the boy ran off because he thought they were after him for skipping school. "Then I had it that the kid was trapped," said Vidmer, "taken to the dressing room, and the Babe gave him half a dozen autographed balls and the kid cried. Naturally, I had the story exclusive, since I'd made it up, and the next day my office wired that I was being put in for a bonus!"

Ruth needed 17 homers during the month of September, better than one every other day, to break his record of 59. But he kept up the torrid pace. His 56th homer, on September 22, was a dramatic ninth-inning blow that ended the game in the Yankees' favor. To avoid having his favorite bat snatched by one of the fans streaming from the seats, Ruth carried it around the bases with him. As he rounded third, a young fellow wearing knickers caught up with him, pounded his broad back and then grabbed hold of the bat. "At last sight," said one observer, "the youngster was like the tail of a flying comet, holding on to the bat for dear life, and being dragged into the dugout" as Ruth hastened to escape the "swirling crowd of juveniles."

Only three games remained in the season when the Yanks met the Washington Senators in New York on September 29. The Babe was just three homers shy of a new record. He caught hold of Horace Lisenbee's two-strike curve ball in the first inning and winged a low line drive into the right field seats. That was number 58. With the bases loaded in the eighth inning, relief pitcher Paul Hopkins tried to sneak one past him and Ruth slammed it half way up the right field bleachers. That was number 59. Only 7,500 fans were present, but, according to John Drebinger of the *Times,* "The crowd fairly rent the air with shrieks and whistles as the bulky monarch jogged majestically around the bases behind the other three Yanks."

Ruth had two more games to reach the magic number 60. The next day, September 30, subway cars heading to the stadium buzzed with talk, and piles of money changed hands on bets whether Ruth could break his record that afternoon. The Senators elected veteran left-hander Tom Zachary, who had allowed Ruth only two homers during his career. In his first three trips to the plate, Ruth hit two singles and walked. In the eighth inning, with the score tied 2–2, Mark Koenig led off with a triple and the 10,000 spectators stirred as Ruth walked up, swinging his big bat. Zachary's first pitch was a fastball, strike one. The next was high, ball one. On his third delivery, he fired the ball low and inside. The Babe stepped slightly away, took a vicious uppercut swing and golfed a line drive that hugged the foul line and landed fair by a foot, halfway up into the right field bleachers. Zachary, a picture of dejection, threw his glove to the ground. The Babe made his triumphal tour a slow one, jogging around the bases, savoring every moment as the cheering fans tossed hats and scorecards into the air. The Yankees were all on their feet, pounding their bats loudly against the wooden dugout floor. Charlie O'Leary, the third base coach, was so touchy about his bald head that whenever the national anthem was played he hid in the dugout rather than doff his cap. But now he was jumping up and down and screaming; he threw his cap into the air, and his naked dome gleamed in the sunlight. And there was Gehrig, his wide grin mirroring the Babe's, his bat on his left shoulder and his right hand extended in a handshake at home plate—a tableau made classic by so many photographs. When Ruth trotted to his position, the right field bleachers were a dizzying blur of white as the fans rose and waved their handkerchiefs; time after time the Babe lifted his cap and punctuated his mincing stride with a series of snappy military salutes. They ate it up; they cheered themselves hoarse.

Later, in the clubhouse, the Babe inhaled a hefty pinch of snuff and boomed out: "Sixty! Let's see some sonofabitch try to top that one!"

John Kieran echoed the thoughts of millions of Americans when he wrote in his column for the *Times*: "It will be a long time before anyone else betters that home-run mark, and a still longer time before any aging athlete makes such a gallant and glorious charge over the come-back trail."

The next afternoon, the final day of the season, the Yanks won their 110th game, but Ruth was unable to hit another homer in three times at bat. Even *he* couldn't top it.

*　　*　　*

The 1927 World Series was the first that would be a broadcast on a nationwide radio hookup; by then about one-fourth of the country's 27 million homes had radio sets, and the listening audience was estimated at 35 million people.

The Yankees checked in at the Roosevelt Hotel in Pittsburgh two days before the Series began. Later that afternoon the drinks were flowing fast and free in Ruth's suite when some of the Pirates dropped by to say hello. Among them the Waner brothers, short, slender young men who were two of the finest outfielders in the game. Wearing a "giddy dressing gown and gay slippers," and holding a highball in his hand, Ruth looked down at them and blinked, saying, "Why, they're just kids! If I was that little, I'd be afraid o' gettin' hurt!"

Lloyd and Paul Waner did fine, but the Yankees easily won the first two games, and the action switched to New York.

Persistent showers the night before threatened cancelation of the third game on October 7, but when the gates opened at 11:30 A.M a line of 10,000 fans reached along River Avenue from 157th to 161st Street and back again. An hour before game time, more than

30,000 seats were filled. Just then, a report spread among the spectators that Babe Ruth had been killed or severely hurt in an auto crash. As usual, all news about Ruth was exaggerated. He had been driving to the game and was crossing the McCombs Dam bridge, two blocks from the Stadium, when a car in front of his veered on the slippery trolley tracks. The two vehicles crashed, and the left front fender of Ruth's car was dented and part of the bumper torn off. The Babe didn't even bother to stop. "I didn't feel anything," he said later. That day, Herb Pennock threw a fine three-hitter against the Pirates, and the Babe led the Yankee attack with a home run, the first hit by anyone in that Series.

In the fourth and final game, Ruth's scorching single in the first inning knocked in a run that tied the score at 1–1. In the fifth, he hit a "terrific wallop" into the right-center field bleachers with a man on base, that put New York ahead, 3–1. It was his tenth World Series homer, and as he went out to his defensive spot "the crowd in the bleachers rose up and cheered madly." Pittsburgh tied the game, but the Yanks won in the last inning on a wild pitch by Johnny Miljus that scored a runner from third base. As the Yankees ran into their clubhouse, the Babe "beamed all over the place . . . like an overgrown schoolboy . . . his booming voice rang above those of the other players, in that wild, thunderous outburst of celebration." What a season! People couldn't recall a stronger team. The Babe had reached his zenith with 60 home runs, and added two more for good measure against the Pirates. He was on top of the world.

* * *

Christy Walsh lost no time in capitalizing on Ruth's and Gehrig's fame. Three days after the series, they were off on a cross-country barnstorming tour that covered twenty-one cities in nine states and drew nearly one-quarter of a million paying customers. The Babe appeared in a picturesque uniform: white cap and stockings and a black suit with the words "Bustin' Babes" emblazoned across his broad chest. Gehrig sported a white uniform, with the lettering "Larrupin' Lous." Thirteen of the twenty-one games ended early because "fidgety fans" rushed out on the field to touch their heroes. In the first game of the tour, for example, Babe and Lou joined up with a team of locals in Trenton, and Ruth smashed three homers. The first two times, hundreds of boys swarmed onto the field and ran the ninety feet from third to home in stride with "the King of Swat." After his third homer, there was such pandemonium that police couldn't clear the field. The next day, at Dexter Park in Brooklyn, a handful of desperate policemen tried to contain a crowd of 20,000. After eight innings, and no homers by Ruth, the fans became restless.* Ever the showman, the Babe took to the mound and pitched. In the ninth, when he returned to the mound, the fans stormed the field and carried the smiling Babe on their shoulders to the clubhouse. Two days later, in Asbury Park, 7,000 fans clapped for an hour as the game was delayed. Ruth sat in a big armchair at the Berkeley-Carteret Hotel and blithely refused to budge until the local promoters came up with their agreed advance: a $2,500 cashier's check. The game lasted only six innings. Ruth and Gehrig knocked several balls into nearby Deal Lake. The rest were stolen by youngsters, who roamed about the field snatching at everything that was hit, fair or foul. There were so many children on the field that Ruth stood in the outfield with his mitt in one hand and a fountain pen in the other to sign autographs. "After each inning," said one reporter, "he half-carried dozens of small boys who surrounded him on the trips from the bench to the outfield and vice versa."

In almost every town they visited, hordes of fans milled about their hotel lobby. Once they reached the "royal suite," Ruth would order a meal that required "two waiters and three trays" and would attack it with gusto as local celebrities filed in to pay homage and ask the same questions over and over.

"You guys," the typical visitor would say, "gave those Pirates a terrific beating in the series."

"Yeh," Ruth would respond, chewing at his food.

"Four straight games, a terrible beating."

"Yeh."

Yeh, yeh, yeh, *yeh,* the Babe would grunt, while the visitors droned on. Gehrig, sitting on a sofa out of view, made stropping motions with his right hand on his left sleeve, meaning that the visitor was a "barber," an endless talker. If a hippo-like yawn wasn't enough of a hint, Gehrig would sneak off to the bedroom and call on the phone, telling Ruth he was urgently needed somewhere else.

They were given countless gifts. An Indian presented them with headdresses, christening the Babe "Chief Big Bat" and Lou "Chief Little Bat." A meatpacking company gave Ruth a huge ham with his name spelled out in cloves.

Throughout the trip, Lou submitted gracefully to the Babe's paternal instincts. When women phoned their rooms, Ruth warned him

---

* After a game in Iowa that October, the Des Moines *Register* reported with a top-of-the-page headline: "RUTH-GEHRIG FAIL TO HIT HOMERS."

of the dangers involved. In Chicago they attended a banquet given by local reporters, and Ruth was asked to speak.

"It's a pleasure and an inspiration," he boomed into the microphone, "to have a fellow like Gehrig as a runner-up in the home-run race. Lou's a great first baseman."

There was loud applause.

"And he protects his father and mother."

More applause.

"Gehrig," continued the Babe, "is a darned good fellow . . . he protects his father and mother."

There was more applause, but someone tugged politely at the Babe's sleeve and whispered, "You said that once."

"Lay off! *I'm* making this speech!" the Babe barked. He went on: "Lou Gehrig is a wonderful guy to room with. He doesn't snore, and he could sleep on a meat hook."

As the applause exploded once more, Ruth added, "and he protects his mother and father."

Ruth's cut of the barnstorming tour was $70,000, including $10,-500 in a single game—his share of a spectacularly successful charity game arranged in Los Angeles by Marion Davies. As they sat in their train compartment, Christy Walsh prevailed upon the Babe to save some of the money earned during the tour. "You're doing swell, Babe. Why not sock away a few thousand in your trust fund?"

Biting at his cigar, the Babe said, "Aw, shut up."

"But in a year or two you'll have $100,000 in that trust fund, Babe. That's a small estate. Lots of men who live in swell apartments on Riverside Drive and have cars and chauffeurs don't leave estates that large."

"Aw, don't give me a pain," said the Babe.

But later, in the club car, the Babe looked at young Gehrig and said, "A young guy like you should be saving his money."

"Yeh?" said Gehrig.

"Yeh. You've got ten years ahead of you in the big leagues. Save your dough now. Start one o' those trust funds, and push away the dough you're making out of a racket like this. Every dollar you sock away now'll be one more laugh when your playin' days are over."

"Yeh?" Gehrig said.

"Yeh," said the Babe.

At the end of the long tour, when their train pulled into Grand Central Station in November, the Babe and Lou stepped down to the platform, nicely browned by their days in the sun. "Lou, first thing we do," said Ruth out of the side of his mouth, "is go to the

Yankee offices with this coat o' tan. The big-money boys listen to reason when players look fit."

That winter the Babe and Lou made a few vaudeville appearances on the East Coast. Brief snatches of their routine were recorded, preserving Gehrig's high-pitched, nasal New York accent and the Babe's deep, side-of-the-mouth growl:

> LOU: Say, Babe! You've taken off a lotta weight in the last few yee-ahs.
>
> BABE: Look at my figure, kid.
>
> LOU: All you gotta do now is to diet for ten or fifteen more yee-ahs, and you'll almost look hoomin'!
>
> BABE: Boy, I'm careful o' what I eat these days.
>
> LOU: Lissen, Babe, you have a fahm wheah you grow your own food, donchyou?
>
> BABE: Yes, I have a farm.
>
> LOU: What do you raise theah?
>
> BABE: Lotsa things. Cel'ry, f'rinstance.
>
> LOU: Celery? You raise celery?
>
> BABE: Of course! Why the surprise?
>
> LOU: I though Colonel *Roo*-pit was the fellow who always raised your celery.
>
> BABE: I said *cel'*ry, not *sal'*ry!

Needless to say, they were paid a gorgeous celery for all this corn.

"I'm a Friend of Al's"

Shortly before celebrating his thirty-fourth birthday in 1928,* Ruth strode on stage at the Knights of Columbus Hall in New York, bowed to the applause, and lifted a baton that looked like a sliver of straw in his beefy hand.

He faced fifty-two boys from the Saint Mary's Industrial School, who were about to give a concert to raise money for the school building fund. Smiling proudly, Ruth put them through the paces of a few instrumentals. Then, while some of the boys tooted and drummed and sawed away, others rose and sang "The Battering Babe," an original tribute to the conductor that brought the house down:

> Look at him now!
> And think of all the games that Babe has won,
> And how he whacks a homer
> When the Yankees need a run!

> We know he's broken records,
> We're sure he'll break some more,
> Can't you hear those bleachers roar,
> Yow!

> He hits the ball
> And then the ball is sailing in the sky,
> A mile away it kills a cow,
> Wow!

---

* He was actually thirty-three, but there was a foul-up with his birth records that was not yet corrected.

173

And if a bandit on the border
Gets a baseball in the eye,
Put the blame on Babe,
Look at him now, wow!
Look at him now!

He was at the peak of his fame. A magazine survey listed him as "the most photographed person of the day," ahead of President and Mrs. Collidge, Queen Marie of Rumania (who had recently toured the United States), the Prince of Wales, Benito Mussolini, Jimmy Walker, and Gene Tunney. Ahead, even, of Mickey Mouse, who made his debut that year.

Trainer Doc Woods now spent half his time imitating Ruth's flowing signature on baseballs to keep up with the demand. Ruth used a secret exit to escape the mobs after a game at Yankee Stadium, making a mad dash for his car, which was guarded by a policeman. Late at night, when the Yankee train stopped at small towns, Ruth would be playing cards and peer out the window to see several dozen fans waving from the platform. He would step outside, wave, and yell good-naturedly, "Why don't you folks go to bed? Don't you ever sleep around here?"

Even his bats had acquired heroic stature. There was "Black Betsy," the big hickory wood weapon, now retired with a nasty split. His current companions at the plate, said the writers, were "Big Bertha," an "ash blonde," and "Beautiful Bella," a "Titian type."

He even seemed to be above the law. One evening that May he was stopped for speeding near Weehawken (a great speakeasy town). A few days later a crowd of youngsters waited outside Weehawken police headquarters, expecting Ruth to show up and answer the summons. But the summons was mysteriously withdrawn. Police Chief Patrick Dolan gave a knowing wink to a reporter and explained, "The Babe's the greatest player in the world, isn't he? And he's Irish, isn't he? And we have to stick together, don't we?"

Not only was he at the height of his fame, but his finances and physique were also in fine shape. He had saved $70,000 the previous year, and Christy Walsh said Ruth was assured of a "comfortable old age" thanks to annuities and trust funds that were "so tied up that neither Ruth, lawsuits, investments or anything will be able to touch the principal." Artie McGovern, the guardian of his body, claimed that Ruth was "five to ten years younger than two years ago" now that he'd cut down on coffee (which he used to drink "by the gallon"), pastry, and rich foods. He was down to 225 pounds, and his waist, said one reporter, was a "sylph-like" 39 inches.

He was feted and toasted and even made a member of the Elks. That year, *Babe Ruth's Own Book of Baseball,* a ghostwritten auto-biography with plenty of tips for kids, was published by G. P. Put-nam's. A short time later, Ruth admitted it was the only book he'd ever read cover to cover. When a skeptic expressed disbelief, Ruth yelled, "Goddammit, I read it *twice!*"

Even newspapers rarely drew his attention. Sometimes, however, a friend would show him a critical story and he would explode. Once in New Orleans, recalls Marshall Hunt, he was walking through the hotel lobby "all gussied up" on his way to a nice evening somewhere in the French Quarter. He spotted Bob Boyd of the *Evening World* and complained about an article in which he'd been allegedly ma-ligned.

Just then Tom Meany came by, heard the complaint and said, "Oh, you must mean Marshall Hunt's story." Then, with gestures of his hands, Meany explained, "Look, Babe, not all papers are the same. Boyd works for a great big one, like *this.* Hunt works for a little one, like *this,* what we call a tabloid."

Ruth listened, nodding, and said, "Well, all I can say is that you fellas have to be more careful." Then he was off to see his date, and Meany stood there, overcome with laughter.

Though he'd calmed down somewhat, Ruth still enjoyed his eve-nings on the town. In Saint Louis one night, he had several too many while making the rounds of a few speakeasies and could barely return to his hotel. Leo Durocher, then a rookie shortstop, gave him a helping shoulder through the lobby and to his door. The next day Ruth discovered that his wristwatch was missing. Forgetting about all his stops the previous night, Ruth was convinced that Durocher—the last man to be in his company—was the culprit. Some days later, the Yanks played an exhibition game in Scranton, where the coal miners gave Ruth a huge mantel clock made of coal. As the players dressed before the next game in Yankee Stadium, Ruth placed the big timepiece atop his locker and yelled, "By God, here's one that slippery-fingered sonofabitch won't steal!"

He'd worked like the devil to get in shape at Saint Petersburg that spring. Wearing his rubber shirt over his uniform, he smacked one ball after another over the fence and into Crescent Lake. Then he pitched batting practice. When he was done one day, with rivulets of sweat pouring down his face, "he looked like a man who had held his head under the town pump." He tottered to the bench for a drink of water and sat down, moaning with fatigue.

A reporter told him that if he choked up his bat and hit to left field, he could hit more than .400 the next season.

The Babe grunted.

"Wouldn't you rather hit .400 than sixty-one homers?" the reporter asked.

"Hell, no! The fans'd rather see me hit one homer to right than three doubles to left. And besides," he added with a grin, "there's more jack in it for me in this home run racket."

He was right. The turnstiles at Yankee Stadium and other American League parks revolved at a record pace when Ruth was in the lineup, swinging with all his might. He was hitting the ball so far that a *New Yorker* cartoon that June showed a Ruth "goodwill homer . . . leaving Yankee Stadium for Nicaragua."

That September, Republican Presidential candidate Herbert Hoover came to see the Yanks play in Washington and sat in a field box with Senators owner Clark Griffith. A request was forwarded to the Yankee clubhouse, asking Ruth to pose with Hoover. He was ready to go when one of his teammates said, 'Jidge, you better be careful, you're a buddy of Al Smith's and he wouldn't like that."

"Gee, I never thought o' that," said Ruth.

Minutes later, a messenger from the Washington club asked him to come along.

"I changed my mind," said Ruth. "Tell Hoover if he wants to meet me, I'll be glad to get together with him under the stands. But not in public. I'm a friend of Al's."

"BABE RUTH REFUSED TO POSE WITH HOOVER," said the next day's headlines. "It's a matter of politics," Ruth was quoted as saying to Clark Griffith. Manager Huggins tried to calm the brouhaha, saying there had been a "misunderstanding." No one knows how many secret phone calls and private talks ensued, but the next day Ruth's advisers released a statement:

> When the photographer asked me to go to Mr. Hoover's box yesterday, I labored under a misunderstanding and deeply regret that I did not avail myself of the opportunity of meeting him. I hope Mr. Hoover will be gracious enough at some future time to permit me to present myself to him. Politics had nothing to do with it. The ballgame was about to start, Mr. Hoover was the center of attraction, and I thought it would look odd for me to go to his box at that time.

Hoover smiled when he saw the statement and replied, "As an earnest baseball devotee, I long have admired Babe Ruth's batting ability and I look forward with pleasure to meeting him."

By early September, Ruth was running about even with his previous year's home run output; he lacked only 14 homers to set a new record with 28 games remaining. But in 1927 the Yanks had romped easily to a pennant. Now, the Athletics were breathing down their necks. "As long as the A's are close," said Ruth, "I'm going to be swinging for hits into left field. I can't hit 'em as far there, but that's what wins ball games." Taking a pinch of snuff, he said, "You can break a home-run record with a last-place club, but you can't get into a World Series except with a winner." And he wanted to win. He confided to one reporter that he had played in eight series thus far and wouldn't rest until he had made it ten.

Ruth had a fine year, batting .323, driving in 142 runs, and smashing 54 homers; none was more crucial than the one he delivered September 11 when Philadelphia came to Yankee Stadium, only 1½ games behind the league leaders. Lefty Grove had won his last fourteen games, and a midweek crowd of 50,000 fans came out to see him pit his blinding fastball against the bats of Murderers' Row. The game was tied 3–3 in the eighth inning when, with Gehrig on base, the Babe swung and "a cracking sound split the tense silence." The ball sailed high and far toward the bleachers, and then "the thunder broke loose" as the cheering fans rained straw hats and paper onto the field. "It was Ruth, the whole Ruth and nothing but the Ruth!" exulted one paper.

The 1928 World Series was billed as a "grudge match," because Saint Louis had beaten the Yankees two years before. The Cardinals were 5–4 favorites to repeat, because Ruth's knee had bothered him in the final weeks of the season, and both Lazzeri and Combs were also lame. But the Yankees were not concerned about these handicaps. A writer that year said the New York team had "poise, aplomb, insouciance—a calm sure faith in itself that is radiated to the other team and the enemy crowd."

Fans all over the country tuned their radios to the opening game in Saint Louis. Many schools brought radios into their auditoriums, to insure against a rash of absences caused by sudden illness.

Ruth limped out onto the field, looking "slower than a decrepit turtle," but he whacked two doubles and a single and scored on Meusel's homer, which was enough to give the Yanks a 4–1 victory. In the second game, a mighty home run by Gehrig with the bases loaded provided the crusher, and Ruth added two more hits. The victim this time was Grover Cleveland Alexander, the whisky-guzzling oldtimer who bear the Yanks twice in the 1926 Series. Reporters cornered old Alex after the game and asked what happened. He answered dourly: "They made too many base hits."

After a long train trip to Saint Louis, the Yankees made it three straight, thanks largely to a pair of awesome homers by Gehrig. But the real break came in the sixth inning, with the score tied,

3–3. Gehrig was on first and Ruth on third when Meusel hit an apparent double-play grounder. Gehrig bulled into Frankie Frisch at second base and knocked the Cardinal infielder to the ground. Despite his painful knee, Ruth gathered up steam and headed for home. The throw beat him, but, half-sliding and half-falling, he hit catcher Jimmy Wilson like a ton of bricks; Wilson was staggered and the ball squirted from his fingers. Ruth lay prostrate across home plate. Meusel raced for second, and Wilson's throw bounced into the outfield as Frisch (a casualty of Gehrig's rough slide) was unable to reach it. To pour salt on the Cardinals' wounds, after Lazzeri walked Meusel made a beautiful hookslide steal of third, and Lazzeri stole second. When the wild inning was over the Yanks led 6 to 3, and they stayed ahead.

The fourth and last game of the 1928 series has often been regarded as Ruth's greatest single day.

Even in batting practice, his first swing resulted in a line drive that nearly tore the pitcher's leg off. The next three pitches were propelled over the right field pavilion.

In the first inning, however, the fans had a great laugh at Ruth's expense when he was blinded by the sun in left field and let a fly ball drop behind him for a Saint Louis double. He came to bat in the fourth with the Cardinals ahead 1 to 0, eager to rectify his mistake. On a count of two balls, one strike, Willie Sherdel threw him a low curve half a foot inside the plate, but it was in the Babe's power zone; he stepped away and sent it whistling over the right field pavilion to tie the score. But Saint Louis scored again and led until the seventh inning. That's when the roof fell in on the Cardinals.

Ruth came up with one out. Sherdel curved two slow strikes across the plate and the Babe let them pass. Immediately after the second pitch, without taking a windup, Sherdel whipped the ball over the plate for an apparent third strike. Umpire Charles Pfirman refused to allow it. He ruled the "sneak pitch" illegal because prior to the Series both clubs had agreed to bar such a delivery. Sherdel rushed in from the mound. Half the Saint Louis dugout emptied and formed an angry circle around the umpire. Ruth stood on the fringe of the angry Cardinals, smiling and applauding their histrionics. The game was resumed. Sherdel wasted two balls. He tried another curve and Ruth smashed it so far over the right field pavilion that it was seen later bouncing along Grand Boulevard. As he trotted around the bases, the Babe mockingly waved his hand at the hostile Saint Louis crowd. He passed second base and saluted the occupants of the left field bleachers. He turned toward home, still waving derisively at the crowd, which was too stunned to respond. Gehrig shook his hand, stepped up to the plate and hit another homer, right atop the pavilion. Moments later, old Pete Alexander shuffled in to relieve Sherdel, but he was no more effective. New York led 5 to 2 when the inning ended. Ruth swaggered out to his spot in left field, where the fans—still furious over the "third strike" that was disallowed—booed and hissed him. A few pop bottles were thrown out on the grass. Soon there was a full barrage of bottles, "ranging shots" that came closer and closer to the Babe. Finally, the Babe bent over, picked up a bottle, and with a grandiose motion pretended to fire it back at his hecklers. Half the people in the nearby bleacher seats ducked. Then they all erupted in laughter when they saw the Babe grin, toss the bottle gently to the edge of the outfield grass, and trot back to his position. Later, one writer called his action "a masterpiece of mob control." His grin, said someone else, was so big that "it deserved a world's record for the standing broad grin." "First he cowed them, then he won them over," said another man.* In the next inning, the Yanks added some insurance when young Cedric Durst hit a homer off Alexander. Ruth came to the plate seeking his third homer of the game. He was striving to achieve for the second time what no other man had ever done. Alex got one called strike past him. Then he tried an inside curve ball, and Ruth smashed it atop the pavilion. It was an incredible moment. But he wasn't done. With two outs in the last of the ninth, Frank Frisch of Saint Louis hit a high foul close to the left field stands. Ruth, driving his aching knee forward, ran parallel to the seats, his gloved hand outstretched for the ball. The Saint Louis fans whipped up a blizzard of flying newspapers and scorecards to obscure his vision, but, while running full speed, he reached over the railing, snared the ball in his glove, and never broke his stride, running straight toward the dugout, his arm triumphantly aloft in a magnificent gesture of glee and defiance. What an exit! The game and the Series were over.

The Babe thundered into the Yankee clubhouse, his gloved hand still raised, clasping the ball. He was perspiring, panting, and joyous. "There's the ball that says it's all over! There it is, right where I grabbed it outa the air! What a catch! Jesus, I practically grabbed it from between some broad's legs! You guys shoulda heard what she yelled at me!"

* Ruth had an amazing knack for taming belligerent fans. Once in New Orleans, when a fan kept booing him, Ruth looked at the man and wiggled his finger, saying "c'mere." Apprehensively the man walked onto the field. Ruth pulled a baseball from his pocket, borrowed the man's pencil, signed the ball and gave it to him. That shut the man up for the rest of the day!

The players rushed to undress and shower, hurdling benches and trunks strewn about the floor. Suddenly, out of the commotion, someone began to sing, "East Side, West Side, all around the town . . ." and they all joined in, creating an ear-splitting din; the Babe's booming voice could be heard above all. Then someone yelled, "Ruth for president! Vote for Ruth!" The excited Babe yelled, "Jesus, I told these friends o' mine out there in the bleachers I'd hit two homers this game! Wow! I got three, and all off hooks!"

"Hooray!" someone shouted. "Ruth for sheriff!"

Afterward, humorist Will Rogers said in his nationally syndicated column: "You know, it just don't seem like we have any game in America where one man stands out so prominently . . . as Babe Ruth does in baseball. . . . He is the Abraham Lincoln of baseball. It just don't seem right that a pitcher should be made to have to stand out there in front of him and have to throw baseballs at him and take the/ chance of being murdered when they come back at you."

Ruth and Gehrig had made the most powerful two-man offensive in Series history, whacking 16 hits between them for a total of 41 bases. Three of Ruth's 10 hits were home runs. He had batted .625, set a record for runs scored in a Series (9) and for career Series homers (13).

The Yankees' train ride back from Saint Louis that night was a wild experience. Ruth had brought a big supply of spareribs and beer aboard, and numerous bottles of bootleg whisky were already circulating. A long conga line, led by Ruth and Gehrig and joined by many players and writers, snaked its way from car to car raising hell. Half-naked torsos flashed up and down the aisles as grown men turned into howling maniacs. Even Miller Huggins, a normally quiet drinker, by next morning would be seen groping about, muttering, "Did anybody see my teeth?" The Babe was a master of sneaking up on a man, grabbing his collar, and with one violent tug pulling his shirt off. Soon everyone was doing it, and the car was filled with shrieks, the sound of ripping silk, and laughter. Almost every man on the train was down to his underwear when Ruth began searching for Colonel Ruppert, who had locked himself in a private drawing room with an old friend, Colonel Wattenberg, a hops salesman from Louisville. Ruth banged at Ruppert's door, and the club owner yelled, "Go away, I want to get some sleep."

"This is no night for sleeping!" Ruth yelled.

"Go away, Root!"

Ruth and Gehrig crashed against the door with their massive shoulders and shattered a panel. The Babe reached in, unlocked the door

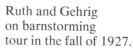

Ruth and Gehrig
on barnstorming
tour in the fall of 1927.

Photo: National Baseball Hall of Fame

Ruth campaigning
for Al Smith.

Photo: National Baseball Hall of Fame

Ruth with his second wife, the
former Claire Hodgson.

Photo: National Baseball Hall of Fame

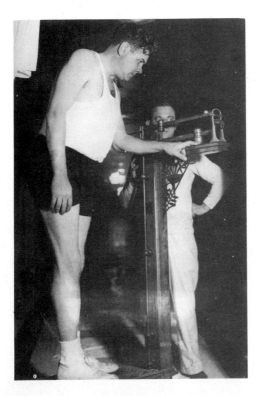

Checking his weight
at McGovern's Gym
in 1932. Scales tipped
at 225½ pounds.

Photo: New York Daily News

Ruth at bat,
around 1929.

Photo: Culver Pictures

Ruth stealing home
during a game at
Yankee Stadium in 1932.

Photo: Wide World Photos

Crossing the plate
at Detroit on
July 13, 1934, for
the 700th home run
of his major league
career.

Photo: Wide World Photos

As a coach
for the
Dodgers.

*Photo: National Baseball
Hall of Fame*

During the filming of *Pride of the Yankees*

Ruth with Claire
in 1943.

*Photo: Frederick Lewis
Photographs*

As a wrestling
referee in 1945.

Photo: Wide World Photos

Giving tips on batting to William Bendix, who portrayed the Babe
in *The Babe Ruth Story*.

Wearing No. 3 for the last time during ceremonies marking the twenty-fifth
anniversary of Yankee Stadium.

Fans pay their last respects to the Babe at Yankee Stadium in 1948.

and edged up to Ruppert as a howling band of Yankees urged him on. Ruppert was wearing a silk pajama coat. "Don't, don't, Root," he warned. "This is custom-made silk."

Ruth grinned and came closer. Sternly, Ruppert said, "Mister Root, you're suspended."

"Gee, Colonel," he said, "I only want a little piece of it . . ." There was a loud ripping sound, a moan from Ruppert, and a triumphant yell from the band of raiders. Gehrig got away with old Colonel Wattenberg's pajama top.

Ruth marched up and down the careening train in his underwear, gnawing on a sparerib and holding aloft a tiny fox terrier, which had been a going-away gift in Saint Louis. He walked into the dining room, which was filled with drunken players and writers, all making speeches to no one in particular. Three songs were being sung at once. The victory train stopped several times along the way—Shelbyville, Mattoon, Terre Haute, Muncie, Buffalo, Rochester, Syracuse, Utica—and everywhere groups came down to the station to cheer the world champions. At Mattoon, the Babe stepped out on the platform and yelled, "Three cheers for the Yankees! Three cheers for Al Smith!" About 2,000 fans were waiting in Terre Haute when the train arrived. Grasping a sparerib in one hand and a pitcher of beer in the other, the Babe went outside and raised them aloft. "Three cheers for Babe Ruth!" someone shouted. Lazzeri and Gehrig stood next to him, and the Babe yelled back, "Three cheers for Lazzeri!" He got them. "And now three cheers for Gehrig!" They responded loudly. "And now folks," Ruth said, "wottaya say? Let's have three cheers for my good friend Al Smith!" This was Hoover country, and he might as well have said Benedict Arnold. A scurrilous campaign had been waged against Smith's Catholicism. It was even said that, if elected, he would build a tunnel from the White House to the Vatican. There was a funeral silence. The Babe waved a sparerib at the crowd and said, "Aw, if that's the way ya feel, t'hell with ya!" and stalked back into the car.

When the train reached Grand Central Station, the Babe took Gehrig and Ruppert over to the Hotel Biltmore to greet Al Smith, who was preparing to catch a train of his own on a nationwide campaign tour. The Babe gave Governor Smith the baseball he had caught for the last out of the Series, after autographing it for his favorite Presidential candidate.

Smith said, "Babe, if they hollered for me like they do for you, I'd be sure to get elected."

He was probably right. The next afternoon, when Ruth's car stalled on a main street in Union City (he was returning from a visit to an orphanage in Paterson) and he stepped out to lift the hood, a crowd of 1,500 amateur mechanics gathered within minutes. When he entered a corner candy store to call for a tow truck, the pressing mob nearly shattered the store's window.

Ruth and Gehrig left on another barnstorming trip and drew 22,000 fans to their first game. A few days later they were in Montreal, where 14,000 fans surged onto the field after Gehrig's ninth-inning homer; the same happened in Trenton, where 3,000 school children broke a police cordon in the eighth inning to touch their heroes. Ruth took every opportunity during his tour to boost Al Smith's Presidential chances. In New York, on station WJZ, he made a long address, noting that: "On the Yankee train coming back from Saint Louis we made stops at many cities and I did a little speech-making for Governor Smith. We found, of the first 9,000 letters and wires received, 7,000 congratulated me for my home runs and my speech . . . only 200 letters criticized me for talking politics. That's a nice proportion for Smith—7,000 for him, 200 against him. . . . The other day I took a ride down to Oliver Street just to look at the little 'two-by-four' home that Governor Smith was born in. It reminded me of my own in Baltimore. And what a wonderful thing it is to think that whether you were raised by poor parents in Oliver Street, New York, or by poor parents on the riverfront in Baltimore, there is a chance for every boy to get to the top in America, whether he wants to be President or a ballplayer." This was a ghost-written speech, of course, but the Babe learned to deliver it with force and sincerity. Another time, on a more informal radio program, the Babe appeared with Tony Lazzeri. He claimed that all athletes were for Smith. "For instance," he said, "here's Tony Lazzeri. Now, Tony, who're the wops gonna vote for?"

SEVENTH INNING

We in America today are nearer to the final triumph over poverty than ever before in the history of any land. The poorhouse is vanishing from among us. We have not yet reached the goal, but, given a chance to go forward with the policies of the last eight years, we shall soon, with the help of God, be in sight of the day when poverty will be vanished from this nation."

Presidential campaign speech
by HERBERT HOOVER, September, 1928

The Crash

Most Boston readers missed the page-three item in the *Globe* of January 12, 1929, with the one-column headline: "WOMAN DIES IN FIRE AT WATERTOWN HOME." The victim was a Mrs. Helen Kinder, twenty-eight, wife of Dr. Edward H. Kinder, a dentist, and mother of Dorothy, nine, a student at a private parochial school in Wellesley.

The night before, a Friday, a neighbor saw a flickering light in the lower front room of the wood frame house at 47 Quincy Street. The glow became a glare. He ran across the street and hammered on the front door, when he heard the crackling of flames. Then he rushed to the corner and sounded the alarm. When firemen arrived, they hurried upstairs to a smoke-filled second-floor bedroom and found Mrs. Kinder face downward on the floor. Her mattress and bedclothes were burning. She was still alive, but she died soon afterward at a neighbor's house. Doctor Kinder was attending the boxing matches at Boston Garden with his brother and father. When he was paged, he rushed home and collapsed when he learned of his wife's death. Death was said to be caused by "asphyxiation and incineration." Police said the fire apparently began in the wall of the living room downstairs, where a radio and several lamps were plugged into a single wall socket and had caused an overloaded circuit. Some of the wires looked frayed. It appeared to be an open-and-shut case.

By Monday morning, no reader could miss the headline atop the *Globe's* front page: "VICTIM OF WATERTOWN FIRE BABE RUTH'S WIFE!" The story was all over the country. A New York paper screamed out: "MRS. BABE RUTH DIES IN LOVE NEST FIRE!"

Ruth first learned of the tragedy on Saturday night, about twenty-four hours after it occurred. He was at a party in Joe Dugan's house up in Scarsdale when the phone rang. His old friend Art Crowley, son of Boston Police Superintendent Michael H. Crowley, had placed the call. After he hung up, he burst out crying. Someone drove Ruth home and on to Penn Station to catch the Boston train, which left at 1:15 A.M.

He looked disheveled and bewildered when he stepped off the train six hours later at Boston's Back Bay station. When Crowley walked up to him, he said, "It isn't true, Arthur! It can't be true!"

He demanded to know, "Where's my little girl? I've got to see her!" Crowley assured him that Dorothy was in good care at her school and persuaded Ruth to go with him to the Brunswick Hotel, where he'd reserved the Babe's old suite, Room 574.

At 8:45 A.M., Crowley drove Ruth to nearby Saint Cecilia's Church, where all through the Mass Babe recited his rosary beads in a deep monotone, giving way to an occasional sob. Two close friends—attorney John P. Feeney and realtor Thomas G. McEnaney—were waiting when they got back to the hotel. At Crowley's insistence, Babe lay upon his bed, still wearing his rumpled clothing, and lapsed into a brief, fitful sleep while the men scribbled a statement for the press on a sheet of hotel stationery. When they awakened him, Ruth took the draft and walked over to the window, where he lit a cigar, puffing great clouds of blue-gray smoke. Finally he said, "Let it go at that." One Boston reporter was allowed in to see him.

His eyes red, his hands trembling, Ruth held the piece of paper and said to the reporter, "Don't ask me any questions. Let me read this to you and then you go away and let me alone."

He began to read: "My wife and I have . . ." but his voice broke and he dropped the paper. Picking it up, he read again, quickly, woodenly: "My wife and I have not lived together for the last three years. During that time I have seldom met her. I have done all that I can to comply with her wishes. Her death is a great shock to me." He crumpled the paper in his fist and threw it into the unlit fireplace. Then he returned to the adjoining bedroom and locked himself in. His friends rapped at the door, but there was no response. That afternoon, Helen's sisters, Catherine and Nora, came to the hotel to discuss funeral arrangements. Later in the day Ruth left the hotel to visit a friend, and from there went to the Watertown morgue, where he sadly confirmed that the dead woman was his wife, Helen.

The story took a confusing, ugly turn. Helen's brother Thomas, a former policeman, told a Boston *Post* reporter: "I have reason to believe that Mrs. Ruth was the victim of foul play, that the police don't have all the facts . . . what is there to prove that the house wasn't fired . . . that she wasn't murdered?" Stories that claimed his sister "was carrying on a love affair with Doctor Kinder are a lot of rotten lies," he insisted.

A flurry of puzzling—sometimes contradictory—statements was issued. Ruth's lawyer admitted that Doctor Kinder and the Babe "were friends in the past; they still are friends as far as I know." He said that an expensive Doberman Pinscher dog owned by Kinder was a gift from Ruth, bred on the Babe's Sudbury farm. The doctor's father, William F. Kinder, insisted that his son married Mrs. Ruth more than a year before in Montreal. Then he threatened, "If Babe Ruth or anyone else mixes my boy into any scandal, I'll tell a story that will blow the top of Ruth's head right off."

But Doctor Kinder finally appeared at Watertown police headquarters and admitted that he was not married to Helen, although the deed on his home, purchased in May of 1927, listed them as husband and wife. When reporters pressed for what else Kinder had said, the Watertown police chief replied with asperity: "He said some other things, but not of public interest."

Another brother of Helen's, attorney William J. Woodford, said, with tears streaming down his cheeks, "Helen was a good girl, but she was secretive. For a long time my mother and my sisters wondered what was the matter with her. But now I guess I have the key to those words she said to me, 'I have found a doctor who will give me opium tablets.' I wondered what in the world she could mean . . . but I couldn't worm another word out of her." (Recently, one source said: "According to Boston writers, she hooked up with this Doctor Kinder because he was a dentist and could get the dope that she wanted.") Neighbors said the Kinders lived "a quiet life," although a woman who lived nearby recalled that at one time "she became acquainted with a group including many Boston jazz musicians." The whole truth was never revealed, but Helen had obviously been a very sick woman. Just four months earlier she had been admitted to a Boston hospital with a nervous breakdown; although doctors insisted that she be given institutional care, she had left after a week.

There were numerous stories of when the Babe had married Helen. Stories appeared that they married in a double ceremony with friends in 1915 in Providence, Rhode Island. Another version mentioned Boston; still another said Quebec. On Monday afternoon, January 14, Ruth received about thirty reporters in his suite. He sat in a chair by the fireplace, nervously clenching and unclenching his hands.

"I'm in a hell of a fix, boys. . . . All I want, to say is that . . . it was a great shock to me." Then the tears streamed down his cheeks.

He fumbled for a handkerchief. "Please," he pleaded, "let my wife alone; let her stay dead." Everyone in the room knew this wasn't the polished statement "they" had prepared for the Babe. But it was all that he could say. He sat there, crying, and the reporters were silent. One man quietly asked him to clear up the question of his marriage date. Ruth took a sheet of paper from his pocket and read, "October 13, 1914. I got the license. Married October 18 at Ellicott City, Maryland. The priest who married us was the Reverend T. F. Doland." And what about his daughter, Dorothy? "I'd rather not mention anything about that." The reporters filed out, and left him alone.

The same day, Helen's nineteen-year-old sister, Nora, dropped a bombshell. "In my opinion, my sister did not die as a result of an accident. Three weeks ago, I went to New York with my sister. It was December 10th or 17th maybe. She said she wanted me there as a witness. We went to the offices of Christy Walsh, and he was there with the Babe. The Babe said, 'I've got to have a divorce.' He said he wanted to marry this other woman. My sister said, 'I'm willing to get a divorce quietly in Reno, in order to keep things out of the newspapers . . . but I won't do this unless you give me $100,000 to protect Dot and myself, and pay my expenses to Reno.' Then the Babe got mad and said, 'I won't give you another cent, but I want a divorce.' He told her to go to hell, because he'd given my sister enough money already. They couldn't come to any agreement and they said good-by. . . . Of course, this meeting didn't end until after about two hours of quarreling and during that time the Babe was very mean to Helen. Mister Walsh tried to settle the argument but he didn't have much luck. . . . And there's one other thing . . . the Babe threatened Helen with a gun while they were at the Sudbury farm about three years ago. He chased her all over the farm at the time and said he'd shoot her. I don't know what the trouble was about that time."

The Babe vehemently denied the sister's story. Major Judson Hannigan—counsel for Mrs. Ruth's family—said, "The charges were made by a member of the family unauthorized to talk for the family or for Mrs. Ruth. As such, we must repudiate it in its present form. . . . We are interested in according Mrs. Ruth a quiet burial."

But Helen's sixty-three-year-old mother claimed that Nora had told her of the December visit to New York. With a fierce gleam in her eyes, she said, "Helen never died by accident! She was done to death!" There were grumblings that Ruth had "connections" with Boston "big shots" and that the truth was being covered up.

The Boston district attorney halted plans for the funeral and ordered an autopsy and an investigation of the fire, saying "We're going to sift this thing to the bottom." "SEEKING POISON IN MRS. RUTH'S BODY," said the Boston *Post,* which reported that the Harvard Medical School would examine the contents of Helen's stomach for possible "traces of poison." In the meantime, a New York paper printed a photo of Mrs. Claire Hodgson, with the headline, "BABE RUTH TO WED BEAUTY." Other accounts said that Mrs. Hodgson had "vanished" from her 79th Street apartment, where for the past two years Ruth's car had been parked "nightly." Another story said that Mrs. Hodgson "has had a great influence in taming the Babe from an erratic playboy to a disciplined and valuable baseball property." There were stories, too, about Helen's poor health in recent years, her frequent hospitalizations, often for "nervous disorders."

At the same time, a fight broke out for custody of little Dorothy. A New York paper claimed it had located her birth certificate and that she was born February 11, 1920, at Saint Vincent's Hospital, with the parents given as "G. H. Ruth and Helen Woodford Ruth." A handwritten notation on the certificate said, "infant baptized by Catholic priest three days after birth." Ruth would neither confirm nor deny his parentage of Dorothy. Another report said the child was taken from a Brooklyn orphanage "to fill the gap in their lives when the first Dorothy died in infancy." Helen's brother William said Dorothy was indeed born to the Ruths: "Anybody could tell it was the Babe's child, her features and build." But it was then "firmly established" that the child had been taken from the Catholic institution in Brooklyn, that she was "on extension" and could "be recalled at any time if not given proper care."

Ruth met with members of the Woodford family at his hotel. Helen's mother said she would like to adopt the child, that he wasn't "suited to be the child's guardian" because he traveled eight months of the year.

He replied angrily, "You can never have Dorothy! That much I'll tell you right now! I'll stand for anything but that!" Members of the Woodford family hinted that they would "expose" Ruth after the funeral, detailing his affairs with other women, which caused the separation between Helen and him. Helen's brother again promised a "red hot exposé." The press spoke of a "mysterious wooden box, or cupboard drawer," in the custody of the police, which held personal records, jewelry, a diary, and "intimate letters." Ruth denied everything, even denied that he knew Doctor Kinder, contradicting his own lawyer's statement a few days before. He also denied that he was seeking a divorce in order to marry another woman.

Suddenly peace came on Wednesday, January 16, when the medical examiner confirmed that Helen Ruth had died in a fire caused by "accidental overloading of frayed electric wires," and the autopsy found no evidence of narcotics or poison. The district attorney said the case was closed as far as his office was concerned, "and I hope, for the sake of the unfortunate woman who cannot speak for herself, that it is closed as far as anyone is concerned." The Woodford family agreed to abide by the medical examiner's findings.

That night, Helen's body was brought to the Woodford home in an $800 bronze casket purchased by Ruth. It was placed close to a blanket of roses and lilies that nearly filled the room. Outside, more than 1,000 persons waited, hoping to catch a glimpse of the Babe. A detail of twenty-five policemen drove the crowd back time and again and finally established lines some distance from the house. It was very cold, but they waited. About midnight a car pulled up and Ruth got out, dressed in mourning. "There's the Babe! The Babe!" came a rumble from the crowd, and dozens of flashlights sought him out in the darkness.

He removed his hat and entered the house, together with Police Superintendent Crowley, young Art Crowley, his lawyer, and other friends. Helen's mother motioned him into the parlor, where he knelt at the bier, holding the rail in front of the bronze casket and making the sign of the cross.

Then he began to moan, and his shoulders shook convulsively. Beads of perspiration rolled down his forehead. His right arm trembled as he took the rosary beads from his coat pocket. For about five minutes he moaned and cried. When he tried to rise he collapsed, and friends reached for him, carrying him toward the door past the weeping members of the Woodford family. Strong arms propped him against a wall, and John Feeney pinched his cheeks and said, "Babe, everything's arranged for the funeral in the morning. You won't have to wait. We're going to take you away now."

Opening his eyes, Ruth blurted, "What funeral?"

He stared ahead blankly and was half carried to the car outside, moaning in a deep voice.

It was snowing the next morning and the skies were sullen, as the cars drove from the Woodford home to Old Calvary Cemetery. In the third car with the Babe were Helen's mother, her sister Josephine, and Police Superintendent Crowley. Babe leaned over, patted Mrs. Woodford on the knee, and inquired solicitously, "How is everything; is everything all right?"

"Yes, Mister Ruth."

"I want everything to be all right."

"You've done very nicely towards us."

"I want to do right by you."

The cars reached the cemetery. The Babe got out, removed his black fedora, and took his mother-in-law's arm. They stood next to the grave and the coffin, which was covered with flowers. As the snow fell, the Reverend Richard Burke spoke a brief prayer. And then Helen was lowered into the earth while the Babe, bareheaded, wept profusely. Afterward, he was taken to Crowley's home, where for the first time in days he slept.*

*   *   *

After Helen's burial, Ruth returned to New York and spent the next few days jumping from one hotel to another to avoid the press. But within a week strollers in Central Park were startled to see him, in heavy sweat clothes, jogging along a path. Some days later he was down in Saint Petersburg, celebrating his thirty-fifth birthday with a luncheon at the Jungle Country Club, where he played golf day after day. He also appeared at a charity benefit for children in West Palm Beach and, with W. C. Fields as referee, boxed a "two-round draw" against Jack Dempsey. In early March, the Yanks began to train at Saint Petersburg, and for the first time fans saw numbers on the backs of the players' uniforms. Barrow had decided to assign the numbers according to lineup position, and Ruth was given the number 3, which he made famous.

While in Florida, Ruth kept in touch with Claire. He was "distraught and frantic" about his daughter Dorothy, she recalled, and although "he never wrote," his phone bill during spring training was $1,600.

They decided to marry. Typical of the Babe's flair for the dramatic, he chose April 17, the opening day of the 1929 season, for the ceremony. But he wanted to protect Claire from the glare of publicity. "If I'm getting married, it's news to me," Ruth said a few days before the wedding. But late the next afternoon, as the clerks at the New York Marriage License Bureau were about to close their ledgers, he and Claire entered and filled out applications. He wrote

---

* Some days later, Helen Ruth's will was made public. She left Babe five dollars and asked that her estate go to her "beloved ward and charge, Dorothy, the former Marie Harrington." Her estate was said to be worth $50,000, but when Helen's bank deposit box was opened there was only a bank book with savings of $1,000 and jewelry worth about $3,000. The settling of the estate, however, revealed a suit for $30,000 against an unnamed party in New York City (which some speculate was instituted by Ruth himself) that was awarded to young Dorothy.

that he was born in Baltimore, said he couldn't remember his mother's maiden name, and listed his occupation as "playing ball." The news of his visit to the license bureau was all over town that evening. A reporter friend dropped by Claire's apartment and found Ruth sitting in the living room, wearing slippers and a great red bathrobe. "Congratulations," the man said.

"My God," Ruth roared. "Did they find that out? Say, tell them fellers down there on the sidewalk to lay off the pictures. The girl is afraid of them damn flashlights."

It rained heavily the morning of April 17, canceling the ball game but not the ceremony, which was set for the Roman Catholic Church of Saint Gregory the Great on West 90th Street. To avoid crowds, they announced the time for 7 A.M. but got to the church at 5:45. Despite the ungodly hour, there was a knot of reporters waiting, and by the end of the ceremony about 150 people collected outside the church.

At the altar, the hulking 230-pound Ruth dwarfed his petite wife-to-be. During the ritual a flashbulb boomed in a corner of the church, bringing a quick angry glance from Ruth, whose ears reddened. Moments later they left the church, man and wife, and a bunch of young boys yelled, "Good luck, Babe!" evoking a smile and a wave from the nervous bridegroom.

They hurried back to the builiding on West 88th Street where Babe and Claire would occupy an eleven-room apartment on the seventh floor, a few steps away from the apartment of Claire's mother. There was a large reception where, as one guest recalled, "the 18th Amendment did not apply." It went on and on, with music supplied by their friend, composer-pianist Peter de Rose, and the ukelele and songs of de Rose's wife, May Singhi Breen.

The next day Claire got her first taste of being an idol's wife as New York opened its season against the Red Sox before 35,000 fans in Yankee Stadium. When the Babe walked over to the box behind third base, where Claire sat huddled in a fur coat, a riot almost broke out. He came to bat in the first inning, and with the count two balls, two strikes, gave her another wedding present, lining a terrific smash into the left field stands, 402 feet away. As he rounded second base he looked her way, smiling and doffing his cap with a flourish.

Recalling those early days of her marriage, Claire once said she knew the Babe could be "tamed" but not "caged," so she gradually instituted a few reforms. He ate and drank too much, he hated going to bed, and his many friends offered ample excuse for not retiring early. Claire established a 10 P.M. curfew for parties at home and dropped a few of Ruth's more boisterous companions from the guest lists. It was tougher when they attended parties elsewhere. One host even set the clocks back, but Claire had her own wristwatch. If Ruth grumbled about offending the host by leaving early, she replied, "You strike out four times tomorrow and *you'll* feel badly, not him."

During the season she tried to keep him away from hard liquor but always kept a large stock of beer available. Once a year, she allowed a "no holds barred" party, after which, one guest recalls, "the apartment looked as though it was swept by a Florida hurricane." The Babe loved to gather up the flashbulbs on the floor, walk to the window, drop them seven stories to the street, and listen to the loud pops.

One week after the wedding, a reporter visited their apartment and found Ruth "just an old married man, domesticated as any husband could be, and twice as contented." Describing her husband's new diet, Claire said that potatoes, white bread, butter, and desserts were "out." From now on, the Babe would get plenty of lamb, beef, chicken, fish, and fresh vegetables.

"That's what I always eat," Babe murmured.

For fear that he might injure himself, Claire took charge of opening tin cans and stuck windows. She changed the blade when he shaved on Sundays and sent him to a barbershop the other six days of the week. When his toenails needed trimming, he went to a chiropodist.

To curb his free-spending habits, Claire handled the checkbook. He was given all the money he wanted, $50 at a time. "Lord, how that man could eat up $50 checks!" she once declared.* But the system worked. They lived very well on a monthly budget of $1,500; the income from his endorsements was more than enough, and they banked much of his salary. Between 1920 and 1929, Ruth had bought at least one fancy car a year, and sometimes more. The 1929 model lasted until 1940.

They didn't skimp on clothing, however. He still bought the finest silk shirts, and his few dozen suits cost $250 apiece. Claire had a hand in choosing his clothes, and writers soon took note of his improved taste for wardrobe, with much emphasis on rich shades of brown. She even tried to get Ruth to stop wearing caps, his trademark, but gave up when he tried on a hat. With his big round face, he looked "hilarious," she admitted.

When Christy Walsh came by one day, terribly excited about a deal that could mean at least $100,000, Ruth cut him off, saying, "Talk to Claire about it, 'The Lone Ranger' is on." After Claire and Christy

---

* After Ruth's death, Claire sent out hundreds of those canceled, endorsed $50 checks to fans requesting her husband's autograph.

settled the details, the Babe signed the contract without reading it, and without missing a moment of his favorite program.

Although some of the other players' wives didn't like it, Claire accompanied her husband on road trips. Colonel Ruppert encouraged the idea, saying it might be a "good influence." So Babe and Claire slept and ate in their private drawing room on the Pullman car. He often left the compartment to play cards with the other players. Sometimes they would hear, "Come on, Babe, time to go to bed."

"All right, mom, just one more hand."

Late at night, he would slip into his berth and in the morning whisper to a friend, "She didn't even hear me."

In Saint Louis, when he suffered terribly from the heat—it reached 106 degrees once—Claire spent the whole night applying cold compresses to his forehead.

The Babe, she later recalled, had "unbelievably strong" impulses for "wine, women and song." He "brought out the beast in a lot of ladies," she said, adding that "I have no boudoir secrets . . . beyond the fact that . . . I envy no woman in the world." She took all of his phone calls and once remarked, "He certainly was called by an awful lot of women." At first she assumed these were "vestiges of his gay bachelor days," and later she said, "There's no reason to assume that a lot of them weren't exactly that." She changed their phone number in New York so often that even she couldn't remember it.

Some weeks after the marriage, while Ruth was taking batting practice in Saint Louis, a member of the Browns walked up smiling and asked, "Is the wife with you this trip?"

"Sure," said Ruth, spitting a gob of tobacco into the air.

"Having a hard time dodging the old phone calls?"

"Aw, go to hell!"

Given his previous carefree life, one might expect Ruth to rebel against all these restrictions, but a friend swears, "I never even heard him grumble." Now he was a family man, with two daughters (Dorothy, who was nine, and Julia, Claire's daughter by a previous marriage, who was fourteen). Claire was better educated, more cultured, and more practical than the Babe. Although he was seven years her senior, she was not only his wife but also the mother he never had for much of his childhood. He was in his mid-thirties now, and the stable home life that he had spurned a decade before now had its attractions. From all accounts, it was a happy marriage.

*   *   *

Early in June of 1929, Ruth fell ill with a severe cold (there were also rumors he'd suffered a heart attack), and after one day in the hospital he was ordered to rest at home for a week. A reporter from the *Sun,* one of New York's more playful dailies, went to see the ailing star.

He found the Babe reclined upon a chaise longue "over which was spread a pale violet coverlet of heavy silk." The drawing room "compared for size . . . with the rotunda of the Grand Central Station and for gorgeous ornateness with some of the more splendid apartments at the chateau at Versailles." The walls were paneled in green silk, the "noble purple" rug was deep-piled and imposing, and at Ruth's right hand was "a green tabouret, upon which rested a vase of pink roses." Near the window overlooking the Hudson stood "one of the biggest grand piano in the civilized world."

Ruth wore "a Paisley dressing gown of the stuff and design so beloved by our maiden great-aunts, and upon his small feet were fawn-colored slippers." Glimpses could be had of "silken, peach-colored underwear," and of "deep golden yellow" silk socks.

The reporter had been told by Ruth's doctor that "certain abstentions" would speed the Babe's recovery.

"Yeah," Ruth growled. "Do ya know what the guy has laid out for me? Babe, you'll have to cut out smokin', he says, and the chewin' as well. And I don't wantcha to take a pinch o' snuff until I say you can. Not a pinch! And no liftin' the old elbow, Babe, he says. What's a guy gonna do? You get sick o' readin' and there ain't much in the papers outside o' the baseball news."

A few days later, his doctor said the cold was responding to treatment, but Ruth himself hinted that it was more than a cold, saying, "All I want is a few days away, where I can be alone and get my nerves in shape."

Perhaps it had been the combined strain of Helen's death and his new marriage. Perhaps it was a recurrence of some old illness. No explanation was ever given. Babe and Claire drove south and spent a quiet week fishing and swimming at a friend's summer cottage on Chesapeake Bay a few miles from Annapolis, Maryland.

He returned to the Yankee lineup in late June, and his health seemed to be fully restored. That season, to compensate for advancing age and the slowing down of his reflexes, he experimented with a modified batting stance: He stood about a foot farther from the plate, and when he leaned in toward the pitch the weight of his body supplied extra power. It seems to have worked. He wound up the season with a .345 batting average and, although he missed 19 games, led the league for the fourth consecutive time in home runs (46).

On August 11, before an overflow crowd that formed a crescent across the left field grass in Cleveland's Dunn Field, Ruth came to bat in the second inning. He was hot, having hit six homers in the past seven games. He swung at Willis Hudlin's first pitch and sent the ball whizzing over the right field fence. It was the 500th homer of his career. This time the writers took notice. The slugger nearest to his record was Cy Williams, the Philadelphia Phillies veteran, who had hit 237 thus far. As Babe trotted past third base, he yelled to a field detective, "I'd kinda like to have that one!" Ten minutes later, Jack Geiser, a middle-aged man from New Philadelphia, Ohio, was ushered into the dugout, looking slightly dazed. He had been visiting relatives in Cleveland and was going to catch a bus near the stadium when the ball rolled up to him. Ruth shook hands, posed for a photo, gave Mr. Geiser a pair of autographed balls in exchange for Number 500, and then slipped the man a $20 bill for good measure. He had quite a story to tell his family when he got home to New Philadelphia that night.

Hitting 500 homers was such an unheard-of feat that the New York *World* said, "It is to be bracketed with our skyscrapers, our universities, our millions of automobiles as a symbol of American greatness. . . . This is no mere record about to be marked up in perishable chalk. It is the middle of an epoch."

He set other records that year. Before a game at Yankee Stadium that August, he took part in a fungo-hitting contest and whacked a ball 447 feet; the longest previous shot, 418 feet, had been made in 1912 by Ed Walsh. That same month, while playing at the Saint Albans Golf Club, he drove a golf ball 325 yards, according to witnesses. Like many Ruthian drives, however, it landed in the middle of a pond.

Despite Ruth's fine year, the Yankees slumped and fell far behind in the pennant race. "They're becoming glutted with success," complained manager Huggins. "They've been in three World Series in a row . . . they have stock market investments, and when they pick up the paper now, they turn to the financial page first and the sports page later."

About two weeks before the end of the 1929 season, Huggins looked quite ill. His appetite was poor, and it seemed as though his eyes were shrinking back into his head. There was a sore under one of his eyes that appeared to be a carbuncle. He walked home after the Yankee game of September 20 and saw a doctor. It was serious; he had a rare skin disease known as erysipelas, also called Saint Anthony's Fire, and his entire body was filled with poison. Five days later, he was dead at the age of fifty.

Now the Yankees were without a leader. Coach Art Fletcher managed the team for the final few games of the season to a second-place finish. But Fletcher said he wanted no part of the job for the 1930 season.

A few days after the season, Ruth suddenly blurted to Claire, "Hey, what's the matter with *me?*" After all, he figured, he was a sixteen-year veteran of the major leagues and had spent a decade with the Yankees. He went to see Colonel Ruppert at the brewery, but the Colonel shook his head sadly and replied, "You can't manage yourself, Root, how do you expect to manage others?"

"Listen, Colonel," said Ruth, "I've been through the mill. I know every temptation that can come to any kid and I know how to spot it in advance."

Ruppert promised to think it over. The story soon circulated that Ruth was being considered for the managerial job. Ruth, covering the World Series in Philadelphia for the Christy Walsh Syndicate, issued a statement that people all across the country had asked him about becoming the Yankee manager, but after a "pleasant conversation with Colonel Ruppert," he said, it was agreed that "so long as I can deliver the goods as a player it would not be wise to take on the troubles and worries of a manager." Explaining that he had "at least two or three good years of baseball left," he concluded with, "but don't forget: someday I hope to realize a great ambition by having my name listed in the manager's column." A few days later, pitcher Bob Shawkey was named manager of the club.

And a few days after that, on "Black Tuesday"—October 29, 1929 —the stock market fell and the showbiz daily *Variety* announced "WALL STREET LAYS AN EGG." Just two months before stocks had been at an all-time high, but they were on a long downhill slide toward the Great Depression. It coincided, too, with Ruth's descent. He had joined the Yankees and become a national celebrity in January, 1920—the dawn of that great decade—and now, as America moved into a new, more sober era, his own life moved with that tide.

Puffing a long, black cigar, Babe drove his car down Riverside Drive on his way to talk turkey with Colonel Ruppert. It was early in 1930, and four million Americans were out of work. Just below Riverside Drive, along the shore of the Hudson, hundreds of jobless men hammered sheets of scrap metal and wood into a shantytown village and lit campfires to keep warm and cook their meals. But the nation's leaders had assured everyone that it was just a temporary recession.

"How much do you want, Root?" the Colonel asked.

"A hundred thousand a year."

Ruppert blinked. "You'd have thought I asked for the whole brewery," said Ruth. "He told me I must be out of my mind."

Ruth left for Florida, where he romped about on the golf course in his plus-fours, or at the beach with Claire in his two-piece striped bathing suit. They went to the dog races, and they drove to Tampa, where the Babe loved to sample the spicy Cuban dishes.

At Saint Petersburg, he celebrated his thirty-sixth birthday with a mammoth dinner, the "appetizer" being a large silver tray piled high with telegrams from well-wishers. He hunted for quail, judged a boxing match, hobnobbed with celebrities such as ex-Governor Al Smith, cartoonist Billy de Beck and copper magnate Edward Guggenheim, and appeared totally unconcerned about his contract differences with Colonel Ruppert.

But then he shocked the sports press by issuing a long mimeographed "letter" in which he threatened to quit baseball unless Ruppert gave him a three-year contract for $85,000 per sesson. He claimed to have enough "bread and butter" at home if he never touched another baseball. Without five cents from the Yankees, he said, he was assured of $25,000 per year from dividends and royalties. Claiming he'd saved $150,000 in the past three years, he said, "If you think that figure's padded, call the President of the Bank of Manhattan or the Equitable Life Assurance Company."

When Jake Ruppert came down to Saint Petersburg, he brought with him a peace offering: eight new Ruthian bats, fresh from the factory. But by March 10 both sides seemed intransigent. Exactly how they resolved their differences may be a prosaic tale, but the legend is far more fun. Sportswriter Dan Daniel allegedly got a "hot tip" from Ford Frick that Ruth would refuse to play the next day's exhibition game against the Boston Braves unless he was given an $85,000 contract. Without checking the story, Daniel filed it to the New York *Telegram*. The next morning, however, two hours before game time, Daniel saw Ruth strolling toward the ball park. He walked up to the Babe and blurted out his dilemma.

"Wotta ya want *me* to do?" said the Babe.

"Quit!" said Daniel.

"But I can't do that!"

"Then sign with Ruppert before noon!"

"But I want $85,000 and he's only offerin' $80,000."

Imagining how his "exclusive" story would sound if Ruth played without a contract that day, Daniel spun a long, impassioned tale of hungry people rioting for bread in Union Square, while *they* were quibbling over a lousy few thousand bucks!* Finally, the Babe agreed to accept $80,000. But Ruth wasn't finished. He wanted the Yankees to refund the $5,000 fine that Huggins had slapped on him in 1925 (who said the Babe had a poor memory?). Ruppert hesitated, but Ruth insisted, "You promised me."

Ruppert said, "So long as Huggins was alive, Root, I'd never have given it back, but Miller's dead now and he'll never know."

Later in the day, before a phalanx of news photographers and reporters, Ruth borrowed a pen and signed a contract that guaranteed him $160,000 over two seasons. In terms of today's purchasing power, the Babe's $80,000 per season would be worth about $216,800. (That year, a YMCA official published a pamphlet on how a young man— a teetotaler, of course—could get by in Manhattan on $25 a week. It included such items as "breakfast 25c," "subway 5c," "talkie theater 50c," "ball game $1," "room at Y $1," and "dinner 75c," and even allowed for a Sunday church donation of a quarter.) But it was worth even more. Taxes are far higher today. In 1930, the federal government took only 15 per cent of the Babe's salary, leaving him with $63,360, which is worth $184,280 today. To earn an equivalent income after taxes now, one would need to gross $307,000 a year. No baseball player has ever received that amount.†

Most papers said the Babe was well worth the money. While he earned more than many prominent citizens, said the *Sun*, "what president of a college, governor, or Supreme Court judge ever made 30,-000 Americans spring up as one man in a delirium of delight?" If the Yankees paid Ruth $100,000 a year "for life," said the *Times*, "it would not cut too heavily into the millions he drew to its ball park. If all the leagues contributed to such a pension they would be no more than acknowledging a debt far beyond payment."

Ruth earned about $200,000 in 1930. In addition to his $80,000 salary, he received a percentage of the gate for exhibition games. There were movie shorts (he did a series of two-reelers for Universal pictures with Notre Dame football coach Knute Rockne), ghosted articles, radio and personal appearances, and endorsements. A ciga-

---

* In fact, the next week more than 1,000 men standing on a bread line in New York City rioted, seizing two truckloads of bread and rolls that were being delivered to a Manhattan hotel.

† As of late 1973, the highest-paid athletes in major sports were Wilt Chamberlain (basketball), $600,000; Dick Allen (baseball), $225,000; Brad Park (hockey), $250,000; and Joe Namath (football), $250,000. Basketball is the highest-paying sport, partly because the teams are smaller and have less equipment and lower overhead, and also because of a recruiting war between the National and American basketball associations.

rette firm paid him $5,000 a year, despite the fact that he was one of the world's most famous cigar smokers.

That summer he appeared at the opening of Babe Ruth's Shop for Men, a haberdashery at the corner of Broadway and 52d Street, to which he'd lent his name for a fee. More than 600 persons cheered as Ruth alighted from his auto. Mopping his brow inside the small crowded store, he pressed a button to turn on the purple, green, and blue exterior signs that bore his name. As the cash register tinkled, Ruth was asked if he'd be found on duty at the store during the winter.

"Sure!" he said. "But not all the time. That would kill me!"*

Although Ruth was at his financial peak, he showed signs of slowing down physically. During an exhibition game in Dallas that April, he raced from first to third on a single by Gehrig and suddenly pulled up lame with a torn muscle in his right calf. "Interest in the game passed away as soon as Ruth left the field," wrote one correspondent.

But he recovered from his injury and more than justified his paycheck by thrilling the fans with extraordinary streaks of power. On May 21 in Philadelphia, for example, he slammed three home runs in a single game, inspiring the *Daily News* to splash across the top of the sports page: "HOT BAM—3!" The second homer was called the longest ever seen at Shibe Park; it soared over the right field fence, over the street, over the rooftop of a house where fans sat in improvised bleachers, landed atop a house on the other side of the yard, and was last seen bounding down the street two blocks away.† Still red hot, the Babe played in a doubleheader against Philadelphia the next afternoon and smashed three more homers; a total of six in two days!

By July 2, the Babe already had 31 homers and was far ahead of his record pace of 1927. But he had become more injury prone. In a game at Yankee Stadium, he leaped high for an apparent home run ball, somehow got stuck in the top of the right field screen, and tore the entire nail off the ring finger of his left hand. He fell to the ground in excruciating pain; the players rushed to his aid, helped him off the field, and he was kept out of the lineup for more than a week. Despite

---

* A year later, as the Depression deepened, the store closed for lack of business with $2,500 in royalties to Ruth still unpaid. The store was sold at auction to a new owner, who immediately plastered the windows with signs saying "Babe Ruth Quits!" and "Babe Ruth Going Out of Business!" and offered bargain prices to liquidate his merchandise. The Babe's lawyers sued on the grounds that such use of his name was "vulgar" and designed "to bring the name 'Babe Ruth' into disrepute."

† As if this feat weren't enough, one of Ruth's biographers claimed that the Babe came to bat in the ninth inning, defiantly took a right-handed batting stance while two strikes crossed the plate, and switched back to his normal stance, striking out. But the newspaper play-by-play of the game belies this account.

these catastrophes, the Babe missed only nine games that year, led the league in home runs (49), and batted a healthy .359, although the Yankees finished third behind Philadelphia and Washington.

In late September, when it became obvious that New York couldn't win the pennant, Ruppert and Barrow began searching for a manager to replace Bob Shawkey. The Babe again saw Ruppert and made a bid for the job. Ruppert reached into his files and recited a long list of Ruth's early sins. "Under those circumstances, Root, how can I turn my team over to you?" The Babe cited his good conduct during the past year, but Ruppert would only say, "I'll let you know."

Soon afterward, however, Joe McCarthy resigned from the Chicago Cubs and became the Yankees' new manager. Ruth was resentful. He told friends he was "sure" that Ed Barrow had sold Ruppert on hiring McCarthy. He was right. Years later, Barrow said, "At no time during the years he was with the club was Ruth ever considered a candidate . . . after all, he couldn't manage himself."

Disappointed, Ruth covered the 1930 World Series between Philadelphia and Saint Louis for the Christy Walsh Syndicate. He was still the ever popular Babe. After signing his autograph for more than half an hour on programs, rainchecks, toy boats, notebooks, and even hat bands, the Babe demanded a rest, cracking to a friend, "First thing you know, some bird'll come up asking me to sign his socks!"

A few weeks after the series, Ruth and Claire formally adopted Dorothy and Julia. At that time the Babe finally revealed the origins of Dorothy, who was born Marie Harrington. "I've never known who Dorothy Helen's parents were," he said. "We took her from the Foundling Hospital in New York City in 1922. My first wife never formalized the adoption, but the child has been with me ever since."

"All we want is to make the little girls happy," the Babe said when he signed the papers at a private ceremony in New York's Surrogate Court. He was a warm, loving father. Julia was "Butch," and Dorothy was "Dot." He gave them lavish gifts for their birthdays. He stayed home far more often now, and liked to play bridge with them. He was often whipped by Julia, who once said with affection, "My God, he's an awful bridge player. He believes everything his partner says; he believes anything *anybody* tells him!" As time went by, Julia had young callers. For some reason, Ruth took a great liking to a fellow named Jack and invariably invited him to a game of bridge. "I came to see *her,* not him!" Jack would later protest. But the Babe always brought out the cards, and when the evening was over he'd say warmly, "Good night, Pete." Or Eddie, or Joe, or Bill, or Mike. Years later, the young man, who married someone else but remained a family friend, laughed and recalled, "He never called me Jack in his entire life!"

In February, 1931, Ruth, Claire, and Julia ascended the gangplank of the liner *Shawnee,* which would take them to Florida for the Babe's annual winter vacation. It was his thirty-seventh birthday, and he said, "I don't get the kick out of birthdays that I used to get. I've had too many of them, but I guess I can stagger along with one more."

When he reported for spring training, he took a lot of kidding from teammate Jimmy Reese. The previous season, Hack Wilson of the Chicago Cubs had hit 56 homers, seven more than Ruth. Reese began to call Babe "The Hack Wilson of the American League."

One night that spring, he went fishing in Boca Ciega Bay with Lou Gehrig, Marshall Hunt, and a few other friends. The boat tipped and the Babe went overboard. Hunt wrote a humorous tale about Ruth's evening dip for the *Daily News,* and the next morning Ed Barrow called him from New York, "For Godsakes, knock off for a while, we're not over with spring training and we've gotta get that big baboon back to New York in one piece!"

The first week of the season, when the Yanks met the Red Sox in Boston, Ruth's legs again showed signs of failing him. In the sixth inning he drove in a run with a double. On the next play he slid into third and sprained his ankle.

When Lazzeri hoisted a high fly to right field, Ruth touched up and charged home. The throw came in to catcher Charlie Berry (a former All-American football player) who stood five feet up the third base line.

Berry didn't expect Ruth to try because of his damaged ankle. But out of the corner of his eye Berry saw him making a serious bid to score and screamed, "He's coming in!" Berry braced himself, waiting for the throw and the Babe. He lowered his shoulder and drove upward, sending the Babe flying into the air. Ruth came crashing head first to the earth and was dazed, but he instinctively reached out with his hand and touched home plate. "In spite of all I'd done to him," said Berry, "he'd scored. What a competitor!"

Ruth was groggy when he took the field in the next inning. When a ball was hit toward him, he turned sharply toward it, took a few steps, and went down in a heap, writhing in pain. Four Yankees carried him into the clubhouse, where he boomed, "It's just a charley horse, I'll be okay!" But the doctor said he'd strained a ligament and might be out for several days. The next morning he was in the hospital, his leg encased in an electro-therapeutic device that one visitor described as "an illuminated doghouse." Many players and writers came to see him. Among them was Charlie Berry. While he was there, Mrs. Ruth said, "You wouldn't be here now, Babe, if you'd had sense enough to stay on third base."

The Babe, says Berry, replied with some annoyance: "You don't know what you're talking about. Your ideas of this game are all wrong. There's a lot more to baseball than just hitting home runs."

Ruth spent four days in the Boston hospital. It was more serious than a strained ligament. He had burst some blood vessels in the left thigh, and the leg, in shock, was temporarily paralyzed. When he arrived in New York, he was rolled from the train platform to a waiting car in a wheelchair.

A few days later, Ruth sat on the pale green divan in his living room, an electric pad resting on his thigh. When the photographers finished their chores and prepared to leave, the writers were about to follow. Ruth, tired of being cooped up indoors, yelled, "Hey, you guys don't need to go! Artie, get the humidor and give everybody a cigar." Then, puffing contentedly on a cigar "almost large enough to serve a small boy as a baseball bat," he chattered away, happy to be the center of attention. McGovern commented that his injury would at least give the Babe some rest and "mental relaxation."

"Mental relaxation my ass!" Ruth growled. "I can't sleep thinking about some o' them close ones we lost. Can't eat, can't do nothing but listen to the radio!"

A day later, he hobbled about his apartment with a cane, eager to get back into action. Despite the injury, he missed only nine games that season.

He hit his 600th home run that summer. "Six hundred!" said one writer. "It is doubtful that any one of the vast army of spectators who have watched the Babe make some of these circuit clouts will ever live long enough to see his like again."

Ruth batted .373 that year and hit 46 homers, more than four other teams in the league. But the king was slipping. For the first time, Lou Gehrig tied him for the home run championship.* Never again would Ruth's name be at the top of the home run list.

For the third straight year, the Yankees failed to win a pennant, and defeat fed the growing friction on the club. From the start of the season, some of the players (particularly a few of the veterans who were close friends of Ruth) resented manager Joe McCarthy; they felt that the Babe was entitled to the job.

---

* Unofficially, Gehrig beat him. Near the end of the season he hit a ball that just cleared the fence. The baserunner, Lyn Lary, thinking the outfielder had caught the ball, ran toward the bench. Gehrig was automatically out for passing Lary on the basepaths, and the home run was nullified.

The new manager did little to curry favor. One of his first acts that season was to ban shaving in the clubhouse. He also smashed a card table, saying, "I want players in here to think of baseball and nothing else. I'm no second-division manager, and I won't stand for second-division baseball!" He forbade players to enter a hotel dining room without a jacket. "You're supposed to be champions of the world. Well, go out there and *look* like champions of the world." Everyone had to be at breakfast by 8:30 A.M. McCarthy sat at his table in the morning, eying each arrival over his morning paper. (During Bob Shawkey's brief tenure as manager, he set 9 A.M. as the latest time for breakfast, but Ruth claimed he couldn't eat that early and was exempted, ordering breakfast later in his room. McCarthy allowed no exemptions.) Ruth and his new manager rarely spoke, and their few words were hardly friendly. It got so that even Mrs. Ruth and Mrs. McCarthy didn't speak.

These tensions affected player relationships. Ruth, for example, loved to coach the young players, offering them tips on batting and pitching. Some of them welcomed the advice and struck up warm friendships with the aging star. Lefty Gomez, a rookie from San Francisco, "was one of the few good ones who could laugh, gab with the crowd . . . and still turn in a good game," Ruth said. But others resented his paternalistic attitude. Ben Chapman, a fiercely competitive young outfielder, had also joined the club that year. When he messed up a play in the field one day, Ruth walked toward him in the dugout, and Chapman snarled, "You keep your mouth shut. Nobody asked you to say anything." Ruth uttered a loud curse and walked away.

Life wasn't as much fun any more. While in Los Angeles on a barnstorming trip after the season, Ruth complained to a reporter that he was paying too heavy a price for his fame: "I can't go to the movies. It might hurt my eyes. I can't dance. They tell me it's bad for my legs. I can't go to a nightclub. They'd say I was drinking and carousing. I can't read a book on a train. It's too hard on my eyes and I spend most of my life on trains. I can't gamble. I love to bet on horses—on anything—but if I was seen with gamblers it would start gossip. I can't travel on airplanes. It's against the rules of my contract and my insurance policies. I can't go swimming for fear I'll catch cold. I can't speed in my car, because if I'm hurt my wages get stopped. I can't enjoy golf, because people always follow me for autographs. Dammit, I can't do anything! But wait, in two years I'll be through with baseball. Then I'm going to break loose."

EIGHTH INNING

Will Tony nose Pat out of the national game?
A major league manager was asked whether
the boys of Italian parentage were making
headway in major-league baseball.

"Not a doubt of it," he replied. "They take
to baseball quicker than they take to spaghetti.
. . . My experience with Italians is that when
they are good ballplayers they are very good.
Ten years from now, watch out for 'em. Now-
adays I can't even get a player on my team
with the nickname of Pat. Once they were all
Pats. Better look out for these Garibaldis who
are born in the United States."

Literary Digest,
October 2, 1932

"Lucky, Lucky, Lucky"

As the Depression gripped America, 14 million people (nearly one-third of the labor force) were without jobs. Men sold apples on street corners. Those with jobs were thankful; workers in sawmills toiled fifty hours a week for five cents an hour; many companies had put "Scotch Week" into effect, requiring employees to work one week per month without salary. Not far from the Babe's apartment, the ramshackle huts of the desperately poor continued to spread along the banks of the Hudson.

Baseball revenues were severely hit by the Depression. Colonel Ruppert estimated that Yankee gate receipts fell 12 to 15 per cent during the 1931 season. Losses were more severe for other clubs. The owners of the sixteen major league teams began a joint effort to trim $1 million from players' salaries. They cut the salary of baseball commissioner Landis from $65,000 to $50,000 a year. Umpires took reduced paychecks. Ruth's annual salary of $80,000 for the past two seasons was an irresistible target. If he continued to earn so much, other players would refuse drastic cuts. As one sports editor observed: "A player who's had a good year can always say at contract time, 'I'm no Babe Ruth, but I'm worth *half* as much, or a quarter as much.' " Another writer called Ruth "the logical storm center of this new era." So it wasn't surprising when Colonel Ruppert, in early 1932, said that "baseball can't afford such a salary." Ruth, he admitted, was "a good asset," but he wasn't the only drawing card on the club. Gehrig also brought out the fans, he said, and earned only $25,000, less than one-third of Ruth's salary.

A few days later, Ruth was chewing on a big ham steak at the breakfast table when the mailman came. Ruppert had sent him a one-year contract for $70,000.

"What's a guy gotta do in this league to satisfy people?" Ruth said to Claire. "I hit forty-six home runs, I'm second in the league in batting, and they want me to take a $10,000 cut!"

On his way to the Saint Albans golf course, Ruth personally returned the contract, unsigned, to the Yankee office. He and Ruppert haggled for a while but never fought. The Babe was bored with money—it was more a question of ego—and the Colonel was too much of an aristocrat to show passion over such a mundane topic. During that meeting, according to the legend, Ruppert remarked, "Root, last year you earned more money than President Hoover."

And the Babe is said to have replied, "Hell, I had a better year than Hoover!"*

The next time-honored step in the Ruth ritual was the trip to Florida and his birthday party. His friends set up a huge square table in the patio of the Jungle Club Hotel, arranged to resemble a baseball diamond with flowers for baselines and bases. A mammoth birthday cake, in the shape of a baseball, occupied the center. Twenty-eight guests sat around the table, with the Ruths in the place of honor at "home plate."

Ruppert came down a few days later and, following a long tradition, sat with the Babe at a table on the sunny lawn of the Jungle Club with dozens of reporters and photographers gathered round for the contract signing. The Babe's pale winter complexion, after walking bareheaded on the Florida golf courses for several days, was now a flaming red. Ruth never had a pen, and this time it was supplied by Ruppert's friend, Colonel Wattenberg. He put his signature to the contract, which was for $75,000 a year, plus 25 per cent of the net receipts from Yankee exhibition games. It was the first time in Ruth's long career—since the day in 1914 when he signed for $600 per season—that he had ever taken a cut in pay. The Depression had begun, indeed.

* * *

The routine continued with the invariability of the seasons. Ruth's spring attack of grippe struck during the first week of the season while the Yankees were in Boston. Feverish, coughing violently, complaining of pains in his chest, he sat in his suite at the Brunswick, "a white spread tucked snugly around his great moon-like head." A large bouquet of flowers nearly covered the dresser. He had planned to

---

* Hoover himself once told a reporter that a small boy asked for his autograph during a public gathering in Los Angeles; the lad asked for three copies, said Hoover, and explained, "It takes two of yours to trade for one of Babe Ruth's."

celebrate his third wedding anniversary that evening, but there was no party—only medicines, thermometers, and fruit juice.

"Maybe I'm getting a little old," he said a few days later, complaining that he had "a touch" of water on the knee and playing ball was "tough on the legs." He vowed to give up golf during the season to conserve his energies.

Now after a game he often returned home in agony, and Claire had to call a masseur. "An electric pad on the right knee was standard practice every evening," she said.

He talked more and more of retiring, but not immediately. He spoke of his ambition to be a manager— "and New York or Boston would suit me fine"—but he was still not through as a player.

In fact, despite his aches and pains, he was hitting like the blazes. Although he often left the game in the late innings when the Yankees were ahead, he wasn't far behind Jimmy Foxx of the Philadelphia Athletics in home runs and batting average. Winning another home run championship would have boosted his spirits, but the pitchers were very cautious when he came to the plate. "How am I gonna do *anything* when they keep walking me all the time?" he complained that summer.

During one doubleheader, he missed three innings of the opening game when he rushed one of his daughters to the hospital for a minor operation. In the sixth inning he slashed a line drive to the outfield, where the man got a glove on it, making it hard to decide whether it was a hit or an error. Between games, a baseball writer dashed down to the Yankee dugout to ask about the operation on Ruth's daughter.

"Who went to the hospital, Dot or Julia?"

"Say," said the Babe, "what did the scorer give me in the sixth? Dot. No, wait a minute, Julia."

"What was the operation? They called it an error."

"What the hell is the matter with you guys? Are you blind? Tonsils."

"What hospital, Babe?"

"How's a guy gonna lead the god-damn league if you guys can't see and rob me of hits alla time? French Hospital."

He continued to be plagued by illness. After hitting a home run against Philadelphia on September 5, he felt shooting pains in his right side and stomach. The next day, at an exhibition game in Binghamton, Ruth was his usual jovial self, putting on a show for the army of small boys that dogged his steps. But the side still hurt. When the Yanks arrived at the Book-Cadillac Hotel in Detroit on September 7, he grew fearful of an appendicitis attack. He called Joe McCarthy, who had remained behind to visit relatives in Buffalo, and got permission to rush to New York for a checkup by team physician Dr. Edward King. The Babe and Claire caught an 8:30 P.M. train and arrived at Grand Central Station the next afternoon. "The Babe shows slight symptoms of appendicitis," said Doctor King after the examination. He was kept in bed with ice packs on his abdomen. His wife hinted that possibly more was the matter when she said, "The excitement at Grand Central Station when he arrived wasn't good for him, but the doctor thinks he will be better if he remains quiet for a couple of days." There was widespread speculation in the press that Ruth might miss the World Series, which would begin in three weeks.

It didn't look too promising ten days later when he worked out at Yankee Stadium. He hit a series of looping flyballs and was unable to lift a single one into "Ruthville," his favorite home run territory in right field. "I don't feel as though I could break a pane of glass," he complained. "They had me packed so deep in ice I don't feel thawed out yet."

But thaw out he did. He finished the season with a magnificent .341 batting average and, despite the fact that injuries and fatigue caused him to miss twenty games, hit 41 homers. The Yankees, after three lean years, won the pennant, and Ruth would realize his ambition of playing in ten World Series.

But his days as home run king were clearly over. Jimmy Foxx had led the league with 58 homers and was being billed as "the new Babe Ruth." Probably the most sensitive barometer of Ruth's power was his slugging percentage (total bases divided by times at bat). With the exception of 1925, when he was gravely ill, Ruth led the league in slugging from 1918 through 1931, an unequaled feat. Now he was fading, but he still had a few thrills in store for the fans.

*   *   *

The moment when Ruth pointed to the center field bleachers during the 1932 World Series and then hit a home run ranks in American legend with Washington's hurling a silver dollar across the Potomac, Teddy Roosevelt's wild charge up San Juan Hill, and the defense of the Alamo. Whether he did or didn't point is irrelevant by now. Everyone *says* he did, and if you ask some oldtimer his memory will be hopelessly fogged by nostalgia, cataracts, and wish fulfillment. Here, according to the newspaper accounts of the day, is what really happened in October, 1932.

The Yankees romped through the first two games of the Series with such ease that some writers called it "a burlesque." There was a great deal of name-calling by both teams, and much of the Yankees' kidding was prompted by the situation of their former shortstop, Mark Koenig, who was now a member of the Cubs. The veteran had been brought up from the minor leagues to help Chicago win a tight pennant race. Although he performed brilliantly, the Cubs decided to grant Koenig only half a share in the World Series proceeds.

The Yankees came to their old teammate's defense with a barrage of insults about the miserliness of the Chicago team. The loudest was Ruth, who, whenever Koenig took the field, would bellow: "Hey Mark, how are ya? Who the hell are those cheapskates out there with ya?" The Cubs became infuriated and called Ruth "pot-belly," "balloon-head," and many stronger epithets, referring to his mother, his race, and his sexual preferences.

When the Yankees arrived in Chicago on September 30, prior to game three, one paper commented: "The Chicago public gave the Yankees . . . a welcome befitting conquerors." Conquerors were apparently not looked upon with great favor, because when the men departed from taxis in front of the Edgewater Hotel they were forced to run a gauntlet of hostile Cubs fans. Recalling one band of hysterical women, Ruth said they uttered profanities "even *I* hadn't heard before!" Even worse was the women's spitting, and their bad aim. "Poor Claire," said the Babe, "received most of it."

More than 51,000 fans jammed Wrigley Field to see the third game on October 1, a warm, clear, and very windy day. Two temporary bleacher sections were erected to hold the overflow. Among the dignitaries in the field boxes were Franklin D. Roosevelt, Governor of New York, who was then in the midst of his Presidential campaign. Ruth and Gehrig drew gasps from the crowd even before the game started, as they blasted one batting practice pitch after another into the stands.

Ruth came to bat in the first inning with two men on base and Charlie Root pitching. After two low, outside balls he drove the next pitch to the rear of the bleachers in right-center for a home run. The Cub fans were stunned. The game was just a few minutes old and New York led, 3 to 0. Two innings later, Gehrig leaned into one of Root's pitches and sent it flying into the right field bleachers. But Chicago fought back and drew even at 4-4 in the fourth inning. The tying run for Chicago was scored by Billy Jurges, who got on base when he hit a low line drive to left field; Ruth made a valiant try for a shoestring catch, but the ball bounced past him for a double. The Chicago crowd howled with glee and razzed the Babe, who doffed his cap.

Ruth strode to the plate in the next inning, eager to make amends. The Chicago bench jockeys were really letting him have it; particularly Guy Bush, a pitcher with a raucous voice and a rich assortment of insults. As Ruth stood there, a single yellow lemon rolled up to the plate. The umpire threw it aside. Root hurled a strike across the plate and the crowd cheered. The Babe, in a pantomime worthy of Marcel Marceau, lifted one finger for all in the stadium to see.

Root's next two pitches were wide of the mark. Then he threw another strike, and as the din in the stands became deafening the Babe lifted two fingers. Virtually every man on the Chicago bench had his hands cupped to his mouth, shouting insults, and Ruth jabbered right back at them, a smile on his face. Then he stepped out of the box, placed the bat on his left foot, and raised his finger.

Where he pointed is a subject of debate. Cub catcher Gabby Hartnett claims he waved his hand toward the Cub bench and yelled "It takes only one to hit it." Lou Gehrig, who was kneeling a few feet away in the on-deck circle, says that Ruth pointed at Guy Bush in the dugout and yelled, "I'm gonna cut the next pitch right down your ——— throat." Pat Pieper, the Wrigley Field announcer, says Ruth pointed to center field. John Drebinger of the *Times,* who was in the press box, made no mention in his story that day of Ruth's pointing, but he did say the Babe predicted a homer "in no mistaken motions."

Point or not, Ruth's intention was clear. When Root delivered the next pitch, he swung with all his might.

It was a tremendous smash that tore straight down the center of the field in a great arc, came down alongside the flagpole 436 feet away, and disappeared between the scoreboard and the edge of the right field bleachers, crashing into a small ticket booth at Waveland and Sheffield avenues. It was Ruth's 15th World Series homer and, as one man wrote that afternoon, "easily his most gorgeous."

"Lucky, lucky, lucky," Ruth murmured to himself as he circled the bases in full view of the 51,000 stunned Chicago fans. He was beside himself with joy. Holding up *four* fingers now, to signify a home run, he stopped briefly near third base, looked toward the Chicago bench, slapped his knees, and had a fit of laughter.

Root, badly shaken, now faced Gehrig, who swung at the first pitch and lifted an enormous fly ball that fell into the stands for another home run. That was all for Root, and the Cubs, as the Yankees won the third game 7 to 5.

After the game, seven different fans outside the park proudly claimed they possessed Ruth's home run ball. Among them was the man who worked in the small ticket booth, who swore it had bounced right through his window.*

The following afternoon Guy Bush started for Chicago, and when Ruth came to bat in the first inning he threw a mean fastball that winged him in the right forearm. It hurt, but the Babe dusted himself off and trotted to first base, laughing. Bush didn't last through the first inning, as the Yanks swamped Chicago 13 to 6, taking the series in four straight games. Counting their sweeps in the '27 and '28 Series, they had won twelve consecutive games against the champions of the National League.

The Yanks had only two hours to dress and catch a special 6 P.M. train back to New York, but they staged a riotous clubhouse demonstration. They draped their arms around each other and let loose with a raucous chorus of *The Sidewalks of New York*. The buoyant Ruth momentarily forgot his differences with manager McCarthy; he grasped him by the hand and boomed, "My hat's off to ya, Mac!"

It was a satisfying time for the Babe, who had now played in more World Series than any man and held Series records in almost every major category: most home runs, total bases, long hits, bases on balls, strikeouts, runs scored, runs batted in, most times batting over .300 (six), and most runs batted in during a single Series game.

He had earned a good rest, and he relaxed all that winter. In early December he went on a ten-day hunting trip to North Carolina with his friend Frank Stevens, the stadium concessionaire who sold the hotdogs that Ruth dearly loved. Even a short pleasure trip was magnified into a grand production by the Babe. He took with him to the station three guns, three suitcases, boots, his portable phonograph, and an ample library of music. He insisted on packing his entire record collection in large round cake tins, but when Claire insisted that there were none in the house, he told her to call the local bakery and buy a half a dozen.

"These tins have *cakes* in them, Babe!"

---

* The next spring, Ruth and Grantland Rice attended a supper party on an estate in southern Georgia, where the famed political columnist Walter Lippmann and his wife were among the guests. It was an elegant affair, until Mrs. Lippmann asked Ruth to describe his famous homer of the 1932 Series. "It's like this," he said, puffing a huge cigar, and making good use of his hands to talk. He painted in every detail, including every four-letter word that he and the Cubs had exchanged during that dramatic moment. At the end, he said, "By the time I reach home plate, I'm almost fallin' down, I'm laughin' so ——— hard." The battered Mrs. Lippmann waited for a few minutes to pass and then mumbled something about having to leave. When Rice asked Ruth whether his strong language was necessary, he answered, "What the hell, Grant, you heard her ask me what happened, didn't ya?"

"We can take the cakes out."

Ruth went to the station, leaving Claire behind with thirty pounds of fresh cake. Luckily, he hadn't taken the cakes with him, because the country air improved his already Gargantuan appetite. A few days later, the cook at the hunting camp reported that the Sunday dinner menu consisted of roast turkey that Ruth had shot, roast ham, boiled ham, Irish potatoes, sweet potatoes, collards, cornbread, toast, coffee, cake, and pie. At breakfast, the cook said, Ruth ate "only two eggs" but also had "two or three links of sausages, I don't know how much bacon and about a loaf of toasted bread."

When he came home and walked in to Artie McGovern's gym to start his annual calisthenics program, McGovern eyed him up and down and—more out of wishful thinking than fact—told reporters: "No longer does the Babe eat whenever the spirit moves him . . . calories are counted carefully." He weighed "only 229 pounds," McGovern insisted, but if the figure was true, most of the poundage had shifted to Ruth's midsection.

"Bull in a Bear Market"

As he signed a stack of Christmas cards in McGovern's office (his list had by now grown to more than one thousand recipients) the Babe sounded optimistic about his contract for the 1933 season.

"Just give the Colonel the right to make good beer . . . he'll be so tickled, he'd be a soft touch for me!" Beer did become legal again that April, and Colonel Ruppert also spent $250,000 financing the second Byrd Antarctic Expedition that year (causing the flagship to be named after him) but as a hard-nosed businessman Ruppert kept each of his enterprises separate, and he insisted the Yanks were losing money.

That year brought the first of a series of setbacks for Ruth. The *Sporting News*'s eighth annual poll of baseball writers dropped him from its all-star team for the first time; he was beaten for the right field spot by Chuck Klein of the Philadelphia Phillies, who drew nearly twice as many votes as the Babe.

The Yankees mailed him a contract for only $50,000. "That's not a pay cut, that's an amputation!" the Babe said indignantly as he dropped the unsigned contract back in the mail. Ruth was still unsigned on March 13 when Colonel Ruppert came to see him in Saint Petersburg. Both emerged unsmiling from a private meeting in Joe McCarthy's office at Miller Huggins Field. "We have not come to any agreement," said Ruppert, explaining that he had renewed his offer of $50,000 and Ruth had demanded $60,000. His offer, said Ruppert, was "equal to $100,000 in normal times," but Ruth would only say, "If they're willing to let me quit for $10,000 it's all right with me." Ruppert issued an ultimatum on March 19, warning Ruth to sign in ten days or not accompany the team on its trip north. He even threatened to reduce the $50,000 offer if Ruth didn't come to terms soon. Ruth relaxed his demands to $55,000, but the Colonel was unyielding, stressing that he and the Babe were "on the friendliest terms," but simply couldn't agree on a business matter.

By now, the salary dispute had blossomed into a national issue, as Americans—poorer than they'd ever been—took vicarious pleasure in imagining such sums. When a Salvation Army official in New York heard a number of destitute, jobless men arguing heatedly about Ruth's salary dispute, he took a poll of the shelter's 1,200 inmates, asking them to name those men who deserved $80,000 a year or more. First place went to "any President of the United States." Ruth placed second, far ahead of such men as John D. Rockefeller, Professor Albert Einstein, Henry Ford, William Randolph Hearst, Walter Winchell, Enrico Caruso, Tom Mix, and Benito Mussolini.

Finally, on March 22, Ruppert visited Ruth at his suite in the Jungle Club, and after a ten-minute conference the Babe agreed to sign for $52,000. Ruppert's "sob story," he said later, "nearly had me in tears." Despite the huge salary cut, he remained the highest-paid player in baseball. As the cameras clicked and the Movietones ground away at the contract signing two days later, Ruth said, "I've had three ambitions in my life. One was to hit seven hundred home runs, the other was to play twenty years, and the next was to be in ten World Series. I succeeded in one last year, makin' my tenth series. Next year will be my twentieth season. If I hit forty-eight home runs, I'll have an even seven hundred, and I'll sure be satisfied with everything."

But he was almost forty years old, and he knew that such a total of homers in a single year was beyond his reach. During the 1933 season, his batting average fell to .301 and he hit 34 homers, not bad for an old man. He missed seventeen games due to a variety of ailments and often left the game in the late innings to rest his legs.

No longer could he hit home runs on demand, as he'd apparently done in the 1932 World Series and years before for Johnny Sylvester. That May he visited an orphanage in Passaic, New Jersey, and told the boys "I'll see you before the game tomorrow, and I promise to hit a home run especially for you." The next day, the boys cheered him on, but the best Ruth could do was a hard line drive that was caught several feet short of the wall.

In mid-June he fell sick during a game in Chicago, was removed for a pinch-runner, and was confined to his hotel room with a 102-degree temperature. But he occasionally showed flashes of the old brilliance. On July 6, he played in the first major league All-Star Game at Comiskey Park, Chicago. Some cynics said that the aging slugger had been selected only as a nostalgic gesture. But in the third inning lefthander "Wild Bill" Hallahan fired an inside pitch that Ruth slammed out of the park for a two-run homer that helped the American League to win the game. Afterward, despite his aching legs, he made a good running catch to snuff out the National League's final rally.

When the Babe wrenched his ankle in Chicago late that August and limped to the clubhouse, he told a reporter, "I think I'll just voluntarily retire for a year. I could stand a long vacation and see how things work out."

He came full circle in the final game of that 1933 season. Twenty years before, he had started out as a young pitcher for the Boston Red Sox. Now, since the Yankees had no chance to win the pennant, the bright idea occurred to someone that Ruth should pitch the last game of the year—coincidentally, against the Red Sox. It was a grand day for the 20,000 fans who saw him stride to the mound. Gulping plenty of ice water between innings and pepping himself up with ample pinches of snuff, Ruth managed to stagger through the game, despite twelve hits by the Red Sox. He also batted third and hit a home run. When it was over, New York had won 6 to 5, Ruth was five pounds lighter, and, as he later recalled, "I had such a sore arm I had to eat with my right hand for a week!"

With the season over, the end of his career as a player also seemed imminent. But baseball was all that he knew, and he wanted desperately to stay in the game as a manager. The Yankees said they were satisfied with McCarthy's services, but Barrow did offer Ruth a post as manager of the Newark farm club in the International League. Ruth claimed that he'd be "unhappy" in the minors, closing the only door then open within the Yankee organization. Christy Walsh had also advised Ruth against accepting the Newark offer, thinking that other jobs would be available. Frank Navin, owner of the Detroit Tigers, seemed interested in Ruth as a manager, and Barrow urged the Babe to call Navin. But the Babe and Claire had already made plans to travel to Honolulu in mid-October, and Ruth said there was "plenty of time" to see Navin when he returned.*

The Babe, Claire, and Julia were greeted with tremendous enthusiasm when they arrived for their three-week visit to Hawaii. The public schools declared a half-holiday, and 10,000 fans packed the local park for the first exhibition game. Hampered by a pile of white and yellow flower leis around his neck, Ruth still managed to hit a home run. He played the outfield during the early part of the game

---

* According to one source, Ruth did call Navin from the West Coast just before debarking for Honolulu but was less than tactful. He bluntly asked the Detroit owner to tell him "yes or no . . . right now" if he wanted him. Navin replied: "Since you put it that way, no."

but switched to first base after hordes of youngsters clambered from their seats and ran onto the field bearing baseballs to be autographed.

When he returned with his family to San Francisco on November 10, Ruth learned that Mickey Cochrane had been hired by Navin to manage the Detroit Tigers. Now that he was back on the mainland, rumors surfaced about possible managerial jobs with several clubs, but none materialized.

The Babe returned to New York with numerous souvenirs from the trip, including dozens of phonographs records of Hawaiian music, a lei made from the feathers of eighty-five pheasants, a huge chunk of coral, and three bulbous-eyed Japanese fantail goldfish.

"Lookit the *tails* on 'em!" he told a visitor to his apartment.

"We had four fish originally," said Claire, but one died the second day out at sea. I was dying, too, of seasickness, but the Babe was more upset about the fish."

"Well, gee! After bringin' 'em all the way from Honolulu!"

"In Chicago," she said, "we got off the train to get something to eat. Babe left the fish with the stationmaster, but the bowl broke and the fish were flopping all over the baggage room. The men there chased after those fish as though their lives depended on it. Finally we got them home in a mayonnaise jar."

"All the way from Honolulu," said the Babe, with a grin as wide as when he'd hit his 600th home run.

For the next few days, when reporters came to see him, Ruth greeted his visitors with a hearty "aloha!" and since no managerial jobs were open, said he felt good enough for "one more year" as a player. Then, leaning back in his easy chair and closing his eyes, he listened to the soothing sound of steel guitars and ukuleles on his phonograph.

That winter, Grantland Rice, the Pindar of American sports, composed an ode called "To Babe Ruth—1934":

> Sultan of Swat and Czar of Clout,
> High Mandarin of Maul,
> Assaulter of the well-known snout
> Of each fast-moving ball.
> For twenty years your mighty mace
> Has drummed its battle cry,
> Beyond the azure fields of space,
> In wavelengths to the sky.
>
> Now time, that ancient cockeyed yap,
> Is pointing to the gate,

Where Cobb and Speaker took the rap,
And Wagner met his fate;
Where one by one they passed from sight,
To hear above the roar,
'Game called.' along the rim of night,
That knew their final score.

But not yet Babe. Your blasting bulk
Has one more year of smoke.
Let time the snatcher sit and sulk,
Grab some other bloke.
We need the songs your big mace sings,
The old heart-lifting crash.
We need the melody that rings
Its music from your ash.

"I Want That Ball!"

Fat, pushing forty, and nursing a cold, George Herman Ruth sat up in bed and gazed out the window at the gray cliffs of New Jersey. He craved a cigar, but his throat ached.

He hoped he'd feel better tomorrow, when the photographers would crowd around and snap his fortieth birthday picture. Cards and telegrams were already stacked high in the living room, and more would come today.

Claire was out shopping, and he felt lonesome. He got some music on the radio, picked up the morning paper, and glanced with little interest at the front page. Times were tough all over: Mayor LaGuardia was fighting to settle a taxi strike; a thousand picketing hotel and restaurant workers had rioted at the Waldorf-Astoria; Paris was under heavy guard for fear of riots, too. There was a photo of Mae West, the Bronx Zoo's sea lion, which had died after eating several egg-sized rocks, and a brass button from a U.S. Navy uniform (the paper contained nothing about the birth—the day before—in Mobile, Alabama, of a child named Henry Louis Aaron). Turning to the sports page, he found a one-paragraph item about himself, reporting that he was feeling well enough to make the trip to Saint Petersburg in a couple of days.

He thought of spring training. Jesus, so many pals gone. Who was left from the great bunch of '27?

He felt like the last living dinosaur, tracked by museum curators waiting for him to drop. That week, a gallery in downtown Manhattan unveiled an eight-foot-tall sculpture of a younger Babe swinging his mighty bat, broad-shouldered and thin at the waist. The artist, Reuben Nakian, said, "The Greeks erected public statues to their athletic heroes, so why not Babe Ruth?" The *Times* art critic called it "a very arresting figure," and commented, "He looks like an American Hercules." It could be dangerous being an American institution.

Police that month arrested a man in South Dakota and claimed he was involved in the kidnapping and murder of the Lindbergh baby. In the man's home, they found a file of "famous persons," including a photo of the Babe with a marginal notation suggesting that he might be a future kidnap target.

It was a depressing day, but soon he'd be in Saint Petersburg, and the sun would warm his aching limbs. There would be no protracted salary battle to fill the sports pages this time. He'd already signed in a brief, colorless ceremony at Jake Ruppert's oak-paneled brewery office. Now it was for only $35,000, quite a drop from $80,000 just three winters before. But what could he do? The way he felt, he'd be lucky to play a hundred games this season. There'd been a touch of pathos when he put his name to the contract, but his old buddies from the press tried to put a bright face on things. They toted up all his contracts and World Series shares since 1914 and proclaimed that the Bambino's baseball earnings amounted to $918,477. And they dutifully quoted him when he smiled and said, "I'm making a lot of money outside of baseball now; I can afford to stick with a game that's done so much for me." Now, he even had his own half-hour radio show, "Babe Ruth's Club," three times a week over WOR, sandwiched between "The Adventures of Tom Mix" and "Amos 'n' Andy."

There were rumors that he might quit baseball altogether and become a golf pro. That spring, as the Yankees stopped in Atlanta on the tour north, the Babe played an exhibition golf match against the famous Bobby Jones, and played well. He liked golf, but he couldn't reconcile himself to the fact that his career in baseball, his whole life since adolescence, was coming to an end.

As the team continued north, Ruth dropped in to see his sister, Mrs. Mary Moberly, in Richmond, Virginia, who was recovering from a nervous breakdown. He sat down on the side of the bed, smiled, and said, "You ain't going goofy, are you, Sis?"

Mary could see the age wrinkles and a touch of sadness in his eyes when he said, "Sis, I'm getting old now, past forty, and my old legs ain't what they were."

But that spring the *Literary Digest* said Ruth was "still on his colossal feet . . . still capable of smiting the planetoid into the middle of next week and heaving his gigantic bulk around the bases like a playful St. Bernard pup." It was easy to write such drivel in an office somewhere, but a lot harder to stand sixty feet away from wild rookie pitchers who wanted nothing more than to blaze one past the famous Babe or knock him down and show him who was boss. That June at Yankee Stadium, a young Philadelphia pitcher fired a high hard one that the Babe couldn't duck in time. It caught him on the wrist, and he fell to the ground. As he was helped toward the clubhouse, the 8,000 fans stood in silence, remembering times past.

There arose a wave of nostalgic affection for the Babe even before he was through. That summer, a nationwide poll of writers picked him ahead of all American League outfielders despite the fact that he was only a shadow of his former self. But every so often he made them remember how it once was. On Friday, July 13, almost exactly twenty years since the date that he first put on a big league uniform, the Babe appeared in a game before 20,000 fans at Detroit's Navin Field. When he came to bat in the third inning, Tiger pitcher Tommy Bridges stretched the count to three balls, two strikes. The Babe swatted the next ball *far* over the right field wall. It was his 700th home run, a great ambition realized, and the hit also helped the Yankees to win the game and climb back into first place.* As he rounded third base, Ruth pointed toward right field and shouted to coach Art Fletcher, "I want that ball! I want that ball!"

Sixteen-year-old Lennie Bielski was standing at the corner of Plum Street and Trumball Avenue when he heard a roar from nearby Navin Field. Suddenly, he saw a ball come over the fence, bounce straight down Plum Street, and roll under a car. He dove under and grabbed it, and then a lot of policemen and ushers grabbed him. Bielski, confused and shaken, was half-carried to the Yankee bench, where he saw the rest of the game for free. In the clubhouse later, the Babe said to Gehrig, "Lou, I don't have my wallet here; give that boy a $20 bill." In return for the 700th home run ball, the Babe also gave him a new one, autographed. (Bielski, now a retired employee of the Internal Revenue Service, still keeps that $20 bill and the signed baseball.) The papers predicted that Ruth's record of 700 home runs "is likely to stand for all time."

He reached another milestone in Cleveland the next day, receiving his 2,000th base on balls, the most telling proof of how much pitchers dreaded his power. Someone calculated that during his career the Babe had "walked" the equivalent of 34 miles from home to first base. But the following afternoon, after singling against Cleveland in the third inning, he was clipped in the right ankle by Gehrig's vicious grounder, and dropped "as if shot." He was carried off on a stretcher. "I'm gettin' outa this game before I'm carried out," said the Babe, while he waited in the clubhouse for the hospital ambulance. Doctors said the Babe might be out for at least ten days.

* Ruth's closest competitors in career home runs were Lou Gehrig with 314 and Rogers Hornsby with 301.

It was about then that Ogden Nash, in an "ode to the crumbling legs of Mister Ruth," wrote:

> Indeed I never understood how even
> in their lusty youth
> Those bantam drumsticks ever held
> up the torso that was Ruth.

The Babe was in a sour, truculent mood when newsmen visited his hotel room. What did they think of Joe McCarthy as a manager? he wanted to know. They believed he was doing a good job.

"Well I don't. If we had a good manager, we'd win the pennant this year."

When the writers argued back, Ruth heatedly insisted that McCarthy was "balling everything up."

Nothing was mentioned in the papers, but the story got back to McCarthy, who remained grimly silent. Some of the younger Yankees were on the manager's side. They even suggested that he could help the club by benching Ruth and putting a faster man in his position. When their comments got back to the Babe, he sat near his locker, close to tears.

In Boston early that August, the Babe said he was "definitely through" as a regular player at the end of the season, and didn't know what the future held for him. But Colonel Ruppert, who was vacationing in Nashville, said, "Don't worry. Ruth will be with us next year. He has many more years up there as a pinch-hitter. Remember, they still like to see him swing that bat."

But fans all around the American League sensed this might be Ruth's last summer in uniform. One Sunday in September more than 46,000 people in Boston turned out for the Yanks' final visit to Fenway Park to bid the Babe farewell. Ruth's eyes were moist when he walked off the field at the end of the game, and the fans gave him a rousing ovation. In the stands was Jim Curley, who that November would be elected Governor of Massachusetts. He turned to his campaign manager, Judge Emil Fuchs (who also happened to own the Boston Braves of the National League) and said: "You've got to get Ruth back to Boston as something or other."

Yankee fans had their last look at Ruth in the team's final home game on September 25. The moment was shorn of all dramatics when he drew a walk in the first inning, limped painfully to first base, and called for a substitute runner. The sparse crowd of 2,000 stood and applauded as he made his way, head down, into the dugout.

There was a warmer sendoff in Washington on October 1, the final day of the season. More than 15,000 people (including many of his friends from Baltimore) turned out to say goodbye. Before the game, the band from Saint Mary's Industrial School played a brief concert. Then he was given a voluminous scroll bearing the signatures of President Roosevelt, members of his Cabinet, other government officials, and thousands of fans. But Lou Gehrig was the man who hit the home run that day. Ruth tried and failed three times, receiving polite applause for his futile efforts. He trudged to the shower and removed his Yankee uniform for the last time.

The next day Ruth had a showdown with Colonel Ruppert. He walked into the Yankee owner's office and asked Ruppert if he was satisfied with McCarthy as the team's manager. Ruppert, who knew that McCarthy's contract had one more year to run, replied that he was. "That suits me," said the Babe. "That's all I wanted to know."

Later that week, Ruth sat in a stifling Pullman compartment with journalists Joe Williams, Dan Daniel, and Tom Meany as the train prepared to leave Saint Louis's Union Station for Detroit. The Babe (aided by a ghostwriter) was covering the World Series between the Cardinals and the Tigers for the Christy Walsh Syndicate. It was so hot that Ruth suggested they step out on the platform for some fresh air. A train engineer recognized Ruth and yelled down, "What's the Yankees gonna do next year, Babe?"

"I don't give a damn what they do," Ruth growled. "I'm through with 'em." His three companions did a collective doubletake. Until now, it was assumed that he would stay with the club in some capacity, perhaps as a pinch-hitter.

When Williams inquired about Ruth's plans for 1935, Ruth told them of his "showdown" with Colonel Ruppert. He said he wasn't going to "sit around on the bench" as a pinch-hitter and would decide his future after returning from a trip to the Orient.

The next day's sports pages were filled with the news of Ruth's quitting. But Ruth made no mention of it in his own syndicated column, which triggered angry phone calls and telegrams from editors who were paying top dollar for the Babe's "exclusive" views. That afternoon, Ruth sat in the sweltering press box when a few writers approached, seeking further details on his surprise retirement. He exploded: "You guys get away from me! You're getting me into a transom!"

His retirement had rescued the Yankees from a ticklish dilemma. Ed Barrow later confessed that, due to Ruth's popularity, he wouldn't have known what to do if the Babe merely decided to sit on the

Yankee bench throughout the 1935 season. How could they fire such a man?

Still uncertain about his future, Ruth joined a group of players and their wives on a two-month tour of the Orient, which would include exhibition games in Honolulu, Japan, Shanghai, and Manila. The Babe was "field manager" of the team, and Connie Mack, manager of the Philadelphia Athletics, was the "boss" of the tour.

As a result of this trip, Ruth learned to his delight that he was a year younger. When he was unable to find a birth certificate before applying for his passport, Ruth's sister secured a copy in Baltimore for him. It showed that he was born a day earlier (February 6) and a year later (1895) than he'd always supposed. "I'm only thirty-nine!" he bellowed.

They left from Vancouver aboard the *Empress of Japan* and almost immediately ran into a storm; at one point, only four of the ship's six hundred passengers took their meals in the dining room. But after the Pacific calmed it soon became evident that there was a bit of a squall aboard ship. The tour members discovered that there was a long-standing feud between Ruth and Lou Gehrig, who had married late in 1933 and was taking his wife with him to the Orient on a second honeymoon.

According to Claire, the two men had been "loused up by a flock of gabbing women." Some time before, Claire complained to the Babe that she'd been "insulted" by Gehrig's mother during a visit to the Gehrig home in New Rochelle. It seemed that "Mom" Gehrig had remarked that Claire took better care of her own daughter, Julia, than of little Dorothy. When Ruth heard of it, he became upset, mentioned it to Gehrig, and soon the men weren't speaking. There may have been other contributing factors. Although Ruth's career was on the wane and Gehrig's was in full flower, the Babe never regarded Lou as more than a "junior partner," a younger brother. Ruth often kidded the shy, methodical Gehrig. Once on a train, for example, he told the waiter to serve him a "steak à la Gehrig." When the waiter looked befuddled, the Babe, shaking with laughter, said, *"You* know, good and thick!"

The family feud, which came close to splitting the players aboard ship into two factions, was noticed by Connie Mack, who at one time had considered Ruth as a candidate to manage the Athletics. Mack told writer Joe Williams that he could never make Ruth his manager because Mrs. Ruth had "too much influence over the Babe" and "would be running the club in a month."

After stopping briefly in Honolulu, they sailed to Japan, where the players got an almost unbelievable welcome. The Emperor sent a private railway car to Yokohama to transport them to Tokyo, where thousands met them at the station. They were given a triumphal motorcade down Tokyo's Broadway, the Ginza, where fans massed along the sidewalks and workers in office buildings showered them with paper and tiny packs of chewing gum.

Ruth was thrilled. He stood up waving a Japanese flag in one hand and an American flag in the other. The car could barely move without knocking down some of the frenzied spectators, but, as he recalled, "they would bob right up again like rubber balls!"

The Americans played seventeen games against Japanese teams, including four in Tokyo that drew an amazing 200,000 fans. The Japanese were fascinated by the big Babe, who awed them with several home runs and made them laugh with his pantomime clowning at first base. In Tokyo they stayed at the magnificent Imperial Hotel, where they donned their uniforms before leaving for the ball park, and a detachment of soldiers had to protect them from mobs of autograph seekers.*

On January 2, with the tour completed, most of the contingent returned to the United States, but the Ruths and a few other players and their families went on to Europe via the Suez Canal.

Paris was the first major stop on his European visit, and, despite Claire's and Julia's pleas to come along on tours of the city's delights, he was soon aching to get home.

He simply couldn't get over the fact that he could stroll the boulevards all day without being recognized or that he was ignored completely by Parisian waiters, who knew little, perhaps nothing, about baseball and had never heard of Babe Ruth. What galled him most was a tiny notice in the "unclaimed mail" section of the Paris *Herald Tribune,* inserted by the American Consulate, asking a "George H. Ruth" to please pick up his correspondence. Why, in America little kids in Iowa or Oregon could reach him by simply scribbling "Babe Ruth, New York Yankees" on the envelope! One day, rather than prowl the museums with Claire and Julia, the Babe went over to the American Boys' School, whose students were the children of U.S. citizens residing in Paris. That was better. In the playground, he had one young lad pitch to him and knocked out fly balls to the others. That evening he told Claire, "The kids were real nice." But

* Ruth's visit to Japan made such an impact that two months later Matsutaro Shoriki, the newspaper publisher who sponsored the tour, was stabbed by a radical nationalist, who blamed him for several "unpatriotic acts," including inviting the baseball star to their country and "causing money to leave the country in time of depression."

he was surprised at their ineptness. "How in hell," he asked her, "can an American kid grow up without being able to throw or swing a bat?"

One of his "greatest kicks" in Paris, he said later, occurred one afternoon while he was strolling down a street. Suddenly he yelled for Mrs. Ruth to stop. "What do you think we saw? If I'd of had a camera, I would've snapped it sure. A horse with his hind legs crossed!"

He had a better time at Saint Moritz, where he "dented more than the ski run" and was thrilled by a long toboggan ride. But even more to his liking was London, where he found several friends, in-including former Mayor Jimmy Walker, who was in exile after the Seabury investigations had revealed a number of questionable deal-ings while he was in City Hall.

Many Londoners recognized him, too, and he was even invited to show his skill at a cricket match near the Thames. Donning the leg pads and picking up the strange-shaped paddle, Ruth made a half-hearted try at a conventional cricket stance. But soon he reverted to his familiar baseball style and smashed the offerings of two bowlers for great distances. When he finished, his "bat" was in shambles; the handle was split and chunks of wood were gone from both edges. The Babe beamed at the compliments of the British athletes; he was enjoying himself hugely. He then got into a good-natured de-bate over whether England's best bowler was faster than pitching star Walter Johnson. The Babe, hand at the wallet, was ready to bet any amount! He had such a good time that he was an hour late for lunch with Claire.

As the liner *Manhattan* pulled into its berth at the foot of 19th Street in New York, the ship's orchestra played "Take Me Out to the Ball Game," and the Babe came down the gangplank dressed in what one reporter called "a symphony of brown." After four months of wandering the globe, he was quite fat and blamed it on the rice in Japan, which "puffed" him up.

For the next few days, the Ruth apartment overflowed with friends welcoming him back. He bubbled over with stories about his trip; the beautiful women of Bali who chewed bright red tobacco, the cross-legged horse in Paris, the time in Manila when "those Hawaiians" tried to give him "the business."

"Filipinos, Babe," said Claire.

"Well, anyway, there must've been 30,000 people out there at the ball park. You could see all those heads jammed together. They tried to tell me there was only 10,000. I stood to lose a bundle o' dough, so I said, 'No money, me no play.' I been lookin' at crowds all my life and I know 30,000 people when I see 'em. So this Hawaiian . . ."

"Filipino, Babe," said Claire.

"Yeah. So he says, 'Me no understand.' I took my glove and started for the gate. He understood *that* all right. We played and we got paid."

But when the funny tales were over and the friends said goodbye, the Babe was forced to look ahead. It was already mid-February—he was usually with the Yankees in Florida by now—but he had no-where to go.

There had been a registered letter from the Yankees waiting for him when he returned from Europe. It lay unopened, because the reporters told him what it contained: a 1935 contract offering him one dollar. This was a "mere formality," the Yankees explained. By mailing the contract before February 1, the Yankees retained control over Ruth's future. The ever practical Ruppert was willing to let him go, but not to play against the Yankees in the American League.

More rumors of managerial jobs for Ruth surfaced. When Clark Griffith, owner of the Washington Senators, was tracked down by reporters trying to check out a rumor, he said Ruth was "definitely out of the picture" as far as his club was concerned. During the winter meeting of the baseball club owners at the Hotel Commodore in New York, Joe McCarthy had called Ruppert aside and offered to resign in order to avoid any embarrassing conflict with Ruth, but Ruppert assured him that he had the job.

It was rumored that Ruth's jobs with Detroit and Washington fell through because he demanded a large salary and a percentage of the gate receipts; but the Babe appears to have been so anxious for work that his demands couldn't have been inflexible. Something else seemed to be the matter.

One owner, who demanded anonymity, said he didn't know any-body "willing to undertake the experiment" of Ruth as manager. "The successful teams don't need him, and it's doubtful whether he would exhibit the patience to build up a second-division club. The big question concerns his ability to maintain discipline. He's never had such responsibility."

"I just don't know how the big guy would have done as a manager," said Ford Frick in a recent interview. "Stars generally don't make good managers; they become impatient with mediocrity. What hurt his chances, I think, is that he refused to give it a try first in the minor leagues."

"He could've been a *good* manager," insists Whitey Witt. "His whole heart and soul was in managing. The players liked him, and that's what you need, a guy who can handle men. Who the hell can't manage if you've got good players?"

But, as if there were some conspiracy, no serious offers came. A sports promoter in Iowa wired him an offer of $35,000 to play with the bearded House of David team that toured the country. The Babe wouldn't be required "to wear whiskers," said the promoter.

And while he was off in the Orient an agent for Colonel Zach Miller's Wild West Show approached Christy Walsh with an offer of $75,000 to tour the country with a circus for one year. The Babe, said the agent, "would travel in state in the big parade on top of a sacred elephant preceded by a calliope playing "Take Me Out to the Ball Game." Then, in a "fifteen minute headline act," he would pound out "tremendous fungo fly balls and do other slugging stunts, with a special lecture to kids on how to be a dynamite ball bomber." Mercifully, they never got together on price.

"How Does It Feel, Babe?"

In late February of 1935, Boston Braves owner Emil Fuchs called Ruth and offered him a job. It was almost too good to be true. The Babe would be a player, assistant manager, and vice-president of the Braves; he would share in the club's profits and have the option to buy stock.

Then Fuchs dangled the most tempting bait of all: the chance to manage the Braves in 1936, since the team's present manager, Bill McKechnie, was working on a one-year contract.

Ruth was elated. Suddenly he was converted from a washed-up slugger, a pariah as far as most club owners were concerned, into a baseball executive!

A few mornings later, at the Yankee office in New York, Colonel Ruppert handed Ruth a typewritten sheet of paper; his unconditional release from the team.

"But what is the price, what will the Babe cost me?" asked Fuchs.

"Do you think I would sell this man?" said Ruppert. "If he can better himself elsewhere, the Yankees won't stand in his way." Privately the Colonel was relieved, because Ruth had slipped badly as a player, and Ruppert didn't know what to do with him.

The next step was to secure waivers from the other seven clubs in the American League to permit Ruth's move to the National League. Ed Barrow sent out a flurry of telegrams and got approval in a matter of hours. When one owner balked, hinting he might exercise his waiver option and acquire Ruth's services, Ruppert got on the phone and swore he would "never" allow the Babe to play with another American League club; he would withdraw the waiver offer before it came to that.

The transaction was announced on February 26, 1935, at a press conference in the brewery, where Ruppert, Fuchs, and Ruth—all dressed in natty blue suits—praised each other to the high heavens. The reporters were given copies of an exchange of letters, Fuchs to Ruth, Fuchs to Ruppert, Ruppert to Ruth, Ruth to Ruppert, Ruth to Fuchs, with phrases of goodwill overflowing the paper like honey.

The reporters gagged on some of the cloying verbiage and demanded a few impromptu remarks. Fuchs blew a verbal kiss at Ruppert for his "generosity" in releasing Ruth, and the Colonel, with a sad smile, said he would never stand in the Babe's way. Then Ruth put both hands in his pocket, advanced his right foot and cleared his throat, "Ha-hum!" That was a good start. He said that despite their differences over the years, Ruppert had been "like a Santa Claus" to him, evoking another sad smile from the Colonel. He tried to say that he'd always given his best for the Yankees, and would do likewise for Boston, but he became a bit confused and said "against the Braves," and Judge Fuchs whipped out a handkerchief and nervously mopped his brow. When someone asked Ruth exactly what his duties would be as vice-president of the Braves, he stammered, but Fuchs rushed to the rescue with: "Advisory capacity; be consulted on club deals and so forth."

* * *

"Babe Ruth is coming home!" said an article in Boston the next day. "Home to the folks who love him best, just as that other Boston sports hero, the mighty John L. Sullivan, did so many years ago, when the rest of America told him to step aside for youth." And the Boston *Herald* exulted: "He is that rarest of things, a living tradition!"

The Babe was ecstatic about his new career. "I've always wanted to manage a big league club, and this is my chance." When this statement was published, the Judge, contacted by phone in Boston, protested on the grounds that it was embarrassing to the Braves and to manager McKechnie, who still had a one-year contract. The reporter, told by Ruth that Fuchs had privately assured him of the manager's job next season, asked him directly: "Will Ruth manage the club in 1936?" The Judge shot back: "The letter speaks for itself." The letter was couched with "ifs" and "buts" and words like "mutual interest," but this was mere quibbling. What, possibly, could stand in the way?

That day, the Babe and Claire stepped aboard the train for Boston. Claire said she was "well satisfied" with her husband's new career. They would live in Boston while the Braves played their seventy-seven home games, "then I'll go on the road with them to see that the Babe gets his sleep . . . he gets absolutely no rest unless I watch him." The Babe, for the benefit of his press cronies, turned up his collar and mimed a sheepish expression, as though he'd just been caught with his hand in the cookie jar.

It was like the triumphal return of a beloved monarch when their train pulled into Back Bay Station. A swirling crowd of thousands got beyond the control of police, who formed a flying wedge to protect them. Ruth was sweating freely when he arrived at the Copley Plaza, and moments later he signed a three-year contract with a minimum salary of $25,000 per season.

That night there was a hastily arranged banquet in the hotel, attended by dozens of New England dignitaries, to honor the Babe. But after many sweet words, Braves vice-president Charles C. Adams sounded a discordant note: "Judging from Ruth's past career, we can hardly consider him of managerial calibre now. . . . He has much to learn within the next few months. He must prove himself to be a good soldier." But the Babe was oblivious to all this picayune stuff. Already he was speculating on how he would manage the Braves one day. "I won't apply the whip," he told a reporter. "You can get more out of a fellow by showing him a little consideration and friendly advice." When he was reminded that Bill McKechnie was still manager, he said, "There won't be any problem; he's the manager and I'll work with him." He assured the reporter that he would "never" take the manager's job "unless I'm sure that McKechnie's future is provided for." But a headline in the New York *Post* that day said: "RUTH SEALS McKECHNIE DOOM."

How all this sounded down in Saint Petersburg, where McKechnie was putting the Braves through their spring practice paces, can only be imagined. McKechnie simply said that Ruth would be an "asset" so long as he could swing a bat. He confessed, however, that with three good outfielders and a good first baseman already on the roster, he wasn't sure where to put the Babe. As for the other matter, he would continue to direct the club, because "no ball club can have two managers."

The whole affair seems to have been flawed from the start: by the imprecision of the Ruth-Fuchs understanding over the manager's job and by the fact, not widely known, that the Braves were nearly bankrupt. The club had lost money in 1934, and the entire franchise was valued at a mere $210,000.

But none of these concerns was on the Babe's mind as he and Claire boarded the Orange Blossom Special in New York on March

3. And not in all the years he'd played as a Yankee had there been such a fuss as when the train pulled into Saint Petersburg the evening of the next day. He was given a tumultuous reception by 3,000 cheering, milling, and pushing men and women.

The fans crowded around Babe and Claire on the little station platform, and others watched from the tops of parked cars, empty freightcars, and letterboxes.

"I hope they cheer this loud when I get out there in uniform," the Babe chuckled as he helped Claire through the mob.

The next day, 3,500 fans filled the stands and overflowed onto the field at tiny Waterfront Park. Ruth still had no uniform, and he looked quite a sight, with no cap, a heavy sweatshirt, a pair of coach Hank Gowdy's pants, and a pair of socks borrowed from Shanty Hogan. He waddled out onto the field and was engulfed by autograph seekers. Then he was photographed in every conceivable pose and stood for a number of shots with veteran Rabbit Maranville. Ruth liked to refer to himself and Maranville as "the last of the Mohicans," because between them they had spent nearly half a century playing baseball and raising hell. The Babe walked back to the bench and sat down. Gowdy came over with two dozen baseballs, and Ruth asked, "What are those?"

"Baseballs," said Gowdy. "We practice with 'em."

"Oh," said Ruth, sighing with relief. "I thought I had to *autograph* the damn things!"

"Listen, Ruth," said Maranville, "don't be worrying about autographing baseballs on this club. You start at the bottom like the rest of us, and work your way up!"

"I can still hear the Babe's laughter thundering from the kettledrum he was wearing under his belt," a Boston writer recalled.

As Ruth took his practice swings, McKechnie told reporters that the title of assistant manager meant "nothing in particular," except that Ruth would be consulted on matters of strategy along with the other coaches. If any "trouble" developed between them, said McKechnie, "it won't be caused by me."

Ruth looked strange the next day in the red and gray road uniform of the Braves, but otherwise he resembled "the same old Babe in all his portly glory." Other than a kink in his arm from swinging a bat too hard, he felt fine. By late March, although he was hitting only .250 in the exhibition games, Ruth was batting 1.000 at the ticket office. With only eight of the Braves' twenty-seven exhibition games completed, they collected more money at the gate than during the entire 1934 training season. Ruth had attracted 20,000 customers to those games, and it was estimated that the proceeds would be enough to cover most, if not all, of his $25,000 salary.

* * *

On April 16, "cannons boomed, airplanes roared overhead, and martial strains filled the air" as Braves Field held the greatest opening day in its history. Despite near-freezing weather, more than 25,-000 fans came out to see Ruth in his new uniform (it actually began to snow during the game, and the band struck up "Jingle Bells"). In the stands were Governor James M. Curley, four other New England governors, five mayors, and many other prominent citizens. And the "old Bambino, in the twilight of his career," didn't disappoint them. Coming to bat against Giant pitching star Carl Hubbell, he drew first blood with a single that scored a run. In the top of the fifth, he contributed the game's "fielding gem" when he "raced madly" to short left field and "plunging headlong desperately stuck out his gloved hand to spear a fly ball." In Boston's half of the fifth, with a man on base, Ruth again faced Hubbell and smashed the ball 430 feet into a narrow runway between the bleachers in right and center fields. He had been the "whole show" in Boston's 4 to 2 victory. Later, in the clubhouse, Ruth called himself "the happiest man in Boston."

But the adrenalin was all used up. Within a week, Ruth was home with a cold. By mid-May he had played in only four games. He couldn't shake the cold. His eyes watered so much that he couldn't see well. If he didn't feel better, he said, he would place himself on the voluntarily retired list, and McKechnie concurred. Fuchs claimed he knew nothing of Ruth's plans to quit, but privately he begged the Babe to play on; his argument was that Ruth should shake off his cold and "leave while on top," but he was more concerned about the club's shaky finances.

On May 23, there was a banquet at the Schenley Hotel in Pittsburgh for old Rabbit Maranville, whose days in baseball were numbered. Ruth rose to speak and said, "I've known Rabbit a long time and I love him as my own brother . . ." Then no words came. He seemed to be weeping. There was a long, embarrassed silence. He wiped his eyes with a napkin and muttered, "Dammit!" The orchestra struck up a tune to relieve the tension. But Ruth waved his hand. He wanted to continue. "Baseball can't afford to lose Maranville. If it can't find a place for him, then you'll hear me criticize baseball." He was speaking for himself, too.

Two days later the Babe paced about his hotel room in Pittsburgh, trying to figure a way to bow out gracefully. Claire urged him to simply quit. Christy Walsh called from New York with the same advice. "I *can't* quit," the Babe roared. "Damn it! I gave that double-crossing old sonofabitch my word I wouldn't quit until after the Memorial Day doubleheader in Philadelphia."

That afternoon, by some miracle, the Babe hit *three* home runs against the Pirates. The last one carried clear over the right field grandstand, bounded into the street, and rolled into Schenley Park; it was described as "the longest drive ever made at Forbes Field." After the game a Pittsburgh writer said that "The great man Ruth . . . sent 10,000 gabbing fans out of the ballpark convinced that the Bam's legs may be spavined, his body reaching the age of senility, and his glorious major league career in its sunset stage, but his eagle eye and his coordinated swings are just as effective as the day when he was the greatest home run king of all."

But the next day Cincinnati pitchers struck him out three times, and he limped to the dugout after pulling a leg muscle in the outfield. He did little better in Philadelphia on Memorial Day. In his final at bat, he was out on a squiggly ground ball to the infield. It was an ignominious way to end a big league career. He had appeared in twenty-eight games for the Braves, batted only .181, and hit six home runs.

"It was pretty much of a nightmare," he later recalled. For the first time in his life, baseball had become a drudgery. His legs were killing him, and young pitchers were striking him out on pitches that he would have smashed out of the park a few years before.

Ruth sat on the bench nursing a cold during the next two games against the Giants in Boston. He wore civilian clothes, was wrapped in a windbreaker, and had a Turkish towel around his neck. The third game against New York was rained out.

Then came Sunday, June 2. That morning, Ruth complained to Fuchs that his legs were hurting. The Boston owner reminded him that he was advertised to play in an exhibition game the next day. Ruth said he was "willing to hobble around and please the crowd," but he insisted he wasn't fit to play in the official league games on Tuesday and Wednesday. He asked Fuchs's permission to go to New York while recuperating and "represent the Braves" at a celebration aboard the ship *Normandie.*

"Nothing doing," said Fuchs. There was a heated argument, and Ruth said that he would put himself on the voluntarily retired list and go to New York without Fuchs's blessing.

Just before the game there was a series of bewildering developments. First, handouts circulated in the press box announced that

Judge Fuchs's finances were "exhausted" and that he sought a group of New England "sportsmen" to revitalize the club with more capital.

Then a messenger came to the press box saying that Ruth wanted to see the New York writers down in the clubhouse. When they arrived, Ruth told them he was retiring.

But moments later word came from Fuchs that the Babe had been fired and "is through with the Braves in every way." Ruth's career as a baseball executive had lasted about three months.

As the confused reporters milled about in the clubhouse trying to make sense of the story, manager McKechnie walked over to Ruth, shook his hand, and asked him to autograph a box of baseballs. McKechnie said he agreed with Ruth's idea of retiring, "so that he wouldn't get hurt."

That night, Ruth was in a sour mood. Saying that he was shaking the dust of Boston from his shoes, he claimed he was "given a dirty deal." The next morning he and Claire and Claire's mother checked out of their hotel, got into his brown sedan, and started the seven-hour drive back to New York.

A flock of New York writers was waiting for him when he pulled up at his home on West 88th Street. He was surly and out of sorts and called Fuchs a "double-crosser" because Fuchs had "promised" him the Boston manager's job in 1936. He claimed that Fuchs had talked him into the Braves job and that the "money-hungry" club owner had run him and other members of the team "ragged" by scheduling them to make speeches around town to sell tickets.

But at the same time, up in Boston, Fuchs let loose with a few broadsides of his own. He circulated stories that Ruth was "a shirker and peevish prima donna who guzzled highballs when he should have been in rigid training." The Babe, he claimed, would order his afternoon highball in the dining car of the train, which was "bad business" in the presence of the younger athletes. Fuchs claimed that when he suggested to Ruth that if he wanted to "moisten his whistle" he should do it in the privacy of a drawing room, the Babe answered with a roar: "Sez who?"

Although manager McKechnie had gone to Ruth's Boston hotel to say goodbye, he was pressured into taking sides in the controversy. After Ruth's departure, Fuchs met privately with his manager; McKechnie came out and told reporters that Ruth had been "a detriment" to the Braves and had caused "a lack of discipline" on the club. His pitching staff, he said, had "complained continuously" of Ruth's sluggish behavior in the outfield.

"I can't believe Bill said that," said Ruth. "Well," he sighed, "there's no use kidding myself. I'm through as a day-to-day ball-player. But I'm not through with baseball. At least I hope not."

But the future looked bleak. The Associated Press polled all the big league owners and reported "not a single club in either league manifested anything but academic interest in what Ruth does next." There was only a telegram from a club owner in the tiny North Florida League: "Will you consider management of the Palatka Baseball Club? Wire best terms."

The Babe, says Claire, "was never one to sit around and mope." Seeking an outlet for his competitive nature, he left the house each morning and played golf. He went hunting and fishing. He thrived on competition, even at home. He played cards in the evening with friends. Among the Ruth's closest friends were the songwriting team of Peter de Rose and May Singhi Breen. The Babe loved to stage "scallion-eating races" with May. Claire recalls that they would sit down with a huge bunch of scallions between them and laughingly reduce the pile one scallion at a time.

Eating and cooking were also favorite pastimes. He was an expert at carving venison or fowl and kept a pair of poultry shears in perfect condition for such operations. He enjoyed standing at the head of a dinner table, skillfully slicing the meat and heaping it on his friends' plates. The night before a hunting trip, he would laboriously prepare his own special barbecue sauce by the gallon and carry it along. He also made "the most wonderful spaghetti sauce," says Claire. He went to great lengths to secure the best olive oil, imported tomato paste, and dry mushrooms. Even breakfast involved a complex ritual of cooking the eggs with milk and a variety of condiments on a low flame, so that they came out soft and fluffy. He planned each meal "like a campaign," says Claire, and when he was finished cooking he rolled up his sleeves, grabbed the scouring powder, and left the kitchen spotless.

Dot and Julia were growing up, and he was a strict father. If they went on a date, it was home by eleven, and no argument. When Julia was nineteen, the Babe forced her to break off an engagement on the grounds that no girl was ready to marry until age twenty-five (perhaps he recalled his own first marriage, at nineteen, to a sixteen-year-old girl).*

* * *

It was a pleasant, easy life. He had earned more than $1 million from baseball and—thanks to Claire and Christy Walsh—had saved

---

* Julia finally married at twenty-four, and Dot at nineteen.

much of his money. But money was not enough. Not for a man who had played baseball from March through October ever since he wore knee pants at Saint Mary's Industrial School.

Now, there was no order to the seasons, no structure to his life. The days, weeks, months drifted by. There were no home stands, no road trips. No trains to catch. Whenever the Babe came in from the golf course or some other expedition, he would ask: "Any phone calls?" Sometimes he became enraged at the indifference of the baseball world, but Claire was always there with "a kind word, a kiss, a can of beer."

*   *   *

Ruth did play a few exhibition games in September, 1935, and proved that his name was still ticket office magic. In Minneapolis, 13,000 fans turned out to see the police of that town compete against the police of nearby Saint Paul as the Babe played half a game for each side and walloped balls out of the park in a pregame home run exhibition.

At Dyckman Oval in the Bronx, 10,000 fans overflowed the field to see Ruth play with a group of local semipros against the New York Cubans. The Babe hit a long double during the game and later spent five minutes blasting pitches out of the park. When he ran to his car, perspiring heavily, surrounded by fans waving pieces of paper to be signed, he looked happy; he could still, as he liked to say, "powder that onion." And he could still draw people. At home, there were 35,000 fan letters begging him not to quit baseball. Wasn't the message clear to all those blockhead club owners?

Later that month, while watching the Giants play at the Polo Grounds, Ruth looked like a forlorn figure who "has finally faded into legend." As he sat with his wife and singer Kate Smith, most of the photographers aimed their cameras at Miss Smith.

In late October, after seeing the 1935 World Series between the Tigers and the Cubs, he issued an ultimatum to the club owners, giving them "one last chance" to hire him when they convened in Chicago that December for the major league winter meetings. If not, he threatened to seek work outside of baseball and even hinted that he might go to England to popularize the game there.

He waited vainly for the offers to come. And, recalls Claire, he sometimes sat in his kitchen and wept by the hour.

Out of sheer habit, like some migratory creature, the Babe went to Florida in February, 1936. When he was in Fort Myers to see an exhibition game between the Cincinnati Reds and the Philadelphia

Athletics, Reds general manager Larry MacPhail offered him a
a spare outfielder and pinch-hitter, mentioning that he would be a
"nifty asset" to the Reds, who had finished sixth the year before.
Reacting like a child with a candy bar waved in his face, the Babe
was eager to accept, but the next day he said, "I talked the matter
over with Mrs. Ruth and she convinced me that with all the weight
I'm carrying around it would be asking too much of my legs."

As the teams headed north, Ruth sent the Yankees a check for
two opening game seats, but when he called their office about the
tickets he was told they hadn't been sent out because his check was
nowhere to be found. By contrast, his old friend and former ghostwriter Ford Frick (now president of the National League) had given
Ruth a lifetime pass to all National League games, despite the fact
that he had played only a few months with the Braves. Ruth was
deeply touched by Frick's gesture and wounded by the callous attitude of the Yankees.

So on opening day of 1936 the most famous Yankee of them all
sat in the Polo Grounds to watch the Giants. For fifteen fleeting
minutes before the game, he was again America's idol. The 55,000
spectators let out a tremendous roar when they saw Ruth's bulky
frame move through the crush of people toward his seat. Photographers and reporters came running over.

How does it feel, Babe? "Feels funny, funny," he mumbled, doing
his best to smile, feeling strange indeed at not being out on the field
for the first time in twenty-odd springtimes. The band marched past
his seat with a special salute, and friends waved hello. But suddenly
the crowd rose and became silent as the national anthem was played.
Then the umpire yelled "Play ball!" and the Babe was just one of
the crowd as 55,000 pairs of eyes shifted to the action on the field,
and the cheers went out to younger men.

He saw several games that year. Always there were the introduction,
the cheers, the quick wave and smile to the fans. But being a spec-
tator made him edgy. Without golf three or four times a week, he
admitted, "I would have blown up to 300 pounds; also, I would
have gone nuts."

That summer (with the help of ghostwriter Bill Corum) he
pinch-hit for vacationing columnist Walter Winchell. In the column
he made a sad plea for a manager's job, saying that someday the
"baseball bosses" would think of him not as "a hell-roaring kid" but
as "an old-timer who has learned about self-control."

That October he saw the Yanks play the Giants in the World
Series, and again sat on the Giants side of the field. But when the
Yankees won the series, he showed up at their victory party and

drank and joked with Colonel Ruppert. Cap Huston was there, too, talking about his plans to buy the Brooklyn Dodgers and install Ruth as manager, but nothing ever came of that. Albany of the International League offered him a manager's job, but again the Babe insisted that he was a big leaguer.

He busied himself with trivia that winter. He made a Vitaphone film short for Warner Brothers. At Christmas time he appeared at a special carnival for 4,000 underprivileged children. Cab Calloway had regaled them with "Minnie the Moocher"; Harry Di Dio and his trick poodle Chum had tickled them with their act; and they oohed and aahed at the feats of Madame Sandwina, the strong woman. But when the Babe was introduced "they sat spellbound," and when he got up an impromptu game of baseball with four clowns, "their antics evoked shrieks of merriment."

He sounded cocky in early 1937 when he told a reporter of "all sorts of offers," including a chance to work in the front office of a major league club, but he insisted that after one week in an office he'd be "dead." He needed "fresh air," he insisted, and if he couldn't get a big league manager's job, he would "just take it easy."

He made enough from sidelines, he claimed, to pay all his expenses. There had been $1,500 for a five-minute radio broadcast the other night. He would soon sign a $39,000 contract to broadcast thirteen weeks for the Quaker Oats Cereal Company. During that period he attended a ball game in Newark, where the radio announcer, trying to plug his own sponsor, asked, "Babe, are you a Wheaties fan, too?" Ruth, ever loyal, said, "No, I like Quaker Oats."

The Babe went to Bermuda for a golf tournament that year. And in November he hunted in Nova Scotia and made a dramatic return when the ship pulled in at the North River pier. Lashed across the front bumper of Ruth's car was a big deer. Two bucks were draped over the front fenders. Lying snugly in the rumble seat was a large black bear. He pulled the dead bear out and "wrestled" with it as photographers clicked away.

And so it went, until June, 1938. The Brooklyn Dodgers were having a terrible year, and Larry MacPhail (who had become the club's executive vice-president) walked up to Leo Durocher, the shortstop and captain of the club, and asked what he thought of hiring Babe Ruth.

Durocher later admitted that he couldn't have been more surprised if MacPhail had asked him about "exhuming Abner Doubleday." MacPhail explained that Ruth might help attendance by serving as a coach and "hitting a few out of the park in batting practice." Both

Durocher and manager Burleigh Grimes reluctantly agreed that Ruth might help the gate.

The Babe had just returned from a fishing trip one night when Claire, trying to sound casual, said that Larry MacPhail had called.

Ruth grabbed the telephone, spoke with MacPhail, and hung up. Smiling broadly, he said, "I might be in baseball again!" The door slammed behind him.

He rushed over to MacPhail's apartment in Washington Heights. Durocher, Grimes, and Christy Walsh were already there. Ruth signed a $15,000 contract for the remainder of the season as a Brooklyn coach.

Although MacPhail made no mention of job advancement, Ruth spoke openly about his managerial aspirations. Taking Durocher aside in another room, he said that he would be "boss . . . before too long." This rankled Durocher, who had ambitions of his own. When he let Ruth know that "the line for manager forms at the right," the conversation ended on less than amicable terms.

But when Ruth returned home at 1 A.M. he was happier than ever, telling Claire, "I'll be manager next year!" When Claire inquired about money, Ruth boomed, "Pay? What the hell's the difference?" Later, the Babe would remark that just getting back into a "monkey suit" was compensation enough. "To be part of the club, to hit the Western trips!"

Ruth made his debut on June 19, 1938, and, judging from the cheers of the 28,000 people at Ebbets Field, many had come to see him. The photographers kept him busy for an hour, posing in his tentlike Dodger uniform in the first base coaching box, hands to his mouth, yelling encouragement to batters, hands waving directions to runners, shaking hands with his new Dodger teammates. When a reporter asked if he might be reinstated as a player, he replied, "Sure, but it'd take me a month to get in shape; I'm as fat as a pig."

His new career almost ended a few nights later, as he drove home from a friend's house along a narrow highway in New Jersey. Perhaps he was daydreaming, perhaps he'd downed a few scotches too many, but by some freak accident the front wheels of his new Oldsmobile brushed against the front wheels of a car coming from the opposite direction. This sent Ruth's car into a violent skid; it hurtled a ditch, hit atop a low brick wall and turned over in a field, resting on its side. Miraculously, when the police helped Ruth from his car he was unhurt. So were the occupants of the other car. No charges were filed.

The Babe's billowy form became a regular fixture out near first base. But he wasn't very adept at giving signals—he confused both himself and the batters—so he was made a sort of "traffic cop." But the fans loved him, and each night he autographed several dozen cards to save himself the trouble of signing them on the field.

Because of Ruth, the Dodgers scheduled ten extra exhibition games during the remainder of the season, and they grossed nearly enough to pay his entire $15,000 salary.

It was "a daffy thing" for him to do, he confessed later, because most of the exhibition games were played at night. Ruth had never played night baseball, and to make things worse the games were played in small towns, where the parks had dim lights. Most of the opposing pitchers were eager to strike him out, and several pitches narrowly missed his head.

But he was enjoying himself. One night in Albany the pitcher was blazing them in so hard that it seemed dangerous to stand up at the plate. Ruth let a couple of pitches swoosh by, then lifted a fly ball that towered far above the lights and slowly arched over the fence. The small crowd went wild as the Babe trotted around the basepaths in his unique style, grinning and tipping his cap. It was a good feeling.

The urge to hit was irresistible. He knew that his legs were shot and his reflexes slower, but he could still send a ball a mile when he got his big arms and shoulders moving. Late that July, for example, during a pregame hitting contest in Saint Louis, he competed against such sluggers as Johnny Mize, Joe Medwick, and Dolph Camilli. Each batter was allowed ten swings. Ruth walloped one 430 feet, five feet farther than Medwick's best shot. He grinned all day. Soon afterward, he asked MacPhail to have him put on the active list as a pinch-hitter. But manager Grimes gently put his foot down: "I like Babe Ruth. I care for the Dodgers. In the welfare of both, I'm turning down his request."

The main thorn in Ruth's relationship with the Dodgers was thirty-three-year-old Leo Durocher. They hadn't gotten along well years before, when Ruth was a Yankee star and Durocher was an outspoken rookie. Now, with the tables turned, it was even worse. One day, when the Dodgers won an extra-inning game with a hit-and-run play, a young reporter for the *World Telegram* wrote that coach Ruth had called the signal for the daring maneuver. The next day in the clubhouse Durocher was furious and yelled that Ruth didn't have the brains to give a proper sign. The Babe heard about the remark and said, "Durocher, I've been wantin' to smack you down for a long time." There was a brief scuffle. They were quickly separated, but Ruth wound up with a small mark under his eye.

When the Dodgers finished seventh that season, Grimes was ousted as manager, Durocher was given the job, and Ruth was eliminated from the picture. He wasn't fired, MacPhail hastened to explain: "Ruth could've remained as coach, but he told me he wouldn't be available." Indeed, it's possible that Ruth himself resigned rather than take orders from Durocher.

Unlike the Boston debacle, there were no angry words: Ruth parted with "good luck" to the Dodgers and "best wishes" for next year. Then, in a tone that could not hide his sadness, he said, "No matter what the future holds in store, my heart will always be with the great game of baseball."

NINTH INNING

Some argue that Eros . . . was the first of the
gods since, without him, none of the rest could
have been born. . . . He was a wild boy, who
showed no respect for age or station but flew
about on golden wings, shooting barbed arrows
at random or wantonly setting hearts on fire
with his dreadful torches. . . . The early Greeks
pictured him as a . . . winged 'Spite' . . . in
the sense that uncontrolled sexual passion
could be disturbing to ordered society. . . .
Later poets, however, took a perverse pleasure
in his antics and, by the time of Praxiteles, he
had become sentimentalized as a beautiful
youth. His most famous shrine was at Thespiae,
where the Boeotians worshipped him as a simple phallic pillar. . . . Eros was never considered a sufficiently responsible god to figure
among the ruling Olympian family of Twelve.

ROBERT GRAVES,
The Greek Myths

"Why Should It Happen to Me?"

Time passed, and old friends were dying off. In February, 1938, Ruth's birthday had coincided with the annual dinner of the New York Baseball Writers, and he was asked to speak. Looking out at his audience, he said, "You know what I call this dinner? I call it the 'I Wonder Dinner.' I come here every year and I wonder who'll be missing each year."

Then, jerking a thumb toward Colonel Ruppert and Ed Barrow, he asked aloud, "I wonder if Jake and Ed will be here next year." Glancing down at the wrinkled, white-haired Judge Landis who sat beside him, he cracked out of the side of his mouth, "I wonder if *this* old goat will be here next year!" He went on and on, making the audience howl at his seriocomic remarks.

Now, nearly a year later, the Babe learned that seventy-one-year-old Jacob Ruppert lay on his deathbed at his Fifth Avenue apartment. On the evening of January 13, 1939, doctors had apparently lost hope, removed the oxygen tent from Ruppert's bed, and called a priest to administer the last rites.

When Ruth phoned, he was told to hurry over. The dying man opened his eyes and reached out his hand but was too weak to talk.

"Colonel," said the Babe cheerfully, "you're gonna snap outa this, and we're going to the opening game this season." The Colonel smiled, and when Ruth got up to leave he called out weakly, "Babe . . ." Ruth's eyes were red as he emerged from Ruppert's room. "I couldn't help crying," he said. "It was the only time in his life that he called me Babe to my face . . . he was like a second father to me."

There were more tears that July 4, as 61,800 fans packed Yankee Stadium in a sad farewell to Lou Gehrig, the "Iron Horse," who was suffering from a rare type of paralysis. All spring, teammates and opponents had been puzzled by Gehrig's strange awkwardness,

247

his slowness at bat and in the field. Then came word from the doctors that he didn't have long to live.*

The farewell ceremony took place between games of the holiday doubleheader. More than a dozen men—some bald, some gray, most with growing midsections—hopped spryly onto the field. The crowd roared its recognition of the veterans of the great Yankee club of 1927. A mere dozen years had gone by, but they were like ghosts from the distant past. Down the field they marched—behind Captain Sutherland's Seventh Regiment Band—toward the flagpole in center field to raise the World Series pennant they had won from the Pirates back in '27: Meusel, Pipp, Schang, Bengough, Lazzeri, Koenig, Dugan, Shawkey, Pennock, Scott, Pipgras (now wearing an umpire's suit) and Combs (now a Yankee coach and the only man wearing the team's uniform). There too, in a summer suit with an open-necked sports shirt, was the burly Babe, smiling and waving at the fans.

They paraded back and strung out single file along one side of the infield, facing the grandstand. Now the new Yankees trotted out to join them—young heroes like "Jolting Joe" DiMaggio and a muscular rookie outfielder named Charlie "King Kong" Keller.

The crowd roared again as Gehrig—a lone figure—limped from the dugout to join them. He stood there, trembling, as the speeches droned on. The Yankees gave their doomed teammate a large trophy, an eagle perched atop a silver ball supported by six gleaming silver bats, with their names and a poem inscribed upon it.

There was silence in the vast stadium as it came time for Gehrig to speak. Near collapse, he gulped and fought back his tears, staring vacantly at the ground before him. Ruth recalls that he "looked away" because it was such a painful moment. Then Gehrig, his voice cracking and echoing through the loudspeaker system, spoke slowly and tenderly of Miller Huggins, gone ten years ago, Jake Ruppert, gone just a few months past, and all the men who stood in silent tribute before him.

As Gehrig finished, the Babe, "robust, round and suntanned," was nudged toward the microphone. And, "in his own inimitable, blustering style, he snapped the tears away," called the 1927 Yankees "the greatest team ever" and issued a good-natured challenge to the present New York club. Then, forgetting the feud that had cooled their friendship for the past few years, Ruth draped an arm around Gehrig's shoulders as the battery of cameramen snapped away. All through the long ceremony, Gehrig had tried vainly to smile, but when the Babe whispered something in his ear, Lou

* Gehrig died on June 3, 1941, just eighteen days short of his 38th birthday.

chuckled and the deep dimples for which he was so famous were visible for the first time. Then they both chuckled and the crowd roared. As they stood there, arm in arm, the band struck up "I Love You Truly" and the crowd sang along, taking up the chant, "We love you, Lou."

The spontaneous flood of sentiment from the thousands of fans, said one writer, "was one of the most touching scenes ever witnessed on a ball field, and one that made even case-hardened ballplayers and chroniclers of the game swallow hard." As the music swept over the stadium, tears came to Ruth's eyes. "Dammit," he said later, "I went over there because . . . I wanted to laugh and cheer him up. I wound up crying like a baby." Many wept with him. Jim Bishop was there in the stands and recalls: "They thought the tears were for Babe and Lou. No, the men in the stands were weeping for their own youth."

* * *

The Babe went to Cooperstown, New York, a week later for the opening of the new Baseball Hall of Fame. He was one of the five players initially chosen for membership, together with Ty Cobb, Honus Wagner, Christy Mathewson, and Walter Johnson.

Looking at the plaque bearing his likeness, the Babe—still in his mid-forties—said he "felt like a kind of ornament or antique." He was just that. Some months later, Ed Hughes in *Friday* magazine said there was a "blacklist" against Ruth by the club owners, who resented the fact that he had "automatically raised the pay of every ballplayer in the land." Ruth, said Hughes, was "a one-man union without realizing it. He forced the magnates to shell out players' wages commensurate with the gate receipts they helped to swell." When Hughes sought comment from the Babe, he would only remark, "I don't want to say anything that makes me look like a bad sport. You know—on account of the kids." Earlier that year, the Giants and Dodgers said they would permit radio broadcasts of their home games for the first time. The Yankees were contemplating a similar move. Confessing that "I haven't a thing to do this season," the Babe made a strong bid for a "job at the mike" and said he was sure that his fame and his insider's knowledge of baseball would attract a large listening audience. He probably would have, but no offers were forthcoming.

He rarely went to the games now and virtually dropped from public view. In February, 1940, the papers carried his annual birthday photo, and a small item a few days later said that he'd gone to

Florida to be an instructor at a baseball school. Readers caught a rare glimpse of the Babe in a top hat that May when he attended the wedding of his daughter Julia to a young man named Richard W. Flanders. But during the next few years most of the news about him concerned illness or mishaps.

Ruth had several auto accidents during his retirement years. He was fined for reckless driving in southern New Jersey and was later sued for $5,500 by the owner of the car he hit. He struck a woman one evening in New York City and rushed her to the hospital in his car because she was suffering from a concussion. No charges were filed, because witnesses claimed the woman had stepped suddenly into the path of Ruth's car from behind a parked vehicle. Another time, while driving home from a golf game, he sideswiped a car along Queens Boulevard and kept on going. The police were advised by radio to "stop car license number IN-72-35, heading for Manhattan," driven by "a man in a brown cap and coat." As Ruth approached the Manhattan end of the Queensboro Bridge, two police officers blocked the road; one of them held a rifle. Pulling his car to a halt, the Babe hopped out, hands up, demanding, "What the hell's this about?" The officer's rifle—and jaw—dropped when he recognized his prisoner. At the station house, Ruth explained that it was "just a slight bump" (both cars had dented fenders), and he thought so little of it that he didn't bother to stop. When the owner of the other car arrived, the Babe made a quick cash settlement and was released.

Ruth was rumored to have died of a heart attack in September, 1940, but when a reporter called he moaned, "I'm not dead, only *half* dead after turning in eighteen holes of golf!" That winter he was bedded down with a severe cold and in January was under a doctor's care for an attack of the grippe, complicated by "a touch of sinus trouble."

That summer, when Ty Cobb visited New York, Ruth challenged his old enemy to a series of golf matches. "I was sitting in the Babe's apartment," Cobb recalled. "He was up to around 240 pounds and filled a big easy chair. Babe liked to sit with his feet parked on an ornamental beer keg from Jake Ruppert's brewery. We drank from oversized tumblers, and I will say that Babe's wife, Claire, kept them steadily refilled." Puffing on a big cigar and sipping his scotch, the Babe suggested a best-of-three series with the proceeds going to charity. The newspapers jumped at the story and ballyhooed it as a battle between baseball's two premier stars. The first match was set for Boston, the second for Long Island, and the third, if necessary, for Detroit. Bette Davis, the screen star, would present a trophy to the victor. After splitting the first two, they stopped in Cleveland and then took the boat to Detroit. Cobb recalls: "Babe was all smiling confidence, and he killed a good part of a quart of scotch." The former Detroit star won the final match the next afternoon, which was steaming hot, and recalls that Babe "sweat ferociously; he even looked slightly ill."

In November, when Samuel Goldwyn announced that he would produce a film version of *The Life of Lou Gehrig,* Ruth was signed to play himself for a reported $25,000. He took the assignment quite seriously. Since he was vastly overweight, he went on a crash diet. Just before New Year's Day of 1942, he attended a cocktail party for the press in the Rainbow Club of the RCE building in honor of Mrs. Gehrig, himself, and Paul Gallico, who had written the screenplay. He was in excellent spirits and chuckled at friends' amazement over his trim figure. He admitted that he had dieted off some forty-seven pounds and was down to about 220.

Five days later, an ambulance drew up to the Ruths' apartment building early in the morning, and he was carried out on a stretcher. His doctor, Philip G. MacDonald explained that Ruth had suffered "a nervous breakdown." It was brought on, he said, by "over-dieting" and an "auto smashup" a week before, "which shocked his nervous system badly." The accident was kept out of the papers, but his car was reportedly wrecked when he swerved off a road near Tuxedo Park, New York, to avoid hitting another vehicle. He was spirited away to an unnamed hospital in upstate New York.

But in a few weeks he was out in California toiling hard on the film and in his spare time appearing at local army camps and war bond sales drives. Day after day he worked with Gary Cooper, who played Gehrig in the film, retitled *The Pride of the Yankees.* At Wrigley Field in Los Angeles, where the baseball scenes were shot, he slammed one home run after another into the stands for the benefit of the cameras.

He entered so zealously into the spirit of things that, in the re-creation of the Yankees' boisterous train ride after winning the 1926 World Series, Ruth punched his way through a Pullman car window and gashed his fist.

On April 8, with most of the film completed, Ruth was due at the studio to do a brief scene with Teresa Wright, who portrayed Mrs. Gehrig. But the night before he suffered severe chills; a few hours later doctors said he was "fighting for his life" and had symptoms of pneumonia. The studio shot around him for two weeks until he was released from the hospital.

He was back in New York by the end of the month, registering for military service at Local Draft Board 30 on Amsterdam Avenue. "Uncle Sam can have me anytime he wants me," he said cheerily. But he was hardly in condition to fight. In fact, after his recent illness doctors had warned him to cut down drastically on his ten cigars per day, his nips of scotch, and his frequent visits to the golf courses and bowling alleys. He grudgingly followed their orders but maintained a busy schedule of appearances for the war effort.

The Babe got "the thrill of a lifetime" when the Yankees asked him to appear at a Sunday doubleheader on August 23, 1942. Between games, he would put on a hitting exhibition as Walter Johnson pitched to him, and proceeds of the big day would go to the Army-Navy Relief Fund.

He was "like a child" the morning of the game, said Claire. "Was his uniform back from the cleaners? Had it been pressed just right? How about the cap? Were the spikes shined?" He was worried sick, because he hadn't swung a bastball bat in quite some time.

There was a tremendous crowd of 69,000 people at Yankee Stadium that Sunday. In the runway approaching the field, the gray-haired Johnson said, "Babe, I just want to ask one thing; don't hit any back at me." Ruth laughed and said, "Hell, I'll be lucky to hit one at all, but I'll try to pull 'em down the line." The rusty old Washington pitching star lacked control on the first two pitches, but, when he grooved the third right down the middle, Ruth shot a line drive into the lower right field stands and the crowd gave him a grand hurrah. Johnson kept pitching, and the Babe swung away, spraying the field with line drives. Soon both of them were tired and perspiring heavily. But on Johnson's twenty-first pitch, Ruth said, "all the cobwebs seemed to drop off my baseball muscles." He rared back, swung, and sent the ball soaring into the third deck of the right field stands, a place where few balls ever reached. At the last second, the ball hooked a foot or so foul, but Ruth, thinking to himself, "I'll never top that one," tossed his bat away and circled the bases in the familiar mincing trot, tipping his cap as the applause and cheers fell like garlands of flowers at his feet. He and Johnson disappeared into the dugout, both beaming. Later, he shook Ed Barrow's hand and said, "Thanks for asking me, Ed. It's nice to be back—even for a day!"

With his typical zest for every task, Ruth immersed himself in the war effort. In 1943, he appeared at a series of movie matinees in New York City theaters, standing onstage and imploring people to contribute all salvageable material—stockings, rubbers, copper, tinfoil —"for our guys over there." That summer Sid Mercer wrote in the New York *Journal* that "*some*where in baseball there should be a job for Babe Ruth." Whatever Ruth's feelings were, he kept them to himself and continued his war effort activities. From behind a desk at WABC Radio, he and Giant star Mel Ott "batted out" $25 and $100 War Bonds, answering phone calls from fans who agreed to buy a bond in return for a brief chat. He was on hand to present more than a hundred movie prints of the 1943 World Series to be shipped overseas for the troops. A Pennsylvania Congressman even suggested that it would be "a fine morale-builder" if he were to accompany a group of major league all-stars on a trip to the Pacific. Babe was eager to go but explained that his doctors warned him, "I'd die before I got there." He visited four of five military hospitals a week, talking his deep voice hoarse, slapping backs, shaking hands, signing autographs.

He also launched a career in radio with fifteen-minute shows over WEAF on Saturday mornings, and continued it the next year. One evening he made a special network broadcast with Milton Berle, and *Variety* said: "The Bambino went along with the gags like an old trouper and took care of his lines and biz as easily as he used to take care of those American League pitchers a few seasons back." But best of all were the impromptu Ruthian remarks. Once, on his Saturday morning show, he tried to imitate the sound of a baseball being caught. There was no glove handy, so he picked up his leather jacket and whacked it hard. Then, forgetting his audience, he exclaimed aloud: "Jesus, I broke the god-damned cigars!"

The Ruths had an active social life but preferred to entertain at home, says Claire, because "Babe hated to wear collars and ties." They saw a lot of Peter and May de Rose, who brought music and gaiety into the house. They also saw his lawyer, Melvyn Gordon Lowenstein, and old friends like Paul Carey and Paul Schwepel. Ruth's passion for pranks never weakened. He loved to send telegrams to the De Roses, collect, just for a gag. During the war, Paul Carey was a commander in the Navy. Ruth would hide his cap just when Carey had to report for duty and laugh as the navy man searched frantically all over their apartment. The Baseball Hall of Fame has two old checkbooks of the Ruths for the years 1943 through 1945, and from these it appears that they hosted a number of big parties. During one summer month of 1943 alone, check stubs to the Park Circle Liquor Shop totaled more than $600. That October, two checks to another liquor store added up to more than $500. In quieter moments, said Claire, Ruth loved to hear his favorite radio programs, "The FBI in Peace and War," "The Green Hornet," "The Lone Ranger," and "Gangbusters."

But when a reporter visited the Ruth apartment for his birthday in February, 1944, he described him as "a gentleman of unwanted leisure, restless as a caged bear," who in addition to working for the war effort burned up his nervous energy with golf in the summer and bowling in the winter. That year a friend remarked, "He probably bowled more games than anyone in the city." Virtually every afternoon, sometimes with friends, sometimes alone, he would roll his big blue and black Ebonite ball down the basement lanes of the Riverside Plaza Hotel, not far from his home. The Babe had gained weight despite his constant exercise, and his birthday visitor said "in his lounging pajamas he still looks as if he had been invited to a pot-luck supper and swallowed the pot." Despite the fact that the Ruths changed their phone number every few months, it rang incessantly. The Babe, his voice a hoarse croak, would say, "Tell 'em I'm not in," but each time it was a friend who wanted to wish him happy birthday. They were expecting fifty people at the celebration that night.

A visitor admired the Ruths' spacious new apartment. Through the venetian blinds one could see the trees of Riverside Park, and the yachts in the 79th Street Marina on the Hudson River. The apartment had so many trophies it resembled a museum.

"Show them that little cigar lighter made like a bowling pin you got the other day," said Claire.

Sitting comfortably in an easy chair, puffing on an ornate pipe, Ruth said, "I don't know where it is."

"Why, it's in that suit you wore."

Reluctantly, he got up and slouched across the room.

"And straighten up," she said.

The reporter, an old married man himself, later remarked: "The big guy is just human, after all."

*   *   *

Although Ruth hadn't been active in baseball for nearly a decade, American troops on the front lines at Anzio, Italy, once used "Yankees" and "Ruth" as the daily challenge and password; it was still as natural as "ham" and "eggs." And in March, 1944, a Marine Corps correspondent in the Pacific reported that Japanese troops charged the American lines shouting a strange battle cry: "To hell with Babe Ruth!" When he heard this, he replied: "I hope every Jap that mentions my name gets shot, and to hell with all Japs anyway." He felt very vengeful about the attack at Pearl Harbor and destroyed some of the trophies given him during his trip to Japan in the 1930's. "Every time I see one of our wounded," he said, "it reminds me of my baseball trip to Japan. When we reached Tokyo there must have been a million Japanese lining the streets between the railroad station and our hotel. Every one of them had an American flag in one hand and their own in the other. They called me 'the god of baseball.' Now look what they've done to us."

In June he went to the hospital to have cartilage removed from his painful right knee. It was an old baseball injury that he'd let go for some time. Now he hoped the operation would give him back a few years, so he could enjoy his golf game. Every week that summer, a masseuse came to treat the painful knee.

"It's hell to grow old," he said to veteran reporter Stanley Frank of the *Post,* who commented how "depressing" it was to see the Babe without his old bounce and bawdiness.

His hair was matted with gray, and he still limped slightly from the operation when he walked into a building on West 84th Street that October to register for the 1944 Presidential election. He had never voted before, he admitted, but although he was "always a Roosevelt man" he felt that "sixteen years is enough" and said he would support the challenger, Thomas E. Dewey. But as he and Claire stood in line to register, a policeman said that since they had never voted in the state they would have to produce a high school diploma or take a literacy test. They hurried around the corner to a public school, passed the test, and lined up again. When the Babe's turn came, he confirmed to the registrar that his name was George Herman Ruth.

"Age, please?"

"Over twenty-one."

"Occupation?"

The Babe hesitated and then said, "Retired."

With the war nearly over and the baseball world still apathetic, he *was* retired. But he yearned for action and announced that he would tour briefly as a wrestling referee "to keep in touch with the crowds."

In Portland, Maine, on April 2, the Babe chased a pair of professional wrestlers around the ring as 2,300 fans in the smoky arena screamed their lungs out. The "villain" of the match was 200-pound Manuel Cortez. who specialized in "dirty tactics," and Ruth hammed it up as required. "Several times," it was reported, "the Mexican grappler and the Babe squared off and berated each other in stentorian tones."

Some sportswriters were appalled that Ruth should be forced into the indignity of "rassling," which was little more than burlesque, in order to "keep in touch with the crowds." Jim McCulley of the

Daily News said that since childhood he'd kept Ruth "up on a pedestal" and called the Babe's inability to find a place in baseball a "dark blotch" in the history of the game.

Ruth's fifty-first birthday passed by in 1946 without fanfare. For the first time in decades not even a photo on the sports pages marked the event. Now he was bowling for the March of Dimes infantile paralysis fund. Appearing with Ken Strong, he drew several hundred people to their matches at alleys throughout the city. Once, at Radio City Center, Ruth asked how much had been collected after a contribution box was passed around. It wasn't enough, he said, and made an impromptu appeal that doubled the donation the second time around. Then he emptied his own pockets and had to borrow cab fare to get home.

That spring, after Jacob Ruppert's estate was forced to sell the Yankees, Larry MacPhail was put in charge of the club. Ruth called him and said he'd heard the job as manager of the Newark club (a post he'd refused years before) was vacant. MACPhail seemed pleased to hear from Ruth and told him to "sit tight." Two weeks later Ruth called again. This time MacPhail said that George Weiss was in charge of hiring for the Yankees' farm system, and he'd be in touch. Two more weeks passed, and someone else was hired for the Newark job.

Then the Babe flew to Mexico—and put his foot right in the middle of an international controversy.

Jorge Pasquel, millionaire president of the Mexican Baseball League, had challenged baseball's standard contract, which gave big league clubs the exclusive right to a player's services for the duration of his career. Pasquel and his brothers flashed large amounts of folding money and lured several American players south to the Rio Grande. The major league club owners, all staunch advocates of the free enterprise system, were outraged over the fact that their players should change jobs merely over a question of money. They took the Mexicans to court, declaring that "the great American game as we know it will be destroyed" if the contracts that bound players to a single club were declared illegal. The Mexicans rebutted that U.S. player contracts were "monopolistic, unconscionable, illegal," and that players who signed them were held "in peonage" for life.

It became such a heated issue that one paper commented that not since Mexico's historic oil expropriation of 1938 had any battle so delighted the Mexican ego. Pasquel was depicted as "Saint Jorge," tilting with the "dragon" of American baseball.

Whether he knew it or not, said *Newsweek,* Babe Ruth's visit to

Mexico was "the greatest psychological blow the Pasquels have delivered in their war against the American monopoly."

The Babe stepped down from an American Airlines plane in Mexico City on May 16, 1946, and yelled out something that vaguely resembled *"Qué tal amigos!"* When asked by reporters if the big leagues had tried to dissuade him from visiting the Pasquels, Ruth snapped, "No one asked me not to come—but that doesn't make any difference, because I go where I please anyway."

He insisted that he'd come to Mexico merely to "enjoy golf, bullfights, and baseball games." But one could detect a note of resentment against organized baseball (which had ignored him for so many years) when he said, "The Pasquels are doing a fine thing for baseball and their country. Baseball is a game that should be played all over the world. It keeps kids out of trouble and develops them into better citizens." He said it was "wrong" for American club owners to enforce a threatened five-year ban against players who jumped to the Mexican League.

Later that day after the first inning of a game at Mexico City's Delta Park, there was a roar so loud one would have thought a bases loaded homer had just sailed over the wall. As Ruth, Claire, his daughter Julia, and his son-in-law Richard Flanders made their way to their seats down front, he was introduced as *El Sultan del Bat, El Rey Jonronero* (the Home Run King), and, finally, "El Bambino, Baby Ruth!" The crowd cheered wildly, and Ruth responded with a brief speech, after which he settled back to watch the game. He saw his first bullfight a few days later and was proud of the fact that a *torero* had dedicated a bull to him. Afterward, the Ruths spent a few days swimming and fishing at Cuernavaca and Acapulco (where the Babe got a painful sunburn) and returned to New York. Nothing came of the Mexican trip, nor did the Mexican League succeed in breaking the big league hold on its players, but by his presence there Ruth got some small measure of revenge against the owners who had ignored him for so long.

He went back to his quiet life. Late at night, neighbors saw him walking Bob, his big boxer, in Riverside Park. He would joke, "he's the boy who keeps *me* in shape now."

On the morning of August 10, 1946, Ruth prepared to attend a picnic for 3,000 orphans at Long Beach. He had a blinding headache, but he'd promised an old friend, Ray Kilthau, that he would go. For the past few months he'd suffered pains over his left eye and hoarseness in his throat, but it was worse than ever now.

The Babe plodded through the sand that hot sultry day, signing

autographs and posing for countless photos. That night he was in
agony. Claire called a doctor, who recommended a dental checkup
and treatment of a sinus condition. But the pain grew worse. Each
morning, however, Ruth rose early, ate breakfast, and went out to
bowl or play golf. "Whatever this thing is, it's not gonna lick me,"
he told Claire. "Maybe I can just *work* it off."

That September he wrote to Larry MacPhail, pleading for *any*
type of job with the Yankees, no matter what the salary. When a
letter came from the Yankees the next month, the Babe sensed it
was a rejection: "They write the bad news and telephone the good."
He was right. MacPhail said there was no job at the moment but
added:

> There is an important job to be done in the metropolitan New York
> area in connection with the promotion and development of sandlot
> and amateur baseball. I believe the three major league clubs should
> aggressively support and subsidize these activities. If you would like
> to discuss this with me some time, I would be glad to meet you at your
> convenience.

After reading the letter, Claire says, the Babe walked into the
kitchen and wept again.

Later that month, Howard Hughes Productions bought the rights
to Ruth's biography for "screen and literary purposes" for a reported
$100,000. The Babe appeared with heavyweight boxing champion
Joe Louis at the Hotel Roosevelt as part of the campaign to re-elect
Governor Thomas E. Dewey; they were co-chairman of the Sports
Committee for Dewey and Ives.

But by November 26 the pain over his eye had become so severe
that Dr. Philip McDonald ordered him checked into French Hospital. He was taken there in a wheelchair, and reporters were shocked
when they saw him: The entire left side of his face was swollen,
and his left eye was closed. He couldn't swallow food. The doctors
would only say that "Ruth has been suffering from headaches, and
it was planned to check whether a sinus condition . . . might be
the cause." X-rays were taken. Three bad teeth were removed. Peni-
cillin was administered. One month later Ruth was still in the hospital,
still in pain, and his stay was described as "indefinite."

He had cancer. The malignant tumor had straddled the major
artery on the left side of Ruth's neck. It was pressing on nerves,
which caused severe pain and interfered with his ability to speak
and swallow. On January 5, 1947, in a three-hour operation, Dr.
Hippolyte Wertheim operated to remove the malignancy. To do so,
he had to sever nerves and tie off the artery. The operation did

not completely remove the cancer. It had originated in the naso-pharynx, a part of the air passage behind the nose, in an area beneath the skull that was unreachable by surgery.

Phone calls swamped the hospital switchboard inquiring about Ruth's condition. Lying in his room recovering from the operation, he recalled, "I often felt so alone that tears would run down my cheeks." But Claire cheered him up, bringing in stacks of letters and reading excerpts to him. A seventh-grader from New Jersey sent a religious medal, which was pinned on Ruth's pajama coat. A woman from Indiana sent a small bottle that contained water from the shrine at Lourdes. Hundreds of telegrams arrived, including one from Jack Dempsey that urged him to "keep punching." He received a touching letter from a former schoolmate at Saint Mary's who was now in prison and heard that Ruth was "down with throat trouble":

> Well, it's been a long time . . . since those good brothers used to try to knock some learning into our heads. . . . George, remember the time Brother Sebastian used to walk up and down the big yard, look-ing to catch us smoking? Remember that time in the yard when you were knocking out some balls to us and smacked a hot one down my way and it hit me in the eye? And Brother Matthias gave me a few for missing it?

Although the Babe had no appetite, his friend Toots Shor made an elaborate ritual of sending meals up from his restaurant. By now, May de Rose had enlisted a group of USO girls to help answer the voluminous mail. Ruth signed the replies whenever he could; it gave him something to do. He spotted one letter and remarked to Claire, "Here's a lady who wants to know the name of my doctor. She thinks I have cancer."

"Well, you haven't," said his wife. By now, if Claire didn't know, she must have suspected it, as did others, but not a hint of cancer was ever mentioned in the press.

One week after the operation, Ruth was able to walk feebly along the hospital corridor. He was still in pain and couldn't speak. They were feeding him intravenously, and he'd lost much weight. He had received so many X-ray treatments that the roots of his hair on the left side of his head rotted, and when a nurse combed him the hair came out in chunks. In a few months he had aged twenty years.

Baseball Commissioner A. B. "Happy" Chandler, accompanied by a few members of the press, came to visit him on February 4. When Chandler sat down on the bed, Ruth turned his head and wept. He pointed to his scrawny arms but was too choked up to speak. Chandler

left, dabbing at his eyes with a handkerchief. A reporter stayed behind hoping for a brief interview. But Ruth could say nothing. He
could only look at the man with swimming eyes and again hold out
his shrunken arms.

Two days later Ruth's spirits were lifted when his friends brought
not one but four birthday cakes and a fresh pile of letters, cards,
and telegrams. The doctors let him record a reply for the newspapers and radio. His hoarse voice was heard to say: "I'm fighting
hard and I'll soon be on top. I thank everyone from the bottom of
my heart for their messages and good wishes."

On February 15, Room 1114 of French Hospital was vacated.
About one hundred persons stood outside waving and shouting as
Ruth—wiping away tears in his eyes—was helped by a nurse and a
friend down the steps to an auto. A few of the bystanders had tears
in their eyes, too. The old home run king was perceptibly grayer
and had lost nearly forty pounds. He seemed to have shrunk in
height, and his face was pinched and tired. Finally he sat in the
car with Claire, Julia, and a friend, Charles W. Schwefel, managing
director of the Gramercy Park Hotel. Julia leaned out the car window
and said her dad wanted to relay the following message to the press:
"I'd like to have a change of scenery. I want to look at the river
from my apartment window."

That night the De Roses and a few other friends gave Ruth a
welcome home dinner at his apartment. After the meal they heard
Walter Winchell say on WOR that the Babe's friends had "wept"
when they saw him and that he had shrunk from 225 to 100 pounds.
Ruth was offended and croaked, "I never did believe anything that
sonofabitch ever printed. Hell, when I'm dead my *bones* will weigh
more than that!"

"I'll fix that," said May de Rose. She went to the telephone to
call WOR. She told them about the party and what Babe had eaten
for dinner. Ruth insisted upon staying up until the 11 P.M. news,
and he listened with a smile as the broadcaster said the Babe had
consumed ham, pineapple, sweet potatoes, salad, and more, and
weighed 180 pounds. Still grinning, he walked into the kitchen and
took another slice of ham.

A few days later, a fellow New Yorker dropped by to see the
Babe. It was Hank Greenberg, the American League home run king,
who some years before had fallen only two shy of Ruth's record 60
homers. Now Greenberg was a veteran and had been sold by Detroit
to Pittsburgh.

Ruth was in a jovial mood. "Get a load o' this," he said, standing
and pulling up the jacket of his pajamas. His stomach was gone, it

was flat. "First time I've been able to look straight down and see my feet for thirty years! I'm down to 186, the same as I weighed when I came into baseball thirty-two years ago. Hell, if I could get a steak down me, I'd take on Joe Louis," he said, pounding his stomach with his left fist.

He changed into some maroon lounging pajamas for some pictures. A nurse patted down his graying thin hair. "Darndest thing I ever saw," he said. "Ran a comb through my hair one day and it all come off in the teeth."

Ruth reached for a bat from among his trophies and said, "Going to tell you something, Hank. I'm going to show you the whole secret of how I hit those home runs. Only fellow I ever told it to was Lou Gehrig." He wrapped his hands around the bat handle, with the little finger of his right hand extending down below the edge of the handle.

"Look," he said, lightly swinging the bat. "See how this grip makes your wrists break at the right time? Throws the whole weight of the bat into the ball. You've just *got* to follow through. I kept it secret a long, long time," he mused.

A few days later, Burris Jenkins, Jr., of the New York *Journal-American* dropped by to say hello. By now more than 27,000 messages from well-wishers had arrived at the Ruth apartment. The Babe led Jenkins into the bedroom, where telegrams and letters were stacked high on the dresser and chairs. Stuffing tobacco into his pipe, the Babe looked out the window at the ice-covered Hudson River. Then he turned to Jenkins with a helpless gesture, saying, "I can't understand it! Why should it happen to me?"

Jenkins didn't know what to say. The Babe, anger and frustration in his voice, said, "If only I could manage a ball club for a year— for a *week,* even! They could fire me at the end of a week!"

"Don't Come Back Tomorrow"

The Florida sun felt good. Babe and his wife had been at Ray Kilthau's place since early March, 1947. One afternoon, he pulled in a 50-pound sailfish, but he needed help from his nurse, Sonya Oliker. He was "whipped," he said, adding that the fish "felt like it weighed three hundred pounds."

That spring, the Ford Motor Company, which sponsored American Legion baseball, made Ruth the titular head of the league. His doctors knew it would be strenuous but felt that he would stay happier by keeping active. During the next few months, the Babe, Claire, and a nurse traveled 50,000 miles and made appearances all over the country. In one town, the public schools were closed so that children could see him at the local ball park. Ruth laughed that evening, saying to Claire, "Even if they don't like baseball, they *gotta* like the Babe. Hell, I got 'em the day off!" As she recalls, "He was happy in his pain and weariness.

In April Commissioner Chandler declared a "Babe Ruth Day" throughout America, when he would be honored before a Sunday game in Yankee Stadium. The day before, the *Daily News* decided to "bring a legend to life." They tracked down Johnny Sylvester, the boy whose life had been miraculously "saved" during the 1926 World Series by Ruth's home run. Sylvester, a Princeton graduate and a former navy subchaser commander, was now thirty-two years old, had his own family, and worked as a business executive on Long Island.

"Gee, I hope he remembers me," he said to his wife as they were ushered into the apartment at Riverside Drive. Ruth, wearing lounging pajamas, strode into the living room and said, "Hello, Johnny! Christ, the last time I saw you, you were just a skinny little kid!"

"Well, Babe," said Sylvester, "it's only right that I should visit you after what you did for me." He pulled two old ink-scrawled baseballs from his pocket and said, "I thought you'd like to see these." They were the balls sent to him by the Yanks and Cardinals in 1926. Ruth examined them closely. "Look at some of them names, Gehrig, Meusel, Koenig . . . they were great boys," he murmured, shaking his head sadly.

"When you sent me these baseballs, you were really making dents in them," Sylvester said, laughing.

"Yeah," said Ruth, half to himself. "Those were great days."

There were 58,000 fans in Yankee Stadium that Sunday. The broadcast of the pregame ceremony, handled by Yankee announcer Mel Allen, was piped into all major league parks. Even in Japan the ball parks that day held ceremonies to honor "Babu Rusu." Francis Cardinal Spellman opened with an invocation, and after the speeches Ruth walked out from the Yankee dugout, hunched over, looking shriveled in his camel's hair coat. He removed his cap and waved weakly to the cheering crowd. After receiving several mementoes, he was introduced to speak. He began to cough violently, and doubled over. But he soon recovered and whispered hoarsely into the microphone to the hushed crowd in the same way that eight years before Lou Gehrig had done. It was Ruth, not his ghostwriters, speaking. The thoughts rambled but the sentiment was clear:

"Thank you very much, ladies and gentlemen. You know how bad my voice sounds. Well, it feels just as bad. You know this baseball game of ours comes up from the youth. That means the boys. And after you're a boy, and grow up to know how to play ball, then you come to the boys you see representing themselves today in your national pastime.

"The only real game, I think, in the world is baseball. As a rule, some people think if you give them a football or baseball, or something like that, naturally they're athletes right away. But you can't do that in baseball. You've gotta start from way down the bottom, when you're six or seven years of age. You can't wait until you're fifteen or sixteen. You've gotta let it grow up with you, and if you're successful and you try hard enough, you're bound to come out on top, just like these boys have come to the top now. There's been so many lovely things said about me, I'm glad I had the opportunity to thank everybody. Thank you."

As he walked back to the dugout, tears in his eyes, there was a great deluge of applause for the shrunken giant with the suddenly gray hair.

He returned to Florida in mid-May to fish in the Keys and wander about in the sun with his dog, Pal. They stayed at the Kilthau villa, where Ruth awoke early each morning, slipped into swim trunks, and went out on the dock facing the bay. After breakfast on the screened porch, he religiously scanned the sports pages. Then he puttered around on the lawn with a niblick or cast for snapper on the dock. But suddenly he began to feel worse, and on May 23 they flew back to New York.

His pains were so severe that he could not sleep or swallow solid foods. His jaws were so sensitive that he doubled over in pain if he bit down on the white of a soft-boiled egg. Sometimes he fell forward at the dinner table or crumpled to the floor. Large doses of morphine were administered, but even drugs proved of little help after a while.

On June 25 he returned to the hospital, ostensibly to "take things easy for a few weeks." Doctors felt his case was incurable. He had lost ten more pounds, and his left vocal chord and the left side of his palate were immobile. In desperation, they suggested a new experimental cure, and Ruth agreed. The new drug was known as teropterin (a synthetic relative of folic acid, a vitamin of the B-complex family) which had shown promise in checking cancer in certain species of mice. Ruth was one of the first humans on whom it was tried. He was given the first daily injection of five milligrams on June 29. He also received a blood transfusion. After six weeks, Ruth seemed much better. He had gained weight and felt some relief from his pain. So dramatic was his improvement that his case was the subject of a paper read before the International Cancer Congress in Saint Louis that September. Since the reading of the paper endangered the blanket of secrecy over Ruth's true condition, the science reporters agreed to simply identify the patient as "a nationally famous fifty-two-year-old man."

He left the hospital but continued to receive daily injections. Now he was able, at least, to chew and swallow food. He felt well enough in July to fly to Dallas and speak to a convention of American Legion youths.

He also began to work with Bob Considine on his autobiography, *The Babe Ruth Story*. By now Allied Artists had obtained film rights to the book, and Ruth was paid a reported $150,000 plus a share of the profits.

"It was damn hard to work with a man who was dying," says Considine, and "dying as resentfully as Babe was. He was often in incredible pain." They had to work fast, because the publishers wanted the book for the 1947 Christmas trade. Considine enlisted Fred Lieb to help him put the book together, and they set off in different directions to conduct research. Sometimes while being interviewed, Considine recalls, the Babe "would break off in mid-sentence and say, 'Let's get the hell outa here and hit a few.'" Ruth insisted on driving his Lincoln Continental by himself. On the way to the golf course they would stop at a small Italian butcher shop on Ninth Avenue, where Ruth would buy chopped meat so that the cook at the golf club could prepare hamburgers for lunch. He could no longer chew the steaks he loved so much. Working against time, Considine and Lieb prepared a rough manuscript in about two weeks of feverish dictation, typing, and editing. The only passage Ruth wanted to strike from the manuscript, says Considine, was one dealing with the time bookmakers swindled him at the race-track in Cuba. But the Babe wanted him to leave in the material about his juvenile delinquency "to serve as a warning to the kids."

When the book was published early the next year, Ruth was taken up to New Haven, Connecticut, to present the manuscript to the Yale Library. "You know," he admitted, "you can't put everything in a story, so I left out a few things." Later he said to a friend that perhaps there should have been two books, "one for kids, and one for adults."

Near the end of the book, Ruth was quoted as saying: "I honestly don't know anybody who wants to live more than I do." But all around him was death. That October, Brother Gilbert, the man who helped to discover him, died of a cerebral hemorrhage. They had often kept in touch over the years, and it was a blow to Ruth, who was too weak himself to attend the funeral in Lowell, Massachusetts. But the next day a twelve-year-old boy who lived near Lowell wrote to him:

> I'm sorry your friend died. If you wish, and the brothers will let me go to the mass, I will go for you as I live in Danvers. I will behave.
> Love, Frank Haggerty.

Ruth wired the boy his blessing and then called the family to allow the young boy to represent him. Now that he was in such serious condition, many awards were forthcoming. That November he went to Omaha to receive a scroll of appreciation from Boys Town. Days later, back home, he was given an award by the National Fraternal Order of Eagles. That Christmas he dressed as Santa Claus and appeared at the Hotel Astor in a benefit for the Sister Kenny Foundation to greet forty young polio victims.

The pain continued. Once more he took the train to Florida with Claire and a new nurse, Frank Delaney. When he arrived at Golden Beach shortly before his birthday, he rubbed the left side of his neck and told a reporter in his gravelly voice, "If I get this nerve straightened out, I'll be all right. I'm going to try and get some sun on this old ear of mine." On his birthday a group of reporters and photographers waited outside his house for the perennial picture story. Ruth pushed open the screen door and stepped into the sun, shielding his eyes with his right hand. He grinned widely at a small boy who stood nearby. "Hello son," he said. He walked slowly down the walk as the boy held on to Ruth's slacks.

"Happy birthday, Babe," said a photographer.

His eyes red from fatigue, Ruth said he felt ninety years old. He had slept only a few hours in the past two weeks, he claimed, and "I can't even get that unless they shoot stuff into me." He was in pain "all day, all night," he said, and pounding his knee with the palm of his hand he complained, "I just haven't got the old pepper."

The doctors, he said, claimed they didn't know what was wrong but also insisted that further operations were too risky. "Risky?" the Babe exclaimed. "A man can't go on like this!"

He grinned when someone interrupted with a few funny base-ball stories. Then the photographers snapped Ruth's annual photo. A few fathers brought their children over, and Ruth patted them and smiled. He leaned heavily against a table between shots but straightened up and smiled each time they said, "Just one more, Babe." Then he shuffled slowly back toward the house. As the children continued to play on the grass, one father was asked if his four-year-old son knew who Ruth was.

"No," he said. "I just told him he was a nice man."

Before leaving for Florida, Ruth had told his old friend Frank Stevens, "I haven't long to go; but I'm gonna get outa here and have some fun before I die." That spring Frank Graham saw him in Florida, "almost feverishly searching for fun," visiting the old haunts of his youth.

At Al Lang Stadium in Saint Petersburg, Red Smith asked him about those good old days and Ruth's eyes gleamed "with some-thing like pleasure" when he recalled in his husky voice how he had once got "his adjectival shoulders into a swing and . . . knocked the indelicacy ball against the Anglo-Saxon hotel out there." You'd find him in all the small Florida towns where there was baseball, said Smith, "always with a squad of cops fending off autograph hounds and a horde of junior executives chuffing and scurrying like tugboats around an ocean liner."

Ruth returned to New York on March 24, deeply tanned after six weeks in Florida, feeling "like a new man." After Easter he would go to Hollywood to serve as technical adviser for *The Babe Ruth Story*. The producers, eager for a maximum return on their investment, sensed there wasn't much time left and were filming the picture in great haste. Most of the picture had already been shot when the Ruths arrived, and they never saw any of the scenes being filmed. William Bendix was playing the title role, and the Babe did manage to corner him once and give him some tips on swinging a bat properly.

But soon afterward Ruth fell ill again, and they headed back east by train. He sat in the stateroom, head in hands, silent. Shortly after the train left Los Angeles, a porter knocked, saying that Mr. and Mrs. Fred Astaire were aboard and wanted to say hello. He was tired, but the nurse dressed him, and they greeted each other and posed for photos. When they stayed briefly in Chicago, David Condon of the *Tribune* interviewed him as he sipped beer, the food easiest on his throat. But when the photographers came by, he waved them away. "I don't want the kids to see me drinking beer," he said. By now, he apparently felt some messianic urge to present a clean, wholesome image for "the kids," that vast army of admirers.

* * *

Rain fell in torrents on June 13, 1948, the day chosen to celebrate the 25th anniversary of Yankee Stadium, the House that Ruth Built. He was the guest of honor. The club had invited all members of the 1923 team to play a three-inning contest against a group of Yankee stars from other seasons. The clubhouse that afternoon was filled with laughter, as men who hadn't seen each other in years joked and slapped each other's back. Whitey Witt rummaged around for a pair of size nine shoes; Mike McNally searched for the impossible, a pair of pants with a 48-inch waist. Suddenly there was a hush, and someone said, "Here he is now." The Babe, helped by friends on either side of him, walked in slowly, wearing a dark suit and a white cap. He smiled. Slowly, gently, his friends came over, one by one, to shake his hand and murmur a few words. Many of them hadn't seen him for a few years and were shocked by his ravaged face. His friends helped him to undress and put on a Yankee uniform. Then he sat down to tie his own spikes and the photographers moved in. Minutes later, a garbardine topcoat was draped over his shoulders, and he was led into a dark runway toward the dugout. It was damp and cold. "Better wait inside," someone said, and they led him back to the clubhouse. He sat down on a bench, stooped over, saying nothing.

"All right, they're ready," came a voice. Again they led him out into the third-base dugout. He sat down on the bench and picked up a fielder's glove. "Christ," he said, looking at the large webbing, "you could catch a basketball with this." The players around him laughed, and he held the webbing up against his face as though it were a catcher's mask, evoking more laughter. He spotted Mel Harder, a pitching coach for the Cleveland Indians. "You remember when I got five for five off you?" he croaked. "Yes," said Harder, "I remember." He picked up a bat, a Bob Feller model. "It's got good balance," he said. Then Mel Allen's voice could be heard on the public address system starting the introductions. The players moved away from the front of the dugout, and a platoon of photographers aimed their cameras at him. He let the topcoat slip away, and got to his feet. Allen's voice boomed out: "George Herman Ruth . . . Babe Ruth!" He slowly climbed the steps and walked onto the field; the flashbulbs were like a burst of lightning, and the crowd followed with a long, booming roll of thunder that thrilled him and brought tears to his eyes.

Despite the wretched weather, there were 49,000 people in the Stadium. He walked slowly toward the plate, carrying a bat that was now a cane. And the thunderous applause continued. All the old-time Yankees were there waiting for him. And old "Simon Legree," Ed Barrow, now in his eighties, approached from the direction of the other dugout. They embraced unashamedly at home plate as the wind whipped at the World Series and pennant banners that bedecked the Stadium, and the band played "Auld Lang Syne."

That night and for much of the next day, Claire recalls, the Babe cried bitterly.

A few days later, despite his pain, Ruth went on another tour for the American Legion, appearing in Saint Louis, Sioux City, and Sioux Falls. But on June 23 he entered Memorial Hospital. As he was helped up the front steps, Ruth said to Dr. McDonald, "This is Memorial, a cancer hospital. Why are you bringing me here?" Not all the patients there had cancer, said the doctor. On July 3 it was first revealed to the press that Ruth was receiving "radiation treatments." He was so ill on the night of July 21 that the last sacraments of the Catholic church were administered. But he pulled out of it, and the next morning he joked with a friend, "Say, were you here yesterday when I nearly kicked the bucket?"

On the night of July 26, perspiring heavily, supported by both arms, the Babe walked slowly into the Astor Theater to see the world premiere of his screen autobiography. He smiled wanly at Mayor O'Dwyer, and a flock of sports and theatrical celebrities. Before the film was over, he felt ill and had to leave. He missed nothing.

The picture, says Claire, is "an obscenity, a ridiculous charade."

The next morning, Bosley Crowther of the *Times* said there was "a good bit too much of muchness in the line of heroics and tears," and called even the baseball scenes "patently absurd."

Crowther was mild in comparison with what the film (directed, oddly enough, by a man named Roy del Ruth) deserved. It was atrociously saccharine, a vomitous whitewash of a vivid, fascinating life. There was no mention of Ruth's first marriage or of his family. Facts were terribly twisted. Ruth was depicted not as a spirited, fun-loving idol but as a dull-witted eunuch. His $5,000 fine in 1925, according to the film, was meted out after he hit a foul ball in batting practice that injured a young boy's dog; he rushes to the hospital with the boy and the yelping cur and demands that a surgeon operate to save the animal. He forgets all about the game at the Stadium that afternoon, and is fined by Huggins. In the end, seriously ill, he is wheeled down a hospital corridor to take experimental drug treatments that "will help mankind," with a choir of angels singing in the background.

During the last few weeks of his life, Ruth seemed resigned, more serene. Each day, May de Rose came in with the mail and exchanged jokes and funny gossip with the Babe. Claire had already taken a room in the hospital to be near him. His friends, his daughters, all came virtually every day, smiling and bringing cartoons and funny stories to cheer him. The Babe Ruth Foundation to assist underprivileged children had already been established, and he often inquired how it was going. He lay in bed, half asleep most of the time, listening to the radio. August was a month of death; his mother had died on August 23; his father, on August 25. On August 9, things looked so dark that Ruth signed an updated last will and testament.* He was getting ready. Each day he sank and rallied.

Two days later, he was announced as "critically ill," and only the immediate family and a few close friends were permitted to visit his ninth-floor room. Phone calls deluged the hospital, the Manhattan police headquarters, and the switchboards of the New York newspapers. Hundreds of neighborhood youngsters milled around outside the front of the hospital; children who were born years after he retired asked the nurses, "How's the Babe?" One delegation chipped in and bought a bunch of roses. In the next two days, more than 10,000 telegrams and letters arrived at the hospital. Among them was a letter signed by two hundred baseball fans in Sleepy Eye, Minnesota, who affirmed that his brief visit there years ago was

* Ruth left his family well provided for. His net estate totaled $360,811, including $78,017 in U.S. Savings Bonds and a trust fund set up in 1927 that was appraised at $179,611.

"still the topic of conversation." On August 13 a phone call from the White House advised that President Truman wished him well. People called the hospital to offer blood but were told that none was necessary.

On the evening of August 15, he kissed Claire several times and said hoarsely, "Don't come back tomorrow, because I won't be here."

But the next morning, despite his waning strength, he could still make a joke. Months before, in Florida, Babe had addressed some children, and the master of ceremonies later said, "I want you to meet two other celebrities from New York," and he introduced Ruth's friend Paul Carey and his nurse, Frank Delaney. When they got back to Ray Kilthau's villa that night, Ruth said, "Hey, Clara, Paul and Frank are a couple of celebrities!" Now, on the last day of his life, the two men stood at his bedside. Ruth looked up at one, smiled, wiggled his thumb at the other and whispered, "Celebrity!"

At 6:45 P.M., May de Rose came in to read him a telegram. As she left, Ruth lurched out of bed and started across the room. A doctor and nurse gently led him back.

"Where are you going, Babe?" the doctor asked.

"I'm going over the valley," he mumbled.

Minutes later he fell into a deep coma. At 7:30 P.M., a priest carrying a black bag hurried past reporters and the crowd at the hospital entrance to give him a final blessing. At 8:01 P.M. he was gone.

*   *   *

The next afternoon, Yankee equipment manager Pete Sheehy mopped down the stone floor inside the Stadium near the front ramp that led to the grandstand. There was a large display of ferns and huckleberry sprays, which formed a backdrop for the six-foot catafalque, a crucifix, and a vigil light. Remembering a time in the late 1920's when groundskeepers and equipment men didn't receive World Series shares, Sheehy said, "The Babe went around in the clubhouse with his hat and took up a collection for us; he handed me a few hundred dollars . . . that was big dough then." Wiping his eyes, he said softly, "I'll never forget him. I'll make this space *spotless* for the guy."

A hearse from the Universal Funeral Parlor on Lexington Avenue cruised slowly up to the Stadium, and eight pallbearers helped to place the mahogany coffin upon the catafalque.

Not since the death of President Roosevelt three years before had the loss of a single American so moved the nation. That evening, long lines of people—many of them in work clothes—shuffled along the stone floor past the coffin where Ruth lay, dressed in a simple blue double-breasted suit, a set of black rosary beads wrapped about his left hand. By midnight, when the Stadium gates were closed, more than 25,000 people had passed through. The next morning, some 50,000 more filed by. Many men held young boys in their arms and let them peek into the coffin. Thousands more clogged the sidewalks near Saint Patrick's Cathedral on August 19, the day of the funeral, where Cardinal Spellman presided at the Requiem Mass. It was very hot. Among the pallbearers were Joe Dugan and Waite Hoyt. "Christ," Dugan whispered, licking his dry lips, "I'd give a hundred bucks for a cold beer." Hoyt, nodding at the coffin, whispered back, "So would the Babe." Since no gravesite had been selected, the coffin was put in a vault that afternoon at the Gate of Heaven Cemetery in a little town called Valhalla, a proper resting place for a demigod. After friends and family drove off, thousands of fans stepped over a rope barrier and picked blossoms from the huge floral displays to take home as souvenirs. Two months later, the Babe's coffin was taken from the vault and buried in its final resting place in a simple service attended only by Claire and five friends.

* * *

In the days and years after Babe Ruth's death, the press elevated him to sterile sainthood, much as the film biography had done. A few thoughtful writers, responding to the call of critics who demand of biographers that they offer analysis—Freudian and otherwise—have tried to encapsulate the Babe within some rational formula.

But even they ignore the immensely random quality of life, that vast roulette wheel of genes and chance, which—had some other road been taken—might have cast him in the role of saloonkeeper, tailor, longshoreman, or felon. It defies all understanding. Here was a man with a special gift who broke all the rules with a flourish, triumphed grandly, and suffered a painful, early demise. But within his sadly truncated time span, he soared higher and drank deeper of life—dregs and all—than a hundred ordinary men combined.

Perhaps the best eulogy came a few days after the Babe's death from crusty old "Uncle Ed" Barrow. "I'll miss him," he said. Then, his eyes misted by long-ago memories, he chuckled, shook his head, and added, "I'll miss him because he was more damn trouble than anyone I ever knew."

Ruth's Record

Year	Club	League	G.	AB.	R.	H.	2B.	3B.	HR.	RBI.	BA.	FA.
1914—Baltimore-Prov.		Int.	46	121	22	28	2	10	1	—	.231	.964
1914—Boston*		A. L.	5	10	1	2	1	0	0	0	.200	1.000
1915—Boston		A. L.	42	92	16	29	10	1	4	20	.315	.976
1916—Boston		A. L.	67	136	18	37	5	3	3	16	.272	.973
1917—Boston		A. L.	52	123	14	40	6	3	2	10	.325	.984
1918—Boston		A. L.	95	317	50	95	26	11	11	64	.300	.950
1919—Boston†		A. L.	130	432	103	139	34	12	29	112	.322	.990
1920—New York		A. L.	142	458	158	172	36	9	54	137	.376	.936
1921—New York		A. L.	152	540	177	204	44	16	59	170	.378	.966
1922—New York		A. L.	110	403	94	128	24	8	35	96	.315	.964
1923—New York		A. L.	152	522	151	205	45	13	41	130	.393	.973
1924—New York		A. L.	153	529	143	200	39	7	46	121	.378	.962
1925—New York		A. L.	98	359	61	104	12	2	25	66	.290	.974
1926—New York		A. L.	152	495	139	184	30	5	47	155	.372	.979
1927—New York		A. L.	151	540	158	192	29	8	60	164	.356	.963
1928—New York		A. L.	154	536	163	173	29	8	54	142	.323	.975
1929—New York		A. L.	135	499	121	172	26	6	46	154	.345	.984
1930—New York		A. L.	145	518	150	186	28	9	49	153	.359	.965
1931—New York		A. L.	145	534	149	199	31	3	46	163	.373	.972
1932—New York		A. L.	133	457	120	156	13	5	41	137	.341	.961
1933—New York		A. L.	137	459	97	138	21	3	34	103	.301	.970
1934—New York		A. L.	125	365	78	105	17	4	22	84	.288	.962
1935—Boston		N. L.	28	72	13	13	0	0	6	12	.181	.952
Major League Totals			2503	8396	2174	2873	506	136	714	2209	.342	.968

WORLD'S SERIES RECORDS

Year	Club	League	G.	AB.	R.	H.	2B.	3B.	HR.	RBI.	BA.	FA.
1915—Boston		A. L.	1	1	0	0	0	0	0	0	.000	.000
1916—Boston		A. L.	1	5	0	0	0	0	0	1	.200	1.000
1918—Boston		A. L.	3	5	0	1	0	1	0	2	.200	1.000
1921—New York		A. L.	6	16	3	5	0	0	1	4	.313	1.000
1922—New York		A. L.	5	17	1	2	1	0	0	1	.118	1.000
1923—New York		A. L.	6	19	8	7	1	1	3	3	.368	.944
1926—New York		A. L.	7	20	6	6	0	0	4	5	.300	1.000
1927—New York		A. L.	4	15	4	6	0	0	2	7	.400	1.000
1928—New York		A. L.	4	16	9	10	3	0	3	3	.625	1.000
1932—New York		A. L.	4	15	6	5	0	0	2	6	.333	.889
World Series Totals			41	129	37	42	5	2	15	32	.325	.977

ALL-STAR GAME RECORD

Year	Club	AB.	R.	H.	2B.	3B.	HR.	RBI.	BA.	FA.
1933—American		4	1	2	0	0	1	2	.500	1.000
1934—American		2	1	0	0	0	0	0	.000	.000
All-Star Game Totals		6	2	2	0	0	1	2	.333	1.000

* Acquired from Baltimore, July 11, 1914; optioned to Providence, August 20, and recalled at end of International League season, September 27, 1914.
† Sold to New York A. L. for $125,000, January, 1920.

PITCHING RECORD

Year Club League	G.	IP.	W.	L.	Pct.	H.	R.	BB.	SO.	ERA.
1914—Baltimore-Prov. ..Int.	35	245	22	9	.709	210	88	101	139	—
1914—Boston ....A. L.	4	22	2	1	.667	21	12	7	2	3.91
1915—Boston ....A. L.	32	218	18	6	.750	166	80	85	112	2.44
1916—Boston ....A. L.	44	324	23	12	.657	230	83	118	170	1.75
1917—Boston ....A. L.	41	326	23	13	.639	244	93	108	128	2.02
1918—Boston ....A. L.	20	166	13	7	.650	125	51	49	40	2.22
1919—Boston ....A. L.	17	133	8	5	.615	148	59	58	30	2.97
1920—New York ......A. L.	1	4	1	0	1.000	3	4	2	0	4.50
1921—New York ......A. L.	2	9	2	0	1.000	14	10	10	2	4.00
1930—New York ......A. L.	1	9	1	0	1.000	11	3	3	2	3.00
1933—New York ......A. L.	1	9	1	0	1.000	12	5	3	0	5.00
Major League Totals	163	1220	92	44	.676	974	400	443	486	2.24

WORLD SERIES PITCHING RECORD

Year Club League	G.	IP.	W.	L.	Pct.	H.	R.	BB.	SO.	ERA.
1916—Boston ....A. L.	1	14	1	0	1.000	6	1	3	4	0.64
1918—Boston ....A. L.	2	17	2	0	1.000	13	2	7	4	1.06
World Series Totals	3	31	3	0	1.000	19	3	10	8	0.87